A MARMAC GUIDE TO ATLANTA

by

Susan Hunter Smith

Marmac Publishing Company, Inc.
Atlanta, Ga.

©1984 by Marmac Publishing Company, Inc. All rights reserved, including the right to reproduce this book in whole or in part in any form without permission from the publisher. Printed in the U.S.A.

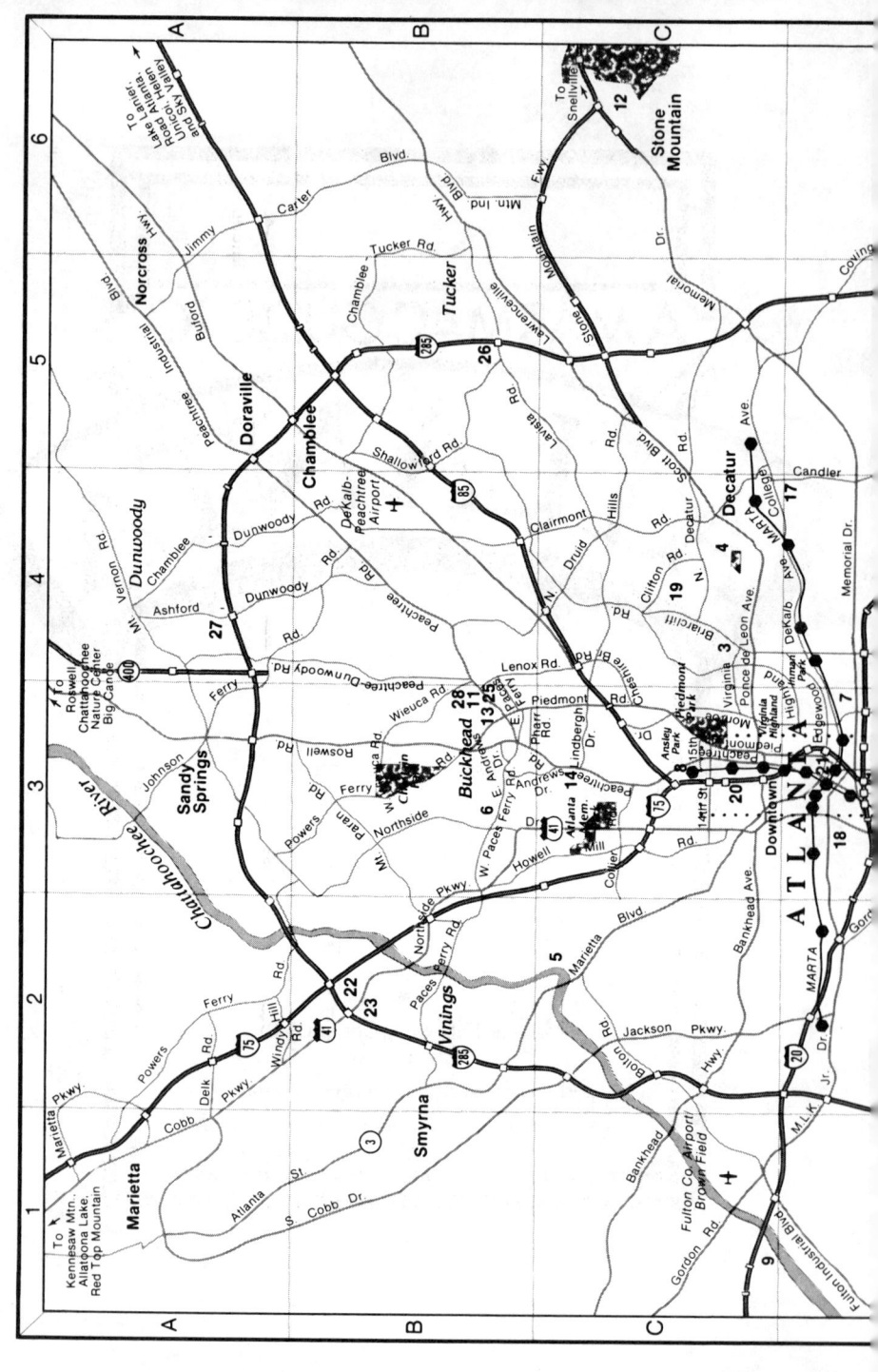

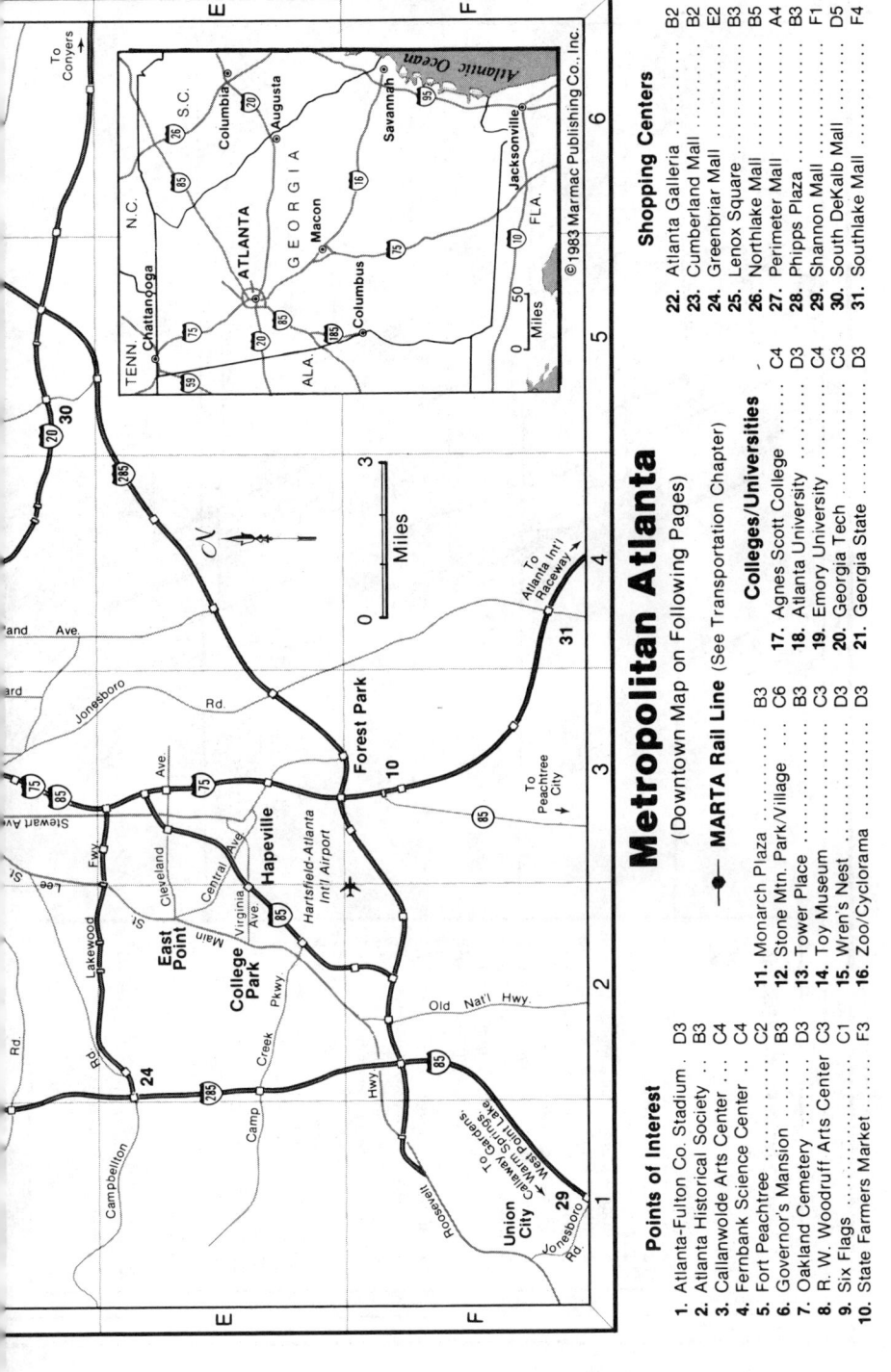

Metropolitan Atlanta
(Downtown Map on Following Pages)

→→ **MARTA Rail Line** (See Transportation Chapter)

Points of Interest

1. Atlanta-Fulton Co. Stadium D3
2. Atlanta Historical Society B3
3. Callanwolde Arts Center C4
4. Fernbank Science Center C4
5. Fort Peachtree C2
6. Governor's Mansion B3
7. Oakland Cemetery D3
8. R. W. Woodruff Arts Center C3
9. Six Flags C1
10. State Farmers Market F3
11. Monarch Plaza B3
12. Stone Mtn. Park/Village C6
13. Tower Place B3
14. Toy Museum C3
15. Wren's Nest D3
16. Zoo/Cyclorama D3

Colleges/Universities

17. Agnes Scott College C4
18. Atlanta University D3
19. Emory University C4
20. Georgia Tech C3
21. Georgia State D3

Shopping Centers

22. Atlanta Galleria B2
23. Cumberland Mall B2
24. Greenbriar Mall E2
25. Lenox Square B3
26. Northlake Mall B5
27. Perimeter Mall A4
28. Phipps Plaza B3
29. Shannon Mall F1
30. South DeKalb Mall D5
31. Southlake Mall F4

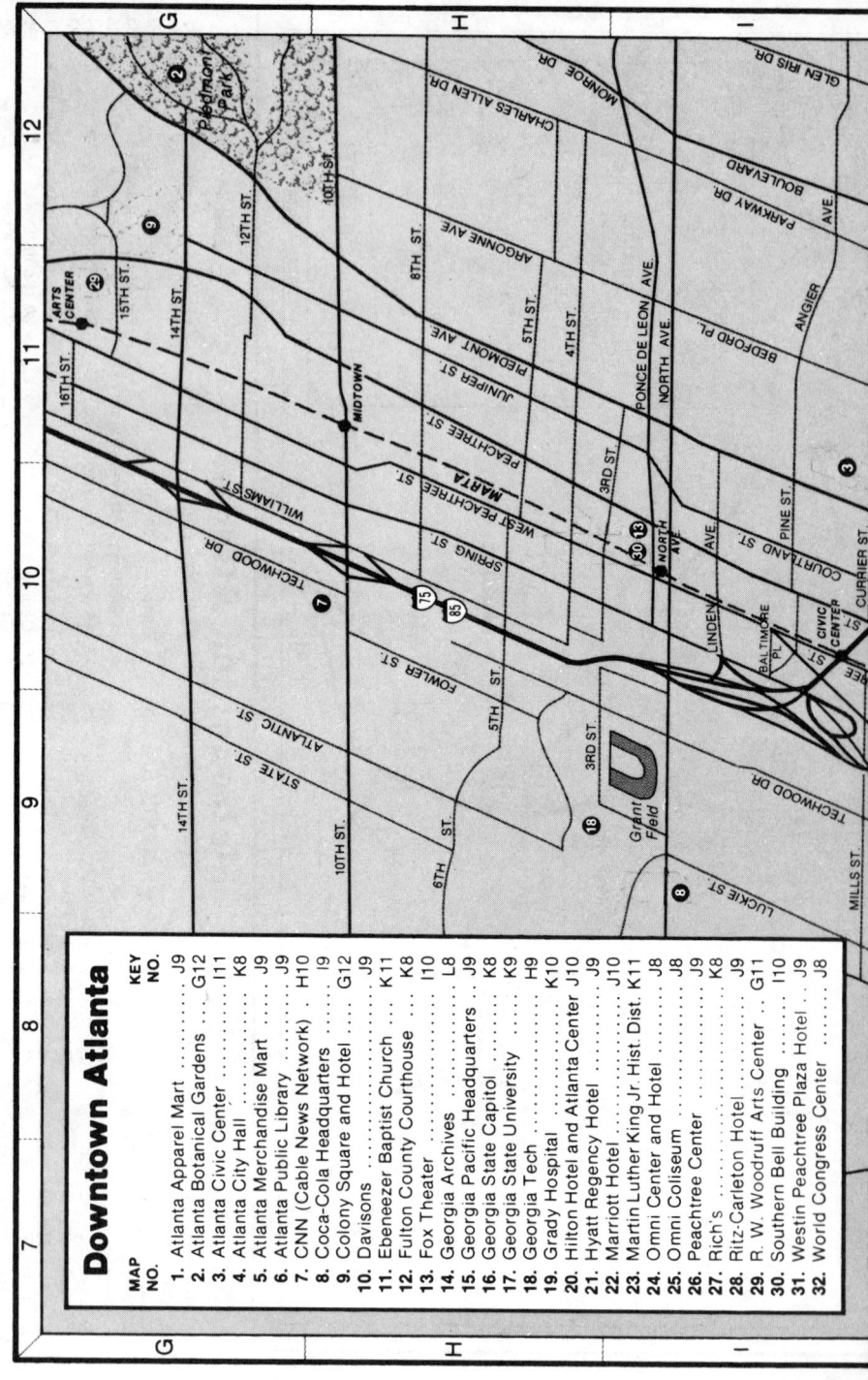

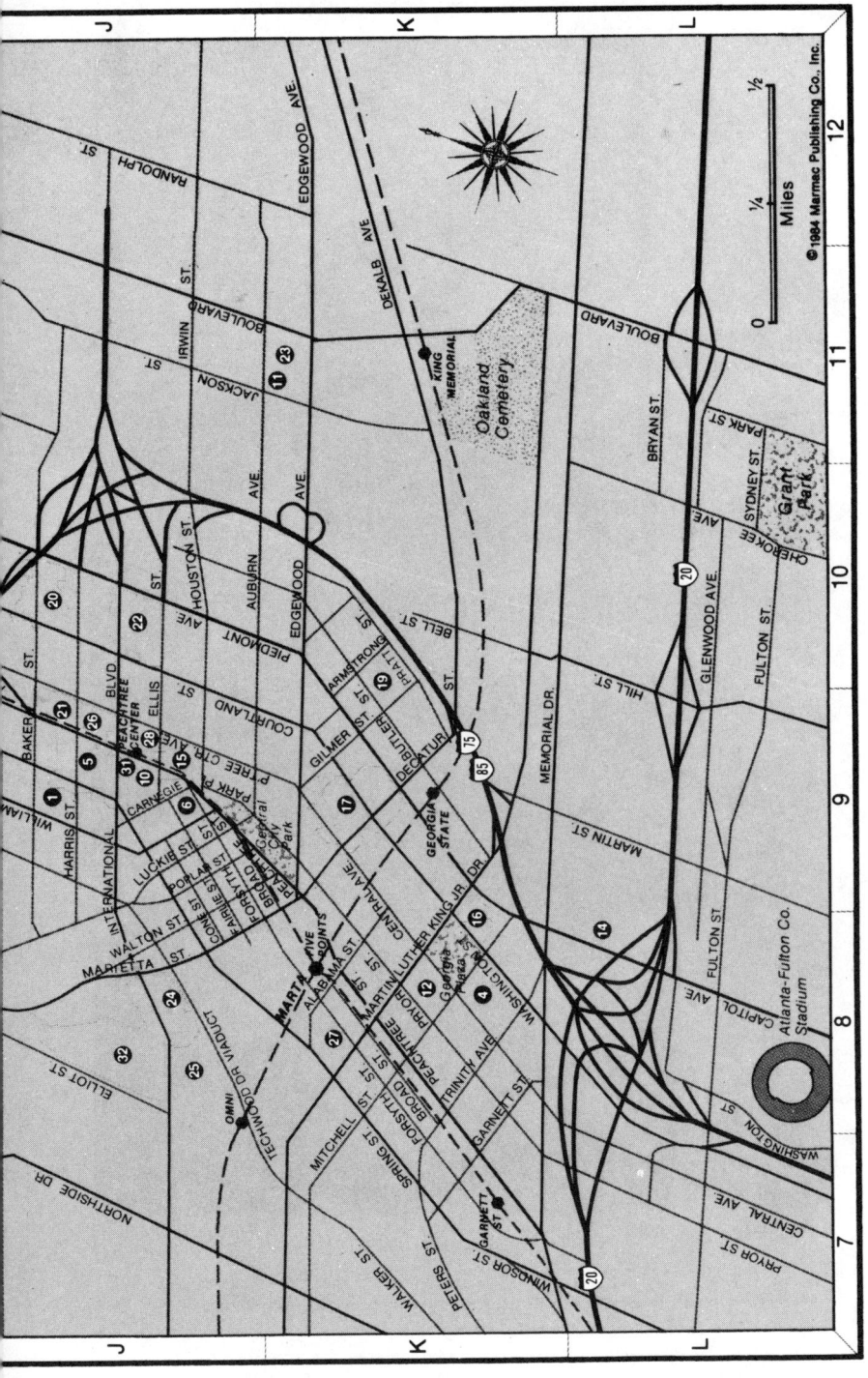

Emerging by Mark Smith　　　　　　　　　　　Courtesy Steven Smith

CONTENTS

FOREWORD	11
ATLANTA PAST	13
ATLANTA TODAY	17
MATTERS OF FACT	24
TRANSPORTATION	26
LODGING	34
DINING	55
PERFORMING ARTS	95
NIGHTLIFE	102
SIGHTS	111
VISUAL ARTS	125
SHOPPING	136
SPORTS	164
SPECIAL EVENTS	178
SELF-GUIDED CITY TOURS	187
ONE-DAY EXCURSIONS	202
NEW RESIDENTS	211
SPECIAL PEOPLE	238
BITS AND PIECES	257
ORDER FORM	

MAPS

Metropolitan Atlanta	2-3
Downtown Atlanta	4-5
MARTA Rail Stations	32
Downtown Walking Tour	188
One-Day Excursions	203
Atlanta Region Counties	228
Georgia in the USA	238

Information in this guidebook is based on personal research and data available at time of printing. Hotels, restaurants, stores, attractions alter their prices and times and open and close all the time. Therefore we ask our readers to bear with us if there are any changes.

Publisher and Executive Director: Marge McDonald
Editor: Elizabeth Speir
Cartography: Frank Drago, Atlanta, GA
Composition: Merck Typesetting, Smyrna, GA
Cover and design: Burton-Campbell Inc., Atlanta, GA
Printing: Murray Printing Co., Westford, MA

ISBN: 0-939944-27-8   ISSN: 0735-827X

KEY TO LETTER CODE

E	Expensive
M	Moderately Expensive
I	Inexpensive
CH	Entrance Charge
NCH	No Charge

FOREWORD

The Marmac guidebooks are designed for the resident and traveler who seek comprehensive information in an easy-to-use format and who have a zest for the best in each city and area mentioned in this national series.

We have chosen to include only what we can recommend to you on the basis of our own research, experience, and judgment. Our inclusions are our reputation.

We first escort you into the city or area introducing you to a new or perhaps former acquaintance and we relate the history and folklore that is indigenous to this particular locale. Secondly, we assist you in *learning the ropes* — the essentials of the community, necessary matters of fact, transportation systems, lodging and restaurants, nightlife and theater. Section three will point you toward available activities — sightseeing, museums and galleries, shopping, sports, and excursions into the heart of the city and to its environs. And lastly we salute the special needs of special people — the new resident, the international traveler, students and children, senior citizens, and the handicapped person.

The key area map is placed at the opening of each book, always at your fingertips for quick reference. The margin index, keyed 1-6 and A-F, provides the location code to each listing in the book. Subsidiary maps include a downtown street map keyed 7-12 and G-L, and intown and out-of-town touring maps.

Please write to us with your comments and suggestions at Marmac Publishing Co. Inc., 6303 Barfield Road, Atlanta, GA 30328. We will always be glad to hear from you.

Downtown Atlanta Skyline

Courtesy Georgia-Pacific Corporation

ATLANTA PAST

Indian Origins

When the U. S. Constitution was ratified in 1788, four-fifths of Georgia was Indian territory. The Creek and Cherokee tribes were both in the Atlanta area establishing trade relationships with the first English traders from Charleston, who were selling cloth goods, hardware, and guns. Present Atlanta was the site of the Indian village called Standing Peachtree, at the confluence of the Chattahoochee River and Peachtree Creek, where there was a natural fording area across the river due to the sandbar at that point. Settlements were made on the high banks of the Chattahoochee, which provided protection from flooding. The sandy flood plain was ideal for hoe agriculture; springs were abundant; the land was rich for growing corn and grain; and the river was the natural mode of transportation to other settlements. This village was on the Indian trail circuit, the Hightower Trail, which ran from Augusta, Georgia through Madison, past Stone Mountain and just north of Dunwoody, crossing the river at Roswell, continuing to the Cherokee town of New Echota and into northern Alabama.

Thus, the first period of Atlanta's prominence as a major crossroad and transportation center began where Indian trails and the Chattahoochee River converged.

In 1813 a Federal Militia outpost, Fort Gilmer, was established at the Standing Peachtree site to protect the state from the Creeks who were sympathetic to the British during the War of 1812. In 1837 the Western and Atlantic Railroad extended its tracks from Tennessee into Georgia and drove a stake into the heart of a new white settlement, Terminus — Atlanta's first name meaning "the end of the line." Just as the natural terrain had influenced the course of the Indian trails and the Indian trails had influenced the direction of the county roads and the county roads had influenced the railroad right-of-way, the railroad also helped to determine the physical configuration of streets in what, in 1850, was commercial antebellum Atlanta and is today the heart of the Central Business District. Even Atlanta's new rapid-transit system is determined by the city's most permanent feature, the original street pattern, and Atlanta's transportation patterns have consistently followed original environmental patterns from the pre-industrial Indians to today. Although the Indians were moved from Georgia to Oklahoma reservations in the 1830s, their names and patterns of movement have been absorbed into the civilization called Atlanta whose main street is still Peachtree Street.

The land rush for former Indian territory in the Atlanta area was stimulated even further by the rapid development of the railroad system which linked Terminus first to Tennessee in 1837, then to Marietta in 1842, and to Augusta, Georgia three years later. In 1843 Terminus was renamed Marthasville after a daughter of former Governor Lumpkin. Then, in 1845, Marthasville became Atlanta, a name associated with the town's first railroad, the Western and Atlantic. From this time to the outbreak of the Civil War, Atlanta thrived — building and creating churches, banks, hotels, a city government, newspapers, fire departments, more railroads, new businesses, courthouses, gas lights, and city directories. By 1862, with a population over 9000, Atlanta was a major Confederate military post, supply hub, and hospital and relief center.

Atlanta Burns

And then the city fell. The Battle of Atlanta in the Civil War was a turning point for both the Union and the Confederacy. Atlanta had to be taken by the Federal forces because of its strategic location for the Confederacy. General William Sherman's Federal Army of 100,000 fought its way from Tennessee to Atlanta in May 1864 following the route of the Western and Atlantic railroad. The city had prepared for siege with 12 miles of formidable trenches circling the city. But the Federal troops broke through from all directions, cutting the major railroad lines to Atlanta. The mayor surrendered in September and ordered civilian evacuation. General Sherman burned the city to the ground and set out on his march to the sea to take General Lee's rebel forces from their own southern flank. Atlanta, the dynamo of the Confederacy, was silenced.

But Atlantans were undaunted, and they came back to build together a biracial city, a new South from the ashes of destruction, a new social, economic, and political fabric. As the building process began again, out of it grew a public school system; hotels; railed streetcars; uniformed police; yet more railroads; public water works; telephones; colleges for women, blacks, and whites; Coca-Cola; a public-health hospital; an opera house; three international cotton expositions; and in 1901 the first Atlanta automobile.

A New South Arises

The 20th century opened the progressive era of continued enterprise.

In the 1920s, Metro Atlanta's population soared to over 200,000; radio stations were established; a municipal airport was begun; the Historical Society and the High Museum of Art initiated their programs; air mail was introduced; the Fox Theater, Atlanta's new movie palace, resembled something from the Arabian Nights; and the present city hall was built the year the stock market crashed.

Atlanta not only survived the Depression of the 1930s — she challenged it. In 1930 Atlanta's own Bobby Jones won the grand slam of golf and both Delta and Eastern airlines initiated scheduled passenger service from Atlanta. President Roosevelt dedicated the first public housing in the nation next to Georgia Tech. In 1936 *Gone With the Wind*, Margaret Mitchell's best-seller during these trying times, flooded the bookstores reminding the nation of its ability to persevere by depicting earlier trauma in its history, the Civil War, and by projecting the image of Atlanta in the character of the upstart but "can-do" Scarlett O'Hara. The burning of Atlanta scene in the movie three years later left an indelible symbol in the national memory of a city that survived its trial by fire.

The TV age came in the 40s after World War II. Atlanta's population had grown from 2500 in 1850 to 331,000 a century later. Although the sixties were an era of intense social struggle for civil rights, Atlantans of both races did not allow the race riots which afflicted other major cities. Dr. Martin Luther King, Jr., Nobel Peace Prize recipient, spoke firmly from the Southern Christian Leadership Conference headquartered in Atlanta. Mayor Ivan Allen, Jr. was committed to the rulings of the Fifth Circuit Court of Appeals upholding the Constitution. And the clarion voice of Ralph McGill was heard in his Atlanta Constitution editorials and nationally syndicated columns calling for affection and unity among the citizens of this model city and our great nation.

This was also a time of building resurgence along with social reordering. The crest of Peachtree Street was crowned with the first new building of Peachtree Center, the Merchandise Mart, and about the same time Marriott opened the first new hotel in downtown in many years.

The building pace continues unabated with hotels, office towers, megastructures, and suburban malls settling on the modern urban landscape. Atlanta, paying homage to her past, now lends an ear and funding to key historic preservation projects and districts to insure the function and pleasure of the places of Atlanta yesterday.

In 1868 Atlanta became the capital of the state, only three years after the city had been leveled by Federal troops during the Civil War. Atlanta, originally the backwoods Georgia trading post for the Indians and then for the colonial traders, took over the leadership of the largest state east of the Mississippi. The city's official emblem is the Phoenix. In Egyptian mythology it is a bird of great beauty said to live 500 years in the desert and then to consume itself by fire, rising from its ashes young and beautiful to live through another cycle. The city's governmental motto "Resurgens" complements the phoenix symbol of renewing spirit; and, in the popular language of today, the Convention and Visitors Bureau grades the city a double A — Amazing Atlanta.

ATLANTA TODAY

"This is Atlanta. This is an uncompleted city. This is the South. It is an uncompleted story."

In 1949 Georgia Governor Ellis Arnall thus predicted the incredible centrality of Atlanta in the regional destiny of what we now call "the Sunbelt," and he also underlined the vast generating capability of this continually rising city. Add to these insights Atlanta's early awareness that she would willfully mold her own image and create her own future, and you are presented with an urban powerhouse supplying the economic, political, and social energy for the southeastern quadrant of the United States.

A Unique International Crossroads

Atlanta has never seen herself as a completed city; she is constantly tempted by the future, by what she can be next. In the 1970s Atlanta designated herself the "Next Great International City." She is well on her way to fulfilling that claim boasting over 40 foreign consuls and trade offices, the largest airport passenger terminal in the world with ever-expanding international flights and carriers, and an increasing influx of foreign visitors, investors, and residents. About 300 of the more than 400 foreign companies in the state are located in the Atlanta metro area and over a dozen foreign banks have begun operations in Atlanta since 1976.

Atlanta is unlike other southern cities that rely on valuable natural raw resources, as does Birmingham, Alabama with its steel industry. She is also unlike southern port cities, such as Jacksonville, Florida or Norfolk, Virginia. And finally, she is unlike southern cities that exhibit the charm of colonial preservation, like Charleston, South Carolina and Savannah, Georgia. Atlanta's uniqueness is predicated on her geographic position as the South's major crossroad, and as the marketplace of the South, the key warehousing and distribution center, the transportation hub, and the financial and communication command post for the region.

This city has never been bashful about promoting herself to outsiders. As early as the 1880s Atlanta boldly declared herself "The Gateway of the South." In 1925 the "Forward Atlanta" public relations campaign — Atlanta's voice in the roaring twenties — began to attract more business to the city. After World War II, the Chamber of Commerce published one of the nation's earlier "city" magazines, *Atlanta*. And in the 1970s the "Atlanta 2000" project involved citizens in future speculation and plans for the "Big A" as it approaches a millenium.

The Corporate Explosion

You are not coming to the sleepy South when you arrive in Atlanta. Although the air may be thick with the scent of magnolias and gardenias, you are coming to the regional headquarters for over 430 of the Fortune 500 companies. Delta Airlines, the Coca-Cola Company, and Georgia-Pacific are three corporate giants with national headquarters in the city. Lockheed, one of the nation's major airplane manufacturers, is also one of Atlanta's main employers. The city is becoming a national influence in the cable TV boom. Scientific-Atlanta, one of the nation's leading makers of cable television equipment and earth stations, is based here. Turner Broadcasting System, the nation's newest broadcasting company is headquartered in Atlanta. Turner's WTBS/TV reaches over 25 million households in 50 states, and his cable-news network (CNN) is the nation's first 24-hour continuous news network. The city is also the financial center of the region, housing within the downtown district over 30 separate financial institutions (banks and savings and loan associations), as well as the headquarters of the Sixth District Federal Reserve Bank and the Fifth District Federal Home Loan Bank.

Identifying With Tourists

Atlanta made a commitment in the last decade to another aspect of its Big Business: the convention and hospitality industry. The monuments to that commitment have literally changed the skyline of the city.

The Peachtree Plaza designed by renowned Atlanta Architect John Portman, is a 73-story, mirrored cylinder with a seven-story atrium lobby, featuring a half-acre lake. It is the tallest hotel in the world, and is topped by a tri-level restaurant and lounge. The pioneer in

Atlanta's splurge of hotels is Portman's Hyatt Regency, with its full-height interior atrium and with a revolving restaurant capping the structure. The blue glass dome of the Hyatt Regency and the shining cylinder of the Peachtree Plaza are landmarks you can easily spot as you enter the city. Newcomers to the hotel industry include the Ritz-Carlton, a luxury hotel whose 25 stories of glass and marble grace Peachtree Street at Georgia-Pacific Plaza, and Days Inn, which has its first downtown location next to the Apparel Mart. Add to these hotels the Atlanta Hilton, the Marriotts, downtown and Marquis, and the Omni International in downtown, plus Colony Square in midtown and you will have a wide choice of hotel rooms in the core city. These hotels mark the first phase of allegiance to the visitor. Hotel and office complexes in the Buckhead area to the north and on the Perimeter encircling the city continue this development into the greater metro area.

Atlanta is also now experimenting with multiple options for accommodating visitors. You can find the small European-style hotel, the apartment-type hotel lodging, and suites for short-term leasing. We will see that you are aware of these special accommodations for your special needs in the chapter on Lodgings.

Atlanta's convention business is heavily dependent on three large trade facilities, as well as the meeting rooms and halls of the hotels themselves. The Georgia World Congress Center is one of the largest single-level exhibit halls in the country. Atlanta's Merchandise Mart is the retail distribution center for the southeast market, and the adjoining Atlanta Apparel Mart places Atlanta in active national competition as an apparel and fashion center. Both marts were designed and developed by Portman as was the recently expanded Atlanta Decorative Arts Center (ADAC) in Buckhead. These two marts together bring more than 250,000 buyers and manufacturers to Atlanta each year.

In addition, the Atlanta Civic Center accommodates trade shows and concerts; the Omni Coliseum and the Atlanta/Fulton County Stadium provide an arena for sports and entertainment for both local Atlantans and visitors. Marts, hotels, restaurants, and exhibit halls combined with professional sports — the Atlanta Falcons (football), the Hawks (basketball), the Braves (baseball) — and a spate of other attractions, all make Atlanta one of the major convention cities in the United States.

Government Center and Academic Forum

Atlanta is the locus of four systems of government: the regional center of the Federal Government, the capital of the State of Georgia, and the seat of Fulton County and the municipality of Atlanta. One of the world's most respected medical research centers is located in Atlanta, the U. S. Public Health Services Centers for Disease Control. Former President and Georgia Governor Jimmy Carter maintains offices in the 26-story Richard Russell Federal Building at the west end of the "Government Corridor," south of the Central Business District. This corridor includes Capitol Hill crowned by the gold-domed state house and the surrounding county and municipal structures. Capitol Hill is a delightful place to visit with gardens, a state museum, restaurant, and outdoor park where you can enjoy your lunch in the arbored sunlight.

Historically, Atlanta has been a thriving educational city, with 29 institutions granting undergraduate and graduate degrees. Atlanta University pioneered college education for blacks in the South immediately following the Civil War and is the largest consortium of predominantly black colleges and universities in the nation. Agnes Scott began education of women in the 19th century. The Georgia Institute of Technology (Georgia Tech), Oglethorpe University, and Emory University are other distinguished and established institutions of higher learning in Atlanta. Georgia State University is now the second largest state university in Georgia with over 20,000 students. Atlanta's colleges and universities keep the city young and challenging. Check their musical programs, lecture schedules, and art museums for a taste of Atlanta's academic life.

Cultural Clusters

The universities and colleges contribute substantially to the total cultural environment in Atlanta through co-sponsorship of special events and joint educational endeavors. In addition, the cultural community has developed umbrella associations and centers for the visual and performing arts throughout the city to pool creative expression, financial support and patronage. The dominant alliance is the Robert W. Woodruff Arts Center, erected in memory of 122 Atlanta art patrons killed in an airplane crash in Paris in 1962. The building is headquarters for the Atlanta Arts Alliance, which includes the Alliance Theatre, the Alliance Children's Theatre, the

Studio Theatre, the Atlanta Symphony directed by the nation's renowned choral director Robert Shaw, and the Atlanta College of Art. The new High Museum of Art building adjoins the Robert W. Woodruff Arts Center, a galaxy of cultural excitement and works.

Smaller arts centers in key neighborhoods provide access to both composite and specialized cultural activities. The Atlanta Jewish Community Center on Peachtree Street, Callanwolde Fine Arts Center in DeKalb County, Chastain Arts Center on the northwest side of town, and Nexus in the Virginia-Highlands section offer both classes, performances, and exhibitions in a wide gamut of the visual and performing arts. The Center for Puppetry Arts and the Southeastern Center for the Photographic Arts, along with the Neighborhood Arts Center which is devoted to cultural activities for the black community in southwest Atlanta, add distinctive focus in the growth of Atlanta's cultural identity.

Transportation Hub

Atlanta's accessibility promotes education, culture, trade and business. The city is the pivotal transportation point in the southern region; the great railroad days which began in 1837 have been superseded by the age of air travel. Atlanta's new Hartsfield International Airport has the world's largest passenger terminal, capable of handling fifty-five million passengers a year, with ease! A special feature of the new structure is an international terminal with the country's largest one-stop federal inspection facility, as well as currency exchange, duty-free shops, and other amenities for the international passenger. With stunning contemporary art incorporated into the massive terminal building, you will find the Atlanta airport a pleasure trip in itself.

Nor is the city's internal transportation lagging. MARTA (Metropolitan Atlanta Rapid Transit Authority) offers residents and visitors the treat of the South's first rapid-rail transit system. The east-west branches opened in 1979, and the first section of the north-south branch began service in late 1982. The full 53 miles will be completed in the late 1980s. MARTA's rapid rail is as much an attraction as a means of transportation. Don't miss it. Take a ride on the North line from Peachtree Center to the Arts Center where you can enjoy the theater, the museum, or the symphony; Colony Square across the street offers lovely dining at the Country Place and other eateries. Or take a ride from the Omni or Five Points Stations east to the town of Decatur. There you can lunch at the delightful restaurant Conversations, right on the square as you emerge from the underground. If you are from a small town, enjoy the Big City train and if you are from New York, Boston, or abroad enjoy the smoothest, quietest ride in the South.

A Word on Climate and Dress

A temperate climate adds to Atlanta's appeal for visitors and for both family and corporate relocation. Atlanta's high altitude of 1050 feet above sea level distinguishes it from most southern cities which experience long summer heat and humidity. Atlanta's elevation allows for four distinct seasons with spring and fall competing for the glory of climatic exuberance. Cold spells are short-lived, although Atlanta occasionally is surprised by an inch of snow in the winter. During the summer's hottest spells, the city averages less than three consecutive days above 90° F. You will find Atlanta informal in attire most of the year, but residents don black tie and flowing gowns for special social occasions. Coats and ties for men are the generally accepted rule although casual dress is accepted now in most establishments. Spring and summer call for lightweight clothes. Ladies should remember, however, the air-conditioned buildings. Autumn requires a light jacket or sweater. Carry a coat in winter. According to the former Mayor Ivan Allen, one of Atlanta's best attractions is her "altitude." Atlanta's weather makes a pleasant course throughout the entire year.

The City's People

Who are Atlantans? The population of the metro area is about 2 million. The local population continues to diversify. Southern accents, midwestern drawls, and northern twangs mix with foreign accents as newcomers move South because of job transfers, business opportunities and personal preferences. Old Atlanta families have a tradition of community service and a refreshing open social acceptance of newcomers from other parts of the country and the world. The city is experiencing moderate, steady immigration, especially among Hispanics, but Atlanta is not characterized by the ethnic neighborhood pattern prevalent in other large urban areas. The Atlanta black community is today a powerful political force in the city. Birthplace and burial place of civil-rights leader Dr. Martin

Luther King, Jr., Atlanta has always been on the forefront of the civil-rights movement in the South and in the nation. With the city's openness to social change and the election of a black mayor in the 1970s, and with its concentration of the largest per dollar investment in black business in the South, Atlanta becomes an attractive home for new black residents.

Who are Atlantans? They are the residents of the New South. You will find Atlanta a fine city to visit and revisit. Southerners have traditionally "gone to Atlanta" to shop, to eat, to attend the Metropolitan Opera, to seek their business fortunes, to be entertained, to meet people from all over the world, and to find new expressions of southern living. Now visitors beyond the South feel the lure of Atlanta, the touchstone of the New South.

MATTERS OF FACT

AAA — Georgia Motor Club, 875-7175.

Ambulance — Grady Memorial Hospital, 588-4141.

Area Code, telephone — 404.

Babysitter — Check with your hotel desk.

Calendar of Events — *Atlanta Magazine* and the Weekend Saturday supplement of the *Atlanta Journal-Constitution* for local daily events.

Climate — Annual Averages
Rainfall: 47.14 inches (120 cm).
Snow or ice: 1.6 inches (4 cm).
Clear days: 220.
Days above 90°F (32°C): 21.
Days below 32°F (0°C): 60.
Dryest month: October.
Rainiest month: March.
Coldest month: January.
Warmest month: July.
Wind: Northwest prevailing.

Dentist — Northern District Dental Society Referral Service, 294-3214 (8:30 am - 5:00 pm weekdays); 688-4234 (evenings and weekends).

Doctor — Medical Association of Atlanta Information and Referral Service, 881-1714 (9 am - 4 pm only; evenings and weekends contact hotel doctor or visit nearest hospital — see below).

Emergency Counseling — Fulton County, 572-2626.

Emergency Rooms — MedFirst (C4), 2945 N. Druid Hills Rd. NE; 325-2100. Sandy Springs Minor Emergency Center (A3), 5457 Roswell Rd. NE; 252-1900.

Fire — 911 or 659-2121.

Foreign Auto Service — Automotive Systems Research (C4), 1784 N. Decatur Rd. NE; 321-9400.

Gas Station, 24-hour — Jim Wallace Service Station (I12), 605 Boulevard NE at North Ave.; 874-6790.

Hospitals — Grady Memorial Hospital (K10), 80 Butler St. SE; 588-4307. Northside Hospital (B4), 1000 Johnson Ferry Rd. NE; 256-8000. Piedmont Hospital (C3), 1968 Peachtree Rd. NW; 355-7611.

Law — 577-HELP (9 am - 12 noon, 1:30 pm - 4:30 pm Mon-Fri), legal information over the telephone.

Lawyer — Atlanta Bar Association Referral Service, 521-0777.

Legal Aid — 524-5811.

Library, Public — Central Branch (J9), 1 Margaret Mitchell Square NE; 688-4636.

Local Laws — Liquor age requirements — must be 19 (18 if in service uniform); no sale of alcoholic beverages in stores, or before 12:30 pm in bars and restaurants on Sunday.

MATTERS OF FACT

MARTA bus and rail — 6 am - 10 pm weekdays; 8 am - 4 pm weekends; 522-4711.

Newspapers — *Atlanta Constitution, Atlanta Journal, Atlanta Daily World, Creative Loafing* (weekly).

Pets — Atlanta Humane Society; 875-0586. Leash Law in effect.

Pharmacy, 24-hour — Treasury Plaza Drugs (C4), 1061 Ponce de Leon Ave.; 874-8660.

Police — 911 or 658-6666.

Population — Approximately 2 million.

Post Office — Central City Station (K8), 183 Forsyth St.; 221-5307.

Radio Stations—
AM—
WPLO (590) Country
WCNN (680) News
WSB (750) Pop/Variety
WQXI (790) Pop/Oldies
WAEC (860) Christian
WGST (920) News
WKLS (970)—Album-Rock
WGUN (1010) Religious
WCGA (1050) Popular
WJYA (1080) Standards
WGKA (1190) Classical
WFOM (1230) Christian
WTJH (1260) Gospel
WCHK (1290) Gospel
WXLL (1310) Gospel
WIGO (1340) R & B
WLAW (1360) Variety
WAOK (1380) Urban-Dance
WMOE (1400) Popular
WAVO (1420) Religious
WDYX (1460) Country
WYZE (1480) Jazz-Gospel
WKRP (1500) Country
WDGL (1520) Christian
WZAL (1540) Popular
WYNX (1550) Christian
WSSA (1570) Christian
WCKZ (1600) Country

FM—
WRAS (88.5) Album-Rock
WRFG (89.3) Diversified
WABE (90.1) NPR-Classical
WREK (91.1) Diversified
WCLK (91.9) Jazz
WZGC (92.9) Top 40
WQXI (94.1) Adult-Rock
WPCH (94.9) Easy-listening
WKLS (96.1) Album-Rock
WSB (98.5) Pop-Rock
WRMM (99.7) Popular
WKHX (101.5) Country
WGCO (102.3) Country-Gospel
WVEE (103.3) Urban-Dance
WJYF (104.1) Standards
WCHK (105.5) Country
WWLT (106.7) Rock/Oldies

Senior Citizens — American Association of Retired Persons, 458-1491.

Social Services — United Way Information and Referral Service, 522-7370.

State Patrol — 656-6077.

Tickets — Omni Ticket Center, 577-9600; SEATS, 577-2626.

Time — 936-8550.

Time Zone — Eastern Standard (Daylight Savings plus 1 hour from April to October).

Tourist Information — Atlanta Convention and Visitors Bureau, 521-6600; Georgia Department of Tourism, 659-7000.

Traffic Laws, State — Right turn allowed on red light, except where posted. Headlights must be switched on when it is raining.

Traveler's Aid — 523-0585.

TV — ABC Channel 2; CBS Channel 5; NBC Channel 11; PBS Channels 8 and 30; WTBS Channel 17; WATL Channel 36; WANX Channel 46.

Weather — 936-8550.

TRANSPORTATION

Atlanta has been the hub of southeastern transportation since its official founding in the railroad era. The city now stars as the air capital of the Southeast. The following information will assist you in traveling to Atlanta by air, highway, rail, and bus and in getting around the metro area.

TO ATLANTA

Air

Atlanta's Hartsfield International Airport (E3) boasts the world's largest passenger terminal and is the second busiest airport in the world. The airport combines efficiency of land use in its relatively small site with both heightened fuel efficiency and maximum productivity, handling over fifty-five million passengers annually.

The airport is located nine miles south of the central city near the southern metro communities of College Park, East Point, Hapeville, and Forest Park. The airport site is in the convenient triangle formed by I-85, I-75, and I-285, with the airport exit on I-85.

The complex consists of the connected North and South Terminals, four domestic concourses, an International Terminal and concourse, and an underground transit mall. Signs, color codes, audio instructions, and space design guide you to your destination point. Remember the space in between the concourses accommodates two jumbo jets. Allow 15 to 20 minutes to proceed from gate to concourse to transit mall, then, via underground train or people-mover, to terminal and baggage claim. Concessions and amenities are located on the two connecting bridges of the terminals and on each concourse. A full-service restaurant, open 24 hours, is located on the eastern bridge.

Two major airlines have memberships in clubs that offer special amenities in their airport club rooms, such as complimentary soft drinks, cash bars, television, and telephone areas. Delta operates three

TRANSPORTATION

Crown Rooms and an International Crown Room in the Atlanta airport; Eastern has two Ionosphere Clubs.

Before you leave the airport, stop at the Georgia Welcome Center located at the top of the escalator between the two baggage concourses. A seven-minute, award-winning travel film will introduce you to the state of Georgia and Atlanta's central position in this context. The quick visual tour is without narrative. You can feel, see, and even smell Georgia's different regions in the multi-media presentation accompanied by a strong musical score. A real treat on your first or next trip to Atlanta.

Atlanta has non-stop air service to over 140 cities nationally, including San Juan, and direct service to 170 other cities, including Honolulu. International flights operate non-stop to such places as Amsterdam, Bermuda, Brussels, Frankfurt, London (Gatwick), Mexico City, and Nassau.

Airlines Serving Atlanta (with reservation and information telephone numbers)

Domestic

Atlantic Southeast.....996-4872	Ozark................688-9565
Delta................765-5000	Piedmont.............681-3100
Eastern..............435-1111	Republic.............762-5561
Frontier.............523-5487	Southeastern.....(800) 732-2000
Northwest Orient......577-3271	Sunbird.........(800) 438-7833

International

Bahamasair.......(800) 222-4262	Lufthansa........(800) 645-3880
British Caledonian.....(800) 231-0270	KLM...........(800) 556-7777
	Sabena..........(800) 645-3790
Delta................765-5000	TWA................522-5738
Eastern..............435-1111	

Ground Services To and From the Airport

Atlanta Airport Shuttle. Leaves airport every 30 minutes to major downtown hotels and Lenox Square. Cost $7.00 to Lenox; $5.25 to downtown hotels. 525-2177.

MARTA Bus. Public bus service between the airport and downtown Central Business District. Bus No. 72 leaves airport North Terminal between hours of 5:53 am and 12:29 am, approximately every 30 - 40 minutes in the morning, every 20 - 35 minutes midday, and every 50 minutes after 7:30 pm, 60¢ each way. 522-4711.

28   MARMAC GUIDE TO ATLANTA

Northside Airport Express. Leaves airport every 30 - 45 minutes to one of four terminals:
1. Presidential Drive (455-1600), Chamblee-Tucker Rd. at I-285 (B5).
2. Radisson Inn (455-1600), Chamblee-Dunwoody Rd. at I-285 (A4).
3. Memorial Drive (455-1600) at I-285 (C5).
4. Windy Hill Rd. (455-1600) at I-285 (A2).

Call terminals for departure times to the airport. Cost $7.00 one way, $13.00 round trip. 455-1600.

Taxi. Atlanta's taxis at the airport are a mixed bag of independent operators and name cabs. More restrictive ordinances recently in effect should make your ride a pleasant one. Cabs line up at the airport taxi stand. The approximate fare from the airport to downtown is about $15.

Animals — Ground Services To and From the Airport

Air Animal, Inc. If you are concerned about taking your pet cheetah or python on the plane with you, call Air Animal, Inc., a company that has the unusual specialty of flying animals around the world. They will take care of the documentation — health certificates and custom papers, provide a special animal crate, and transport your friend to the airport by limousine. Local number 761-0589.

Aircraft Rental and Charter

At **DeKalb-Peachtree Airport** (B4) in northeast Atlanta (457-7236), call **Epps Air Service Inc.** (458-9851), **Executive Helicopters Inc.** (458-6082), and **Dooley Helicopters** (458-3431).

Hangar One Inc. (768-1000) operates out of Fulton County Airport/Brown Field (C1), Hartsfield, and DeKalb-Peachtree airports. They provide charter services and maintenance.

Automobile ─────────────────────

Four interstate highways intersect in Atlanta. Georgia interstates are maintained in excellent driving condition.

I-85 runs Northeast to Southwest from South Carolina to Alabama.
I-75 runs Northwest to Southeast from Tennessee to Florida.
I-20 runs East to West from South Carolina to Alabama.

The fourth interstate circles the city, is approximately 12 miles from the central city, and is designated I-285, "the Perimeter."

We recommend calling your hotel or destination point when you reach I-285 to insure accurate exit directions from the interstates.

TRANSPORTATION

Since Atlanta interstates have both right and left lane exits and compulsory lane exits, specific travel directions coming into the city are very helpful.

Bus

Greyhound and Trailways each have a major terminal in downtown Atlanta. Both terminals are within the same block, next to Peachtree Center.
Greyhound Terminal (J9), 81 International Blvd. NW, 522-6300.
Southeastern Stages is at the same location, same number.
Trailways Terminal (J9), 200 Spring St. NW, 524-2441.

Rail

AMTRAK, 688-4417. Brookwood Station (C3) is at 1688 Peachtree St. NW, three miles north of the central city. The AMTRAK-operated "Cresent" provides the only regularly scheduled passenger service through Atlanta, the evening train leaving for Washington and New York and the morning train departing for New Orleans. Check current schedules.

AROUND ATLANTA

Auto Rental

Rental cars are available by the day, week, or longer. Rental locations include the airport and most major hotels. Major credit cards expedite the procedure. An international visitor's native driver's license is valid for car rental in Atlanta. As prices vary we suggest you call around to check rates that will suit your travel needs.

American International Rent-A-Car	530-2210
Avis Rent-A-Car	530-2700
Budget Rent-A-Car	530-3030
Dollar Rent-A-Car	530-3100
Gelco Leasing	768-8574
Hertz Rent-A-Car	530-2900
National Car Rental	530-2800
Thrifty Rent-A-Car	761-5286

Chauffeured Limousine Service:
Carey Limousine of Atlanta   681-3366
Sun Belt Limousine Inc.   524-3400

Private Car

Atlanta's city streets follow the ecological, curving patterns of the early Indian trails and railroad routes. The hills and winding streets add to the beauty of this tree-lined garden city, but can also add confusion to the traveler or newcomer who anticipates a rigid rectangular layout of the city. Streets sometimes change names at intersections so advance directions are advised. Major north-south arteries are Peachtree Street and Piedmont Road. Major east-west corridors are Memorial Drive on the southside, North Avenue, 14th Street, and West Paces Ferry Road on the northside. All these major streets have a comfortable volume and flow of traffic (even during rush hours) and provide easy access between downtown and the outgoing parts of the city.

The interstates I-75, I-85, and I-20 intersect within the city and also with the Perimeter interstate I-285, making all quadrants of the city and outlying areas accessible to the visitor. During rush hours, 7 - 9 am and 4 - 6:30 pm, the interstate traffic moves slowly, but steadily in and out of the city. Trucks are not permitted on I-75 and I-85 inside the Perimeter except by special permit for deliveries. Because of the speed and convenience of "crossing town" on the expressways, Atlantans use them extensively. With our trusty map and an adventurous spirit you too can traverse metro Atlanta by either street or interstate.

There is ample parking in downtown Atlanta, mainly in parking lots. Always carry sufficient change to cover maximum prepayment at some lots. Many downtown restaurants have complimentary parking with lunch and dinner, so be sure to inquire about this benefit. When necessary have your parking ticket validated by the restaurant or store before you leave.

In case of emergencies or in need of assistance:
AAA (Georgia Motor Club) 1110 Spring St.   875-7171
State Patrol   656-6077
Atlanta Police   658-6600

Public Transportation

MARTA (Metropolitan Atlanta Rapid Transit Authority) is the city's public transit system. It operates 142 public bus lines throughout metro Atlanta and a partially completed rapid-rail system. If your destination is on a MARTA route, we recommend MARTA's reliable and swift service. MARTA has been named the safest bus system in North America (for a population area of one million) by the American Public Transit Association.

Buses and trains sport a rainbow logo of blue, yellow, and orange. The 53-mile (85 kilometer), 41 station rail system is still under construction. However, the East-West line is fully operational, and the North-South line is open from the Arts Center to West End with stops at Garnett Street, Five Points, Peachtree Center, the Civic Center, North Avenue, and Midtown stations. By 1984 the system will be in service between Lenox Square on the northside and Lakewood on the southside. The following year the total MARTA North-South line is scheduled to be completed connecting Doraville and the airport.

Civic Center MARTA station   *Marge McDonald*

Trains run every 10 minutes during the day, every 15 minutes in the evenings and shut down between 1 and 5 am. Maps are available in the stations.

A trip on MARTA East line will give you a panoramic view of the central city and points south and north as you travel east to Decatur, Georgia.

Each MARTA rail station offers unique space design and lively art.

Like the airport, Atlanta's new rapid-transit structures are sights to see in themselves.

Bus stops are marked with concrete pillars or MARTA signs. For schedules and maps of bus routes call MARTA information 522-4711, 6 am to 10 pm weekdays, 8 am to 4 pm weekends.

Fare for both bus and rail is 60¢, exact change only, transfers are free; half dollar coins are not accepted by bus or train, pennies are accepted only by bus. The "Transcard" for unlimited rides on both bus and rail costs $5 per week, valid Sunday through Sunday, or $21 per month, valid from the first of the month, and is also available through branch offices of Georgia Power.

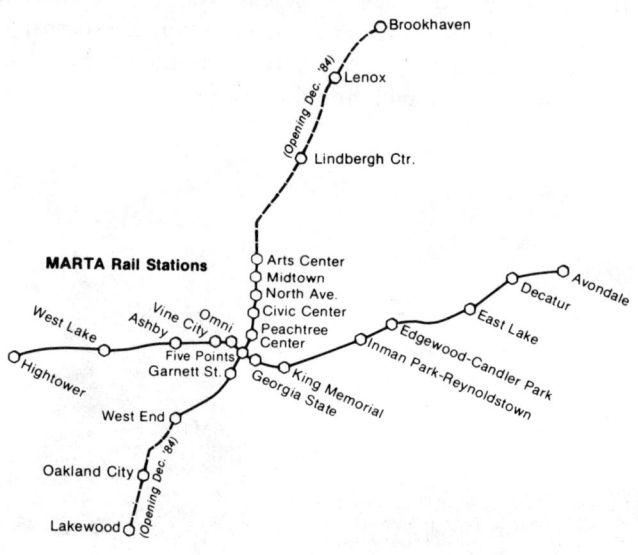

Taxi

Taxicabs line up at all major hotels. They are difficult to hail, so we suggest a phone call.

Cost is $1 plus $1 per mile, plus 25¢ each additional passenger, plus 4% sales tax. Taxi fare to the Airport from the Downtown Convention area for 3 passengers is $4.50 per passenger.

Approximate fares
Airport—Downtown	$14-15
Lenox—Downtown	$10
I-285—Downtown	$16-17

A few suggested Cab Companies
Checker Cab	525-5466
London Taxi	681-2280
Yellow Cab	522-0200

TRANSPORTATION

Tours

Several companies now offer daily sightseeing tours of the city and attractions near the city. Call for time and tours or check at your hotel. **Gray Line of Atlanta Tours,** 767-0594.

For Group Tours only, we recommend **TourGals,** an excellent special guide service available seven days a week, with multilingual guides available. 262-7660.

American Institute of Architects Tours offers group tours (minimum 30) by an architect-guide of contemporary architecture in Atlanta. Tours also tailored to special interests. 873-3207.

Atlanta Preservation Center offers guided and self-guided walking tours in Atlanta's historic districts including Inman Park and the Fox Theater. 522-4345.

Walking

The new breed of walker who enjoys a few hours seeing the city will be delighted with Atlanta's sidewalk ambience and cleanliness. We recommend the daylight hours for walking and taxi service during the evening. An excellent downtown starting point is Five Points at Central City Park. From there you can walk in all directions returning to the park or proceeding north to the arts center in midtown. A downtown walking tour is included in the SELF-GUIDED TOURS Chapter.

Peachtree Center MARTA station with granite walls intact   *Marge McDonald*

HOTEL SAFETY

As a public-safety service we include in this chapter the following guidance in case of a hotel fire. All information is taken from a publication of the National Safety Council.

Preliminary precautions start after you check into your hotel. Check the exits and fire alarms on your floor, count the doorways between your room and the exit, keep your key close to your bed and take it with you if you leave your room in case you need to return. In case smoke blocks your exit, check the window latches and any adjoining buildings or decks for low level escape.

In case of fire, take your key and crawl to the door. Don't stand; smoke and deadly gases rise.

If the doorknob is hot — *do not open* — stay in your room. Then open window, phone for help, hang a sheet from the window to signal for help; turn on the bathroom fan, fill the tub with water, wet towels and sheets to put around doors if smoke seeps in and make a tent over your head with a blanket at a partially opened window to get fresh air.

If the doorknob is *not* hot, leave, close the door to your room, proceed to the exit, counting doorways in the dark, and walk down to ground level. If blocked at lower levels, turn around, walk up to the roof and keep the roof door open to vent stairwell. Wait for help on the roof. **Do not use elevator. Remember to lay low to avoid smoke and gases.**

LODGING

The meeting center of the Southeast is also the prime innkeeper of the region. Atlanta's hotels, motels, and alternate accommodations are the contemporary resting places for both the first-timer and the repeat traveler to this busy city.

Atlanta has been a leader in new lodging concepts at both ends of the hospitality market. The city's unusual skyline is a remarkable testament to that fact. Architect John Portman revolutionized the large luxury-hotel development with his atrium and dramatic cylindrical hotel architecture; Omni International built the first hotel in their rapidly-growing chain; the late Cecil Day founded the Days Inn economy motel chain in Atlanta offering clean, no-frills lodging for the budget-minded traveler; and a new hotel corporation, The Ritz-Carlton, has made its formal entry in downtown and Buckhead locations. Atlanta's hotel development continues unabated as Portman and other developers and chains have announced recent plans to add new hotels within the next two years. Meanwhile, small hotels have sprung up and old ones have spruced up.

Most national and international hotel chains serve the Atlanta area in multiple locations, and there is a place for every visitor in every price range, offering a variety of services and facilities, including alternatives such as the increasingly popular bed-and-breakfast program, short-term leasing, living suite accommodations, home exchange, and a short selection of campgrounds in the metro area. To complete the picture, we list a selection of nearby resort hotels. Our selective listings will help you find the lodging of your choice.

Remember the code letters directly after the name reference each hotel or motel to the maps at the beginning of the book, giving you the section location of the lodging within the city. All hotels have restaurants unless otherwise stated. During weekends, holidays and off-seasons some hotels and resorts offer bargain package visits at greatly reduced rates.

The following key is used where applicable:
- *AP* American Plan (breakfast, lunch, and dinner)
- *MAP* Modified American Plan (breakfast and lunch or dinner)
- *FP* Family Plan (Refers to family room rates; check with individual hotel)
- *PA* Pets allowed
- *E* Expensive, more than $70 per double room per night
- *M* Moderate, $50 to $70
- *I* Inexpensive, less than $50

The listings are in three sub-sections: conventional lodgings — hotels and motels, alternative lodgings including campgrounds, and resorts.

HOTELS AND MOTELS

ATLANTA AMERICAN-QUALITY INN MOTOR HOTEL (J9), 160 Spring St. NW, Atlanta 30303; 688-8600. *M.* The location of this Quality Inn is central to downtown, across from the Trailways and Greyhound terminals, and within a block of Peachtree Center and the Apparel and Merchandise Marts. Facilities include two restaurants, a lounge, and pool *PA, FP.*

ATLANTA CABANA HOTEL (H11), 870 Peachtree St. NE, Atlanta 30308; 875-5511. *I.* This budget hotel has its original Sunset Strip architecture from the 1950s with a fountain in front, flashy chandelier, and white statues of Venus in the courtyard. Amenities include the *King's Inn* restaurant and lounge, pool, and courtesy airport transportation. *PA* Long-term rates available.

BEST WESTERN. *I* to *M.* The Best Western chain, easily identified by its gold crown logo, is the world's largest lodging chain and has numerous locations in metro Atlanta, each near a prime interest site. Restaurant, lounge with entertainment, and swimming pool are standard.

LODGING 37

Best Western Airport Inn (E2), 5021 Old National Hwy.; Atlanta 30337; 768-0040.
Best Western Bon Air Motel (A1), 859 Cobb Pkwy. SE, Marietta, GA 30062; 427-4676.
Ladha Best Western Hotel (J9), 70 Houston St. NE, Atlanta 30303; 659-2660. The Ladha has 233 rooms two blocks off Peachtree and the central business district, a convenient location for moderate downtown lodging with restaurant. *PA. FP* available.
Best Western Midtown Plaza (G11), 1470 Spring St. NW, Atlanta 30309; 872-5821.
Best Western Olde English Inn (D5), 1900 Glenfair Rd. Decatur, GA 30035; 288-7550. *I.*
Best Western Perimeter North Inn (B5), 2001 Clearview Ave. (off I-285), Atlanta 30340; 455-1811 or toll free (800) 528-1234.

BEVERLY HILLS INN (C3), 65 Sheridan Dr. NE, Atlanta 30305; 233-8520. *M.* A former apartment house in the Buckhead residential area has been transformed into a European-style Bed-and-Breakfast inn. The 17 units are decorated with period furniture and have natural wood floors and balconies. Breakfast is served in the Garden Room or on the patio. Fine restaurants are nearby.

CENTURY AIRPORT INN (F2), 1569 Phoenix Blvd. and I-285, Atlanta 30329; 996-4321. *I.* Conveniently located in the airport area, Century Inn provides for corporate meetings with the *Phoenix* restaurant and the lounge *Sam's Place.* Added amenities are a swimming pool and free transportation to the airport. *PA.*

COLONY SQUARE HOTEL (G12), 14th and Peachtree Sts. NE, Atlanta 30361; 892-6000. *M to E.* The Colony Square Hotel is in the midtown section of Atlanta, only a few miles from downtown and from Buckhead. The hotel is situated on the southern end of a beautiful modern complex of office towers, condominiums, retail mall, and restaurants. The AT&T building and the Robert W. Woodruff Arts Center are directly across the street, and the restored Ansley Park neighborhood adjoins the northern flank. The fine Southern Conference Center is available with comprehensive business services. Restaurants include the elegant prix-fixe French restaurant *Toulouse,* the *Trellises,* and the *Crown Room* at the upper level with its Friday special and Sunday buffets. The *Veranda Bar* which terraces from the hotel into the tree-studded mall is one of

Atlanta's most popular after-work meeting places. Weekend packages and multi-lingual staff are available.

COMFORT INN (H9), 120 North Ave. NW, Atlanta 30313; 881-6788. *I to M.* The Comfort Inn is convenient to Georgia Tech, at North Avenue and I-85/I-75. The restaurant is open for breakfast and lunch. Enjoy this small, spiffy hotel with pool and accessibility to the interstates and downtown. The Comfort Inn also rents to Tech students on a quarterly basis.

DAYS INNS OF AMERICA. *I.* These hotels are designed for the budget-minded and the large family or group traveling together. Days Inns maintain a high standard of management; most Inns have outdoor swimming pools, restaurants, gas stations, and playgrounds. Days Lodges offer suites with full kitchens, a living room with sleep sofa for two, and a bedroom with two double beds. For both Days Inns and Days Lodges call 320-2000 for reservations, 320-2020 for group reservations. Check your local directory for toll-free numbers to make advance reservations from your area.

Days Inn (J9), 300 Spring St., Atlanta 30303; 523-1144. *I to M.* Atlanta-based Days Inn has opened its premier inn downtown across from the Apparel Mart, the Merchandise Mart, and Peachtree Center. The 267 units provide exemplary lodging at reasonable prices. A fine restaurant serves breakfast, lunch and dinner.

Days Inn (D4), I-20 and Wesley Chapel Rd., Decatur, GA 30034; 288-7110.

Days Inn Chamblee-Tucker (B5), 2768 Chamblee-Tucker Rd. off I-85, Chamblee, GA 30341; 458-8711.

Days Inn Clairmont (B4), 2910 Clairmont Rd. off I-85, Atlanta, 30329; 633-8411.

Days Inn Cleveland Ave. (E3), 2788 Forest Hills Drive, Atlanta 30315; 768-7750.

Days Inn Old Stone Mountain (B4), 2461 Old Stone Mtn. Rd., Chamblee, GA 30341; 458-9323.

Days Inn Six Flags (D1), 4120 Fulton Industrial Blvd. (off I-20), Atlanta 30336; 696-4690.

Days Lodge Atlanta Airport East (E3), 4888 Frontage Rd., Forest Park, GA 30050; 363-0800.

Days Lodge Buford (B4), 4815 Buford Hwy., Chamblee, GA 30341; 458-8011.

Days Lodge Shallowford (B5), 2792 Shallowford Rd. off I-85, Chamblee GA 30341; 458-8821.

LODGING 39

THE DOWNTOWNER (D3), 231 Ivy St. NE, Atlanta 30308; 577-1510. *I.* This moderately priced hotel is in the downtown convention district next to Peachtree Center. The Good Ol' Days restaurant at the Downtowner is a favorite lunch spot.

DUNFEY ATLANTA HOTEL (C2), 1750 Commerce Dr. NW, Atlanta 30381; 351-6100. *M.* The Dunfey is located at I-75 and Howell Mill Road, convenient by interstate to downtown and the Perimeter I-285. This recently renovated hotel in a contemporarized English country-inn style of half timbers and turrets is a popular convention hotel with four restaurants and lounges, and with recreational facilities including an outdoor swimming pool, tennis courts,

THE EXECUTIVE VILLAS HOTEL (A3), 5735 Roswell Rd. NE, Atlanta 30342; 252-2868. *M.* This attractive hotel at Roswell Road and I-285, features short-term leasing for its one-, two-, and three-bedroom suites. All suites have dining rooms, Thomasville furnishings, designer-selected accessories, and fully equipped kitchens. The Executive Villas Hotel is an excellent choice for families relocating in Atlanta or for the business person on an extended stay. The living room is ideal for comfortable business meetings and receptions. Daily, weekly, and monthly rates are available.

GUEST QUARTERS (A4), 111 Perimeter Center West, Atlanta 30346; 396-6800. *M to E.* This hotel company pioneered the "all suites" hotel in Atlanta with a garden apartment complex. The Guest Quarters in Perimeter off I-285 and Ashford-Dunwoody Road is a luxurious highrise with one- and two-bedroom suites that include a separate living room, dining area, and full kitchen. It is oriented toward personal attention with 24-hour suite service for private dining in your suite, a club restaurant, airport transportation available, comprehensive secretarial services, and a beautiful outdoor swimming pool. Perimeter Center is an exciting area with shops, restaurants, and offices. *PA.* Daily and weekly rates available. Guest Quarters (A3) is also located at 7000 Roswell Rd., Atlanta 30328; 394-6300.

HABERSHAM HOTEL (J10), 330 Peachtree St. NE, Atlanta 30308; 577-1980. *M.* A small, personal downtown hotel, the Habersham prides itself on its location (a block from Peachtree Center) on its executive-size rooms with wet bar and refrigerator, on its Habersham Club in the European tradition serving complimentary breakfast in the mornings and cocktails and hors d'oeuvres in the evenings, and on its professional concierge staff. The Habersham is a quiet refined lodging especially attractive to international visitors who enjoy the personal touch. Dining is easily available within walking distance at Peachtree Center. *FP,* weekend packages, and long-term rates are available.

THE HARLEY HOTEL OF ATLANTA (E2), 3601 Desert Dr. (Camp Creek Pkwy. and I-285), East Point, GA 30344; 762-5141. *M.* This business person-oriented hotel, convenient to the airport, also offers excellent weekend packages for families. Tennis courts, indoor-outdoor pool, and sauna.

HILTON HOTELS. This premier international hotel company has impressive Atlanta credentials. Hilton hotels are stationed in downtown Atlanta, in the airport district, on the Perimeter I-285 next to Northlake Mall, and the newest off I-75 and Windy Hill Road, each a luxury accommodation in the respective areas. Room reservations worldwide (800) 282-5806.

Atlanta Hilton Hotel (J10), Courtland and Harris Sts. NE, Atlanta 30303; 659-2000. *M to E.* The gleaming-white downtown Hilton Hotel is an imposing trylon with the Hilton logo a signal mark in the urban skyline. Inside, the atrium lobby is alive with flowers, sculpture, and inviting seating and meeting spaces, bordered by a promenade of gift shops. On this level is the restaurant *Cafe de la Paix,* downstairs is the world-known *Trader Vic's* restaurant, and atop the hotel is the famous Russian restaurant, *Nikolai's Roof,* plus a glittering disco lounge. This Hilton also offers resort-style facilities including four lighted tennis courts, a health club, and an outdoor jogging track and swimming pool. Foreign languages are spoken in this showcase luxury hotel of 1200 rooms. *PA. FP* and long-term rates available.

Atlanta Hilton Towers Hotel (J10), Courtland and Harris Sts. NE, Atlanta 30303; 659-2000. *E.* The top three floors of the Hilton Hotel downtown are designated The Towers — very special luxury lodging within this elegant hotel. The separate Towers lobby has a living-room atmosphere with help-yourself continental breakfast, afternoon snacks, and a fully-stocked bar available for guests' pleasure and convenience on the traditional honor system. A full-time concierge is on duty for personal attention and for immediate check-in and check-out. Suites available. *PA.*

Atlanta Airport Hilton Hotel (E3), Atlanta Airport, 1031 Virginia Ave., Atlanta 30320; 767-0281. M. This Hilton Hotel services the airport-area visitor with a 24-hour courtesy shuttle to and from the airport. Amenities include an outdoor swimming pool, lighted tennis

LODGING 41

courts, putting greens, and a children's playground. *Lulubelle's Steak House* is the major in-house restaurant. *PA, AP, MAP,* and *FP* available.
Northlake Hilton Inn (B5), 4156 LaVista Rd. at I-285, Tucker, GA 30084; 938-1026. *M.* Convenient to office parks, a shopping mall, and popular restaurants in the area, the Hilton offers a swimming pool, restaurant, and lounge.
Northwest Atlanta Hilton Inn (A2), 2055 South Park Place, Atlanta 30339; 953-9300. *M.* At the intersection of I-75 and Windy Hill Road, another first class Hilton is available for travelers in the northwest metro area. This Hilton offers an indoor-outdoor swimming pool and jacuzzi and three restaurants to choose from, including the gourmet *Landau Room.* Club level suites available.

HOLIDAY INNS. *I* to *M.* This well-established chain will meet your expectations for excellent, moderately priced lodging. All properties have restaurants, pools, and entertainment. One of the newest Holiday Inns deserves special note:
Holiday Inn (A3), Powers Ferry and I-285, NW, Atlanta 30339; 955-1700. This elegant hotel boasts almost 200 rooms and has an indoor and outdoor pool, saunas, game room, live entertainment in the lounge, and direct airport transportation service. *PA.*
Also at the following locations:
Holiday Inn Airport (E2), 1380 Virginia Ave., East Point, GA 30320; 762-8411.
Holiday Inn Airport South (F2), 5010 Old National Hwy. off I-285, Atlanta 30349; 761-4000.
Holiday Inn Downtown (J10), 175 Piedmont Ave. NE, Atlanta 30303; 659-2727. *PA.*
Holiday Inn I-85 Northcrest-Pleasantdale Rd. (A5), 4422 NE Expressway, Doraville, GA 30340; 448-7220.
Holiday Inn I-20 East (D4), 4300 Snapfinger Woods Dr., Decatur, GA 30032; 981-5670.
Holiday Inn Monroe Drive (C3), 1944 Piedmont Cir. NE, Atlanta 30324; 875-3571. (Monroe Dr. exit off I-85.)
Holiday Inn North (A2), 2360 Delk Rd., Marietta, GA 30067; 952-8161. (Exit I-75 just north of I-285.)
Holiday Inn Northwest (C3), 1810 Howell Mill Rd. off I-75, Atlanta 30325; 351-3831.
Holiday Inn Six Flags (C1), 4225 Fulton Industrial Blvd. SW, Atlanta 30336; 691-4100. (One exit from Six Flags on I-20 West.)
Holiday Inn South (E3), I-75 and US 41, 6288 Old Dixie Hwy., Jonesboro, GA 30236; 968-4300.

HOTEL YORK (I10), 683 Peachtree St. NE, Atlanta 30308; 874-9200. *I to M.* The Hotel York is a restored structure in the theater district, directly across from the Fox Theatre in Midtown. The atmosphere is one of personal service in this charming hotel. The Plush Room is one of Atlanta's finest cabarets. The Palms Restaurant is superior and open 24 hours. *FP (12 and under).*

HOWARD JOHNSON'S. *I.* This national company, which pioneered the motor lodge concept across America, has superior facilities in Atlanta at its seven locations. For children, Howard Johnson's has meant an ice-cream parlor of a million flavors, for seafood lovers a plateful of crispy fried clams, and for traveling Americans all across the country a dependable standard of lodging and dining. Standard features include restaurant, lounge and swimming pool. Toll-free (800) 654-2000. *PA. FP* and long-term rates available.

Howard Johnson's (J9), 100 Tenth St. NW, Atlanta 30390; 892-6800.

Howard Johnson's Atlanta West (C1), 4330 Fulton Industrial Blvd. off I-20, Atlanta 30336; 696-2274.

Howard Johnson's Motor Lodge Airport (E3), 1377 Virginia Ave., Atlanta 30344; 762-5111.

Howard Johnson's Motor Lodge Northeast (C4), 2090 North Druid Hills Rd. off I-85, Atlanta 30329; 636-8631.

Howard Johnson's Motor Lodge Northwest (C3), 1701 Northside Dr., NW off I-75, Atlanta 30318; 351-6500.

Howard Johnson's Motor Lodge South (L8), 759 Washington St. off I-75/85, Atlanta 30315; 688-8665.

Howard Johnson's Sandy Springs (A3), 5793 Roswell Rd., Sandy Springs off I-285, GA 30328; 252-6400.

HYATT REGENCY ATLANTA (J9), 265 Peachtree St., Atlanta 30303 (downtown in Peachtree Center); 577-1234 or toll-free (800) 228-9000. *E.* The Hyatt Corporation, now one of the fastest growing hotel chains in the world, gained its impetus for growth with the success of its Hyatt Regency Atlanta hotel in 1967. This hotel with its soaring lobby started the international trend in open-atrium hotel design. The twinkling bubble elevators, interior sidewalk cafe, multi-storied metal sculpture by Richard Lippold, and *Le Parasol* bar make the lobby a thrilling place to meet for business, a social date, or sightseeing. At about 5 pm, the pianist at his grand piano over the front entrance serenades the end of the working day and the beginning of nightlife in Atlanta. Flowers, plants, and birds add a

The Ritz-Carlton Buckhead   *The Ritz-Carlton Buckhead*

natural element to the lobby environment, and the parrots "talking" is a nice touch of humor in such a grand hotel. Fine continental dining is featured at *Hugos,* and a provincial atmosphere with rotisserie and great beef dishes is part of the *Clock of 5's* restaurant experience. Enjoy the *Polaris* lounge view of Atlanta, 41 minutes to turn full circle, and enter the international *Club Atlantis* for some of the most sophisticated shows in the city. Several languages spoken. *PA.*

The Regency Club (J9), 265 Peachtree St. NE, Atlanta 30303; 577-1234. *E.* This club on the 22nd floor of the Hyatt Regency Atlanta is designed exclusively for the VIP traveler. Amenities include two morning newspapers in each room and the traditional Hyatt turn-down service at night, but with cordials and a rose as added luxuries. The club lounge serves complimentary continental breakfast in the morning and hors d'oeuvres in the evening for club guests.

JOURNEY'S END (A2), 1170 Powers Ferry Pl., Marietta, GA 30062; 952-9451. *M.* If you are looking for a relaxed resort setting in Atlanta, you have come to your Journey's End. Here, off I-75 at the Lockheed-Dobbins exit, is a relaxing south-seas setting, ten acres of waterfalls, duck ponds, lush greenery, and rustic architecture. Rooms, suites, and townhouses are available, with fireplaces in each suite.

LANIER PLAZA HOTEL AND CONFERENCE CENTER (C3), I-85 and Monroe Dr. NE, Atlanta 30024; 873-4661. This is an unusual hotel, housing a conference and training center for Lanier, the Atlanta-based high-tech company and also offering convention services and lodging for individuals. The hotel has paid beautiful attention to detail from the landscaping and garden courtyard to the distinctive cuisine in *Seasons, the Steak Club* restaurant and soft elegance of the *Reflections Lounge.*

LENOX INN (B3), 3387 Lenox Rd. NE, Atlanta 30326; 261-5500. *I to M.* This attractive inn, across from Lenox Square, is a pleasant motel for out-of-town shoppers. Amenities include the long established seafood restaurant, the Nantucket Tavern, lounge, pool, and tennis courts.

MARRIOTT HOTELS. The first Marriott downtown was the first bud in Atlanta's blossoming hotel development. The later additions on the perimeter and near the airport maintain the same quality management and guest service. Toll-free (800) 228-9290.

LODGING 45

Atlanta Marriott Hotel (J10), Courtland St. and International Blvd. NE, Atlanta 30343; 659-6500 or toll-free (800) 228-9290. M to E. The wonderful courtyard in southern tradition allows for year-round swimming with its retractable glass roof. Enjoy the health club, sauna, and hydro-therapy pool. Guests are extended tennis privileges at Eastlake Country Club and golf privileges at Fairington Golf and Tennis Club. This Marriott has been since the 1960s a popular place for downtown business lunches and visiting professional athletes. Several languages spoken. PA, AP and FP available.

Atlanta Marriott Northwest (A2), 200 Interstate North Parkway, Atlanta 30339; 952-7900 or toll-free (800) 228-9290. (Off I-75 at Windy Hill Rd. exit.) M to E. Marriott's Interstate North hotel with its entry drive of rolling hills, features a restaurant and lounge, indoor-outdoor pool, tennis courts, and health club. FP, weekend package plan, and longer term rates are available.

Courtyard by Marriott. M. A recent development by Marriott hotels, the Courtyards are smaller hotels designed around a landscaped courtyard. Amenities include king-size beds, a hydro-therapy pool, meeting rooms, a restaurant, and lounge. Three locations are near major hospital and office complexes. **Courtyard Peachtree-Dunwoody** (A4), 5601 Peachtree-Dunwoody Rd., Atlanta 30342. **Courtyard Windy Hill** (A2), 2045 S. Park Pl., Atlanta 30339. **Courtyard Northlake** (B5), 4083 LaVista Rd., Tucker GA 30084.

Marriott Hotel Atlanta Airport (E2), 4711 Best Rd., College Park, GA 30337; 766-7900 or toll-free (800) 228-9290. M to E. Located at I-285 and I-85, the Marriott is the giant of the airport hotels with over 650 rooms, two restaurants, three lounges, and live entertainment. Recreational amenities include indoor-outdoor swimming pools, tennis courts, a weight room, and health club. FP and weekend package plans are available.

Marriott at Perimeter Center (A4), 246 Perimeter Center Pkwy., Atlanta 30346; 394-6500 or toll-free (800) 228-9290. M to E. (Off Ashford-Dunwoody Rd. exit from I-285.) Being situated next to Perimeter Center is a plus for this hotel. Sports facilities include lighted tennis courts, an indoor-outdoor swimming pool, sauna, and hydro-therapy pool. FP and longer term rates are available.

MASTER HOSTS INN I-75 NW (A2), 2375 Delk Rd., Marietta, GA 30060; 952-8141. I. One hundred rooms are available at this location near the Lockheed-Dobbins Air Force exit on I-75. ThermaCuZZi hydro-massage steam baths are special amenities.

THE RITZ-CARLTON. This hotel company stakes out a prominent and prestigious place in the international hotel industry of the 1980s. *E.* (800) 241-3333. Introduced in 1983 the Ritz-Carlton Hotels are sited in two of Atlanta's prime locations, downtown and across from Lenox Square.

Ritz-Carlton, Atlanta (J9), 181 Peachtree St.; 659-0400. The Ritz-Carlton in the heart of the city has rooms and suites tailored to executive clientele as well as individual and international travelers seeking Old World elegance, impressive amenities, and attentive service. A fine gourmet restaurant, two cocktail lounges, and small executive conference rooms are featured.

Ritz-Carlton, Buckhead (B3), 3434 Peachtree St. NE. 237-2700 *E.* The Ritz-Carlton, a contemporary, upscale hotel has three restaurants, two lounges and proudly overlooks the south's honored Lenox Square Shopping Center and is adjacent to Phipp's Plaza. This dramatic luxury hotel with its handsome scalloped tower includes an executive health spa, sun deck, and multiple services and facilities for business conventions and social groups.

OMNI INTERNATIONAL HOTEL (J8), 1 Omni International, Atlanta 30303; 659-0000 or toll-free (800) 241-5500. *E.* The hotel is modern European elegance, with large abstract paintings, marble floors, and oriental vases. The design tone is complemented by a largely European staff and a gourmet restaurant — the northern Italian *Bugatti*. The Omni hotel is integrated into the Omni sports coliseum, the World Congress Center, and the vast shopping mall. *PA.* Weekend packages and a multi-lingual staff are available.

PASCHAL'S MOTOR HOTEL (D3), 830 Martin Luther King Jr. Dr. SW, Atlanta 30314; 577-3150. *I.* Paschal's has been serving the black community and visitors on the southside for many years. Its location is convenient to Atlanta University. Amenities include a restaurant and lounge, an outdoor swimming pool, and free parking. Longer-term rates are available.

POST INN (B2), 1500 Parkwood Cir. off Powers Ferry Rd., Atlanta 30339; 952-9595. *E.* Offering roomy suites in a park-like atmosphere, this new hotel offers complimentary continental breakfasts, whirlpool and spa, tennis courts, a library, and a range of personal aids from secretarial services to babysitters. A relaxed and beautifully landscaped home away from home with the Chattahoochee River Recreation Area only a short walk away.

RADISSON INNS. M. Atlanta Radisson Inns are located on interstate connections and service the business visitor as well as the tourist.

Radisson Inn Atlanta (A4), I-285 and Chamblee-Dunwoody Rd., Atlanta 30341; 394-5000 or toll-free (800) 228-9822. M. Located on the northern arc of the Perimeter, the Radisson is a consistent choice for business conferences in Atlanta.

The Radisson Inn and Conference Center — Atlanta Central (C2), 1750 Commerce Dr. NW, Atlanta 30381; 351-6100. M. The Radisson is located at I-75 and Howell Mill Road. This English country-inn style hotel is a popular convention hotel with four restaurants and lounges. Facilities include an outdoor pool, tennis courts, basketball, and volleyball courts, FP and long term rates are available.

RAMADA INNS. *I to M.* This moderate-price motel chain is known for cleanliness, good management, and strategic location. Toll-free (800) 228-2828.

Ramada Capitol Plaza Hotel (L8), 450 Capitol Ave. SE, Atlanta 30312; 688-1900. M. Across from the Atlanta/Fulton County Stadium off I-75/85 this large hotel is ideally located for sports events at the stadium and for business and pleasure in the downtown area. Free shuttle service is regularly scheduled to the airport and downtown.

Ramada Inn Airport (E3), 845 North Central Ave., Hapeville, GA 30354; 763-3551.

Ramada Inn Central (C3), 1630 Peachtree St. NW, Atlanta 30367; 875-9711. M. The Ramada features a garden courtyard with pool, excellent lodging just off I-85, and a restaurant and lounge with live entertainment. *FP (18 and under) PAC.*

Ramada Inn Marietta (A2), 2255 Delk Rd. off I-75, Marietta, GA 30067; 952-7581.

Ramada Inn Shallowford (B5), 2960 NE Expressway at I-85, Atlanta 30341; 451-5231.

Ramada Inn Six Flags (C1), 305 Industrial Circle SW, off I-20, Atlanta 30336; 691-9390.

RAMADA RENAISSANCE (E2), 4736 Best Rd., College Park, GA 30337; 762-7676. *M to E.* This impressive hotel in the airport area has an elegant lobby, 496 rooms and suites, and an array of amenities including a health club, game room, indoor pool, sauna, and the Renaissance Club level with open bar and 24-hour concierge. Add the *Summerfield's* 24-hour restaurant, the *Lobby Bar, La Martine* nightclub and disco and finally the reservations-only French restaurant, *Le Cygne*.

RODEWAY INN (H10), 330 W. Peachtree St., Atlanta 30308; 577-6970. M. Formerly the Downtown Motel, this hotel has been completely renovated, offering 101 rooms and within a stone's throw of all that's happening downtown. The Rodeway features Atlanta's only 24-hour deli and full-service restaurant, *Ronnie's*, with 450 items on its menu. *PA, FP.*

SHERATON HOTELS. *M to E.* The Sheraton Hotel company has a respected history of fine lodging here and abroad. Expect to find good restaurants and swimming pools in all locations along with personal attention. Toll free (800) 325-3535.

Sheraton-Atlanta Hotel (I10), 590 W. Peachtree St. NW, Atlanta 30308; 881-6000. This large luxury hotel is conveniently accessible to downtown and to I-85/I-75 at the North Avenue exit. Special suites with their own swimming pools are available. Featured on the top floor with a vista of downtown is a superb restaurant with brass decor and the adjoining *Okefenokee Lounge* for cocktails and dancing. Also visit *Ashley's*, the Sheraton's fashionable lobby bar. *PA. FP*, weekend package plans, and longer-term rates available.

Sheraton Century Center Motor Hotel (B4), 2000 Century Blvd. NE, Atlanta 30345; 325-0000. On I-85 at Clairmont Road, the Century Center Complex includes the Sheraton Hotel and a beautifully landscaped and sculpted office park. This is a favorite convention and meeting hotel with an atrium interior, two restaurants, and three lounges with live entertainment. Heated outdoor swimming pool and lighted tennis courts are featured amenities. *PA. FP* and multi-lingual staff available.

Sheraton Cumberland Inn (B2), 1200 Winchester Ave. off I-285, Smyrna, GA 30080; 432-8541. *PA.*

Sheraton Emory Inn (C4), 1641 Clifton Rd. NE, Atlanta 30329; 633-4111. Near Emory University and hospital and across from the Centers for Disease Control.

Sheraton Inn Atlanta Airport (E2), 1325 Virginia Ave., Atlanta 30344; 768-6660.

Sheraton Northlake Inn (B5), 2180 Northlake Pkwy. off I-285, Tucker, GA 30084; 939-8120.

SQUIRE INNS. *I.* These inns, long popular with traveling business people, are known for friendly service and good management.

Squire Inn Northwest (A2), 2767 Windy Hill Rd. off I-75 NW, Marietta, GA 30067; 952-3251.

Squire Inn Sandy Springs (A3), 5750 Roswell Rd. off I-285, Atlanta 30328; 252-5782.

STONE MOUNTAIN INN (C6), P.O. Box 775, Stone Mountain Park, Stone Mountain, GA 30086; 469-3311. *I.* Enjoy this lovely small motel in the southern-plantation style, and the surrounding facilities and attractions of Stone Mountain Park. Swimming pool, tennis courts, golf course, and the lake and its beach await the sportsman, business person, and vacationer. The daily buffet at the Stone Mountain Inn restaurant is superb. *PA. FP,* weekend package, and longer-term rates.

TERRACE GARDEN INN (B3), 3405 Lenox Rd. NE, Atlanta 30326; 261-9250. *M.* The Terrace Garden Inn, across from Lenox Square shopping center and one block from Phipps Plaza, is a contemporary hotel combining informality and sophistication. The *Gardentree Restaurant* allows superb continental dining overlooking a waterfall and flower garden. The lounges are spacious and inviting, swimming and tennis is available, and courtesy transportation to Lenox, Phipps, and Buckhead is available for guests. *PA.* Weekend package plan and long-term rates are available.

TOWER PLACE HOTEL (B3), 3340 Peachtree Rd., Atlanta 30026; 231-1234. *M.* Tower Place Hotel is a medium-size hotel in the Buckhead area near the intersection of Piedmont and Peachtree Roads. It is part of the Tower Place complex of office tower and mall, which is convenient to Lenox Square and Buckhead. The service is especially attentive; expect the nice touch of a complimentary newspaper and turned-down beds. The *Tower Rib Room* is an excellent hotel restaurant.

TRAVELODGE. *I.* This moderately priced national motel chain serves you in three selected Atlanta locations, with complimentary coffee, swimming facilities, and long-term rates.
  Atlanta Central Travelodge (J10), 311 Courtland St. NE, Atlanta 30303; 659-4545. Complimentary coffee and danish each morning. *Good Ol' Days Restaurant* within the hotel.
  Peachtree Travelodge (C3), 1641 Peachtree St. NE (off I-75/85), Atlanta 30309; 873-5731.
  Travelodge at Executive Park (C4), 2061 North Druid Hills Rd. at I-85, Atlanta 30329; 321-4174.
  Travelodge South (F4), 6326 Old Dixie Hwy., Jonesboro, GA 30236; 968-4700.

THE WAVERLY STOUFFER HOTEL (B2), Galleria Parkway, Atlanta 30339; 953-4500 or toll-free (800) 325-5000. *E.* Opened in April 1983 in the majestic Galleria complex, this 14-story, open-atrium luxury hotel has a complete health club for guests, a club level, and over 50,000 square feet of meeting and banquet space. *Cinnabar,* the fine food restaurant, *Petals of Jade* for Chinese cuisine, and *Alfresco* the 24-hour restaurant plus the 5 other eateries provide an array of dining pleasures. The *Ritz* bar features class entertainment. The Waverly is in the fast-growing Cumberland Mall area, popular with tourists, business groups, and shoppers.

THE WESTIN PEACHTREE PLAZA HOTEL (J9), Peachtree St. and International Blvd., Atlanta 30343; 659-1400 or toll-free (800) 283-3000. *E.* The world's tallest hotel, a glass cylinder of 73 stories, the Westin Peachtree Plaza Hotel is John Portman's second hotel extravaganza in Peachtree Center. The lobby lake in the seven-story atrium has scalloped "pods" extending into the water, where you can enjoy your afternoon or evening refreshment listening to the soft music of strolling musicians. The outside glass elevator is a "must" ascent for a panoramic view of Atlanta. Treat yourself at the top of the *Sun Dial* revolving restaurant and cocktail lounges for fine cuisines and a memorable impression of this city. The hotel boasts an outstanding seafood restaurant, the *Savannah Fish Company,* a nightclub with live entertainment, a full health club, and indoor-outdoor swimming. Several languages spoken including Chinese. *PA, AP, MAP, FP,* and longer-term rates available.

Listed below are additional hotels, some for the economy-minded traveler.

Atlantan Hotel (J9), 111 Luckie St. NW, Atlanta 30303; 524-7000. *I.*

Decatur Inn (C4), 921 Church St., Decatur, GA 30030; 378-3125. *I.*

Downtowner Midtown Inn (J10), 1152 Spring St. NW, Atlanta 30309; 875-3511. *I.*

Emory Pines Inn (C4), 1650 Clifton Rd. NE, Atlanta 30329; 634-5152. *I.* Near Emory University, Emory Hospital, and the Centers for Disease Control.

Friendship Inn-Dogwood Motel (B5), 5140 Buford Hwy., Doraville, GA 30340; 457-7246. *I.*

King's Motor Inn (E3), 4772 South Expressway, Forest Park, GA 30050; 363-1100. *I.*

Mark Inn, Southwest (E2), 4498 Washington Rd. off I-285, East Point, GA 30344; 768-8620. *I.*

Matador Master Hosts Inn (C1), 95 Six Flags Service Rd., Austell, GA 30001; 941-2600. *I.*

Northwoods Motel (A5), 5114 Buford Hwy., Doraville, GA 30340; 457-5221. *I.*

Royal Inn of Atlanta, Airport (E3), 301 N. Central Ave. off I-75, Hapeville, GA 30354; 763-2511. *I.*

Sky Host Inn (E2), 1360 Virginia Ave., East Point, GA 30344; 761-5201. *I.*

University Inn (C4), 1767 North Decatur Rd., Atlanta 30307; 634-7327. *I.*

ALTERNATIVE LODGING

Bed-and-Breakfast Atlanta, 1221 Fairview Rd. NE, Atlanta 30306; 378-6026. *I to M.* The British bed-and-breakfast tradition in lodging has come to Atlanta. Fifty Atlanta homes, many of them close to the downtown business area, offer a private guest room with bath and continental breakfast for a moderate fee. The Bed-and-Breakfast organization brings the visitor who wishes to stay in a private home together with homeowners interested in housing guests overnight. Transportation accessibility, language needs, and attitudes about pets and smoking are all taken into consideration in matching host and guest. This is a person-to-person opportunity for Atlanta visitors.

Travelers' Home Exchange Club, Inc., P.O. Box 1511, Denver, CO 80201; (303) 841-4226. This club with a U.S. office in Denver and a branch in England publishes a directory of home exchange listings as well as providing services for rental properties and host exchanges. The charge is about $50 to list your home or to order the directory.

Vacation Exchanges, 350 Broadway, New York, NY 10013; (212) 966-2576. Vacation Exchanges is a home-exchange bureau serving the United States and forty other countries. There is a lister's fee which includes a book listing everyone who is registered. Allow two to three months planning time for vacations abroad. Home-exchange is an alternate form of vacation offering a less expensive and more personal view of the country.

Campgrounds

Atlantans have a number of campgrounds that provide rest and relaxation in a natural setting within an hour's drive from the city. Camping travelers can reverse this flow — come into the city at their leisure and then return to their campsite for lodging. We list three well designed and managed camping areas for your consideration. Rates are nominal.

Lake Lanier Islands Authority, P.O. Box 605, Buford, GA 30518; 945-6701. *I.* Lake Lanier is managed by the Army Corps of Engineers and has 340 campsites for tents and trailers in the coves and on the points of this magnificent recreational lake. Electrical and water hook-ups are available. Lake Lanier is northeast of the city; take I-85 north to GA 365, exit 2 onto Friendship Rd.

Red Top Mountain, Route 2, Cartersville, Georgia 30120; 974-5183. *I.* This campground is 1 ½ miles east of I-75; take the Red Top exit. Red Top has 286 tent and trailer sites, rental cottages, a swimming beach, boating ramp and dock, and water sports. Electrical and water hook-ups available. Check in at the trading posts where you can also secure a fishing license for those over 16.

Stone Mountain Park (C6), P.O. Box 778, Stone Mountain, GA 30086; 469-9831. *I.* This five-hundred-site lakeside campground puts you within easy access of all the attractions and activities at Stone Mountain Park. Electrical and water hook-ups are available. See SIGHTS Chapter.

RESORTS

Resorts around Atlanta encompass every kind of situation, from gardens to lakes to mountains, and are enjoyed by Atlantans as well as visitors. Check with the ONE-DAY EXCURSIONS Chapter for more information on these resorts.

BIG CANOE, Big Canoe, GA 30143; 1-268-3333 or toll-free (800) 241-9361. *M to E.* Big Canoe is North Georgia at its best — 5000 acres of waterfalls, lakes, forests, and natural wildlife with the resort complex settled quietly in the center. Emerald golf greens overlook the blue lake; tennis, swimming, squash, platform tennis, fishing, sailing, and canoeing are offered in this idyllic setting. Treetop Village provides a complete business conference service, and accommodations in handsome one-, two-, and three-bedroom villas and condominiums are leased throughout the year on a daily and weekly basis. Big Canoe, a favorite second home community for Atlantans, 60 miles north of the city, will make you feel at home and at peace. Rates vary according to the seasons, so call in advance for reservations. On season is March 15 through November. Off season is

December to March 15. From Atlanta go north on GA 400, turn left at McFarland, Exit 8, and follow signs.

CALLAWAY GARDENS, Pine Mountain, GA 31822; 1-663-2281 or toll-free anywhere in the U.S. (800) 282-8181. *M.* Callaway Gardens welcomes you into the west Georgia foothills of the Appalachian Mountains. This is a full-service resort with the Gardens an attraction at all seasons and four golf courses open all year.

Callaway Gardens offers excellent tennis facilities, boating, fishing in stocked lakes, quail hunting in season, water skiing, hiking, and a man-made beach on the lake famous for the international water skiing competition every year. During the summer an excellent program for families is available, with a regular day-camp for tots to teens who are instructed by students from Florida State University in everything from nature to water skiing. These students are all members of the Circus Group from the university and perform daily under the Big Top at Callaway for guests and visitors during the summer months.

Hundreds of acres of native southern flowers, plants, and trees are beautifully cultivated in their natural setting. There are world-famous greenhouses and a jewel-like Gothic chapel nestled by a waterfall that offers the serenity many seek today.

The Inn's buffets are popular, and the lounge offers nightly entertainment. Rates vary with facility and season, and we recommend you call for current prices. Inn rooms, cottages, and villas are available. See ONE-DAY EXCURSION Chapter for additional information.

LAKE LANIER ISLANDS, 45 minutes from Atlanta, is a popular recreational haven. Take I-85 north to GA 365, exit 2 on Friendship Rd., turn left and follow signs to Lake Lanier Islands and PineIsle, about four miles. Swimming at the lake beach, tennis, horseback riding, and boat rentals are available. Take your pick of the cottages or the resort.

Lanier Island Cottages, Lake Lanier Islands, Buford, GA 30518; 945-8331. *I to M.* Two-bedroom cottages are available on the lake for weekend packages and weekly rates.

PineIsle, Stouffer's Resort Hotel, Lake Lanier Islands, Buford, GA 30518; 945-8921 or toll-free (800) 325-5000. *M.* Stay at Stouffer's Resort Hotel for excellent cuisine at the *Pavilion Restaurant* and live entertainment; enjoy the active life with outdoor-indoor pools, tennis courts, golf course, health club, horseback riding, sail- and ski-boat rentals, trout grounds, and a super waterslide of 430 feet (131 meters). Rates vary according to seasons.

SKY VALLEY RESORT, Dillard, GA 30537; 1-746-5301. *M to E.* Sky Valley is Georgia's prime snow-skiing lodge in winter and a beautiful North Georgia resort year-round. It is in *Deliverance* country where the Burt Reynolds movie was filmed. And if you saw the movie and like white-water try your skill rafting down the nearby Chattooga River. Guided tours available. The resort offers excellent golf, tennis, outdoor swimming, and horseback riding and boasts a popular restaurant and lounge. Nestled in the Georgia mountains, you can spend several hours nearby browsing and antiquing in the unusual areas and shops. See ONE-DAY EXCURSION Chapter for additional information. *FP,* weekend package plans, and long-term rates are available. Rates vary with season so we recommend you call for current prices.

UNICOI LODGE AND CONFERENCE CENTER, Hwy. 356, Helen, GA 30345; 1-878-2201; call 1-878-2824 for reservations. *I.* This rustic modern lodge of diagonal wood and plate glass has rooms and two- and three-bedroom cottages snuggled into the northern woods. Dining is in the lodge restaurant. It is a mile from Helen and a stone's throw from Anna Ruby Falls. The lake provides swimming and boating, and nature trails abound. Color TV is in the lobby area. During the summer there are classes in pottery, macrame, as well as special dances. Unicoi is a quiet, spartan, and beautiful retreat center at very reasonable rates. Call for seasonal rates.

DINING

Atlanta is presently in the midst of an exciting restaurant explosion, with hundreds of restaurants, a myriad of cuisines, and a range of ambience from a restored excelsior mill to the dazzling pinnacles of the premier hotels, from environmental fantasies to storefront coziness. The restaurant world of Atlanta is flourishing, spinning, and lighting up the eager and hungry faces of Atlanta residents and visitors. We hope that selecting your restaurant in our guide will match the pleasure we have had in presenting these interesting places of dining.

Atlanta has had a small cadre of local restaurants for many years, but the development of the hotel industry has expanded the quality and variety of international menus. Award-winning international chefs preside over class restaurant kitchens within major hotels and have, in many cases, established their own unique restaurants in the city. Atlantans are now enjoying a sophisticated dining scene appropriate to the city's pledge to be a great international city.

In the 1970s small restaurant development escalated and continued into the 80s full speed ahead. Cuisines proliferate including Italian, both southern and northern; French; Spanish; Chinese including Mandarin, Szechuan, and Hunan; Japanese; Indian; Cuban; Mexican; Greek; Russian; Korean; Thai; Vietnamese; Continental; and American. Atlanta's southern cooking institutions have increased in number over the decade, and new Atlantans immigrating from other cities in the United States and from other countries of the world have opened restaurants reflecting their own tastes and cultures.

With a simultaneous rediscovery of Atlanta's neighborhoods, the small and specialized restaurant business has found new places to thrive, new markets of young professionals who like to "eat out" consistently during the week. You will notice throughout this chapter the names of these neighborhood areas — Virginia-Highlands, Inman Park, midtown, and Buckhead. Notice also the names of Atlanta's outlying restaurant districts such as Marietta and the Roswell Road district, and finally Atlanta's shopping malls, many of which have grown at similarly increasing rates. These are alluring places and heady times for Atlanta's small restaurants.

Regional and national chains have also moved to Atlanta. Two national chains, the Waffle House and Chick-Fil-A, deserve special note because they are Atlanta's own. Both originated in Atlanta and maintain headquarters here. Limitation of space does not allow us to include all the very fine chain restaurants; their regional and national reputations will serve as your guide in Atlanta. In an unusual case we reserve the right to make an inclusion. Most Atlanta hotels have quality restaurants that are convenient for the visitor. It is impossible to list them all; we have selected those we feel particularly worthy.

The dining guide includes restaurants, an Etcetera section of hard-to-categorize eateries, cafeterias, and brunch spots.

We include in the Marmac dining guide only those restaurants we can recommend, sketching for you the individual "personality" of each establishment, the raison d'etre among our selections. We include a quick reference for restaurants by area of the city. We have been careful to incorporate restaurants for a variety of occasions and pocketbooks. Our cost categories are listed below and coded directly following the address in the listings.

E   Expensive. Full dinner including appetizer, entree, and dessert (no beverage) over $25 per person

M   Moderate. Full dinner (no beverage), $10-25 per person

I   Inexpensive. Full dinner (no beverage), under $10 per person

RESTAURANTS BY AREA

BUCKHEAD

Anne Marie's, French, M to E.
Anthony's, Continental, E.
Avanti Italian Restaurant, Italian, M.
Bangkok, Oriental, I.
Benihana of Tokyo, Oriental, M.
Bone's, American, M to E.
Brandy House, American, I.
The Brass Key, Continental, M to E.
Bucket Shop, American, M.
Cafe Plaza, Continental, I to M.
Carbo's, Continental, E.
D'Lites, Etcetera, I.
Dante's, American, M.
Darcy's, Continental, M to E.
The Dessert Place, Etcetera, I.
Dos Amigos, International, I.
e.j.'s, American, M.
El Azteca, International, I.
Feedmill Restaurant, Southern, I.
The Fish Market, Seafood, M to E.
Gelateria, Etcetera, I.
Good Ol' Days, American, I.

DINING 57

Grand China, Oriental, I.
Halpern's, Etcetera, M.
Hedgerose Heights Inn, Continental, E.
Houlihan's, American, I to M.
Houston's, American, I to M.
Jalisco, International, I.
JAS, American, E.
Jilly's The Place for Ribs, American, I to M.
Jim White's Half Shell, Seafood, I to M.
Joe Dale's Cajun House, American, M.
La Grotta, Italian, E.
Le Gourmet, Etcetera, M.
Lennox's, American, M.
Longhorn Steaks, American, M.
McNeeley's, American, I.
Maison Gourmet, Continental, M.
Maison Robert, Etcetera, M.
Ma Maison, Continental, M.
Melvin's, Etcetera, I.
Morrison's Cafeteria, Cafeteria, I.
Nakato, Oriental, M.
Old Hickory House, American, I.
103 West, Continental, E.
Pano's and Paul's, Continental, E.
The Patio, Continental, M to E.
Peachtree Cafe and Catering, American, I.
The Peasant Uptown, Continental, M.
Penrods, American, I to M.
Provino's, Italian, I.
Rue de Paris-La Chaumiere, French, M to E.
The Rusty Scupper, Seafood, M.
Sandpiper, American, M.
Sidney's Just South, Continental, M to E.
Swan Coach House, American, M.
Texas State Line Barbecue, Southern, I to M.
Trotters, Italian, E.
Vittorio's, Italian, M.
The Wedgewood, Continental, M.
Zasu's, Continental, M.

DOWNTOWN

The Abbey, Continental, E.
Benihana of Tokyo, Oriental, M.
Brandywine Downs, American, M.
Bugatti's, Italian, E.
Cafe de la Paix, Continental, M to E.
Cashin's Place, American, I.
Coach and Six, American, E.
Crossroad's Restaurant, Seafood, I to M.
Dailey's, Continental, M.
The Diplomat, American, M to E.
The Garden Room, Etcetera, I.
Good Ol' Days, American, I.
The Great Wall, Oriental, I.
Herren's, American, M.
Hugo's, Continental, E.
Ichiban's, Oriental, M.
International Food Works, Etcetera, I to M.
Ivy Street Library and Pub, American, I.
Jonathan's, Continental, M.
The Mansion, Continental, M to E.
Mary Mac's, Southern, I.
Michelle's, French, E.
The Midnight Sun, Continental, E.
Nikolai's Roof, International, E.
Paschal's, American, M.
Pittypat's Porch, Southern, M to E.
Polaris, American, M.
Savannah Fish Company, Seafood, M.
The Sun Dial, Continental, E.
A Taste of China, Oriental, M.
Terrace Cafeteria, Cafeteria, I.
The Varsity, Etcetera, I.

COBB COUNTY (VININGS, MARIETTA, SMYRNA)

Aunt Fanny's Cabin, Southern, M.
Cafe Milan, Continental, M.
Cashin's Place, American, I.
Chicago's, Etcetera, I.
Hennessey's, American, I.
Joe Rigatoni's, Italian, I.

Maximillian's, Continental, M to E.
Old Vinings Inn, Continental, M to E.
Penrod's, American, I to M.
Picadilly Cafeteria, Etcetera, I.
The Planter's, Continental, M.
Round the Corner, Etcetera, I.
The Rusty Scupper, Seafood, M.
Simon's, Seafood, M.
The Waverly, Brunches, E.
Winfield's, Continental, M.

DECATUR

Caravan's Crab Shack, Seafood, I to M.
Claudette's, French, M.
Conversations, Continental, I to M.
Golden Buddha, Oriental, I.
The Lion and The Unicorn, Continental, M.
The Lullwater Tavern, American, I.
Provino's, Italian, I.
Rainbow Grocery and Cafe, Etcetera, I.
Sunday House, American, M.
Williams Seafood of Savannah, Seafood, I to M.

MIDTOWN AND VIRGINIA-HIGHLANDS

The Art of Conversation, Etcetera, I.
Atkins Park, American, M.
B. K.'s Greenhouse Restaurant, Etcetera, I.
Baker's Deli, Etcetera, I.
Blue Nile, International, I.
Brother Juniper's, Etcetera, I.
Burton's Grill, Etcetera, I.
Cafe des Amis, Continental, I.
Capo's, Italian, M.
Cha Gio, Oriental, I.
The Country Place, Continental, M.
The Dessert Place, Etcetera, I.
Don Juan's, International, M.
Eat Your Vegetables Cafe, Etcetera, I.
Gene & Gabe's, Italian, M.
Gregory's, Continental, M.

Le Papillon, Continental, M.
Marra's, Seafood, M.
Milo's, Continental, M.
Mr. B's, Etcetera, I.
The Park, Etcetera, I.
Patrick's, Continental, I to M.
The Pleasant Peasant, Continental, M.
Rousseau, Continental, M.
Seasons, the Steak House, Continental, E.
Silver Grill, Etcetera, I.
The Silver Skillet, Southern, I.
1019, Italian, M.
Toulouse, French, E.
Vickery's, American, I.
Walter Mitty's, American, M.
Zelda's, Continental, I to M.

NORTHEAST ATLANTA

Anarkali's, International, M.
Atlantis Natural Foods Restaurant, Etcetera, I.
Cafe Versailles, Continental, I to M.
Chequers, Seafood, M.
Cognito's, Italian, M to E.
The Derby, American, I to M.
Dos Amigos, International, I.
57th Fighter Group, American, M.
McKinnon's Louisiane, American, M.
Niko's, International, I.
Nino's, Italian, M.
Penrod's, American, I to M.
Petite Auberge, French, M.
Quinn's Mill, American, M.
Savannah The Cafe, Seafood, M.
South of France, French, M.

NORTHWEST ATLANTA

Bernard's, French, E.
Jax, Continental, M.
Red Barn Inn, American, M.
U.S. Bar & Grill, International, I to M.

ROSWELL

El Azteca, International, *I*.
Gene and Gabe's Lodge, Italian, *M*.
La Grotta of Roswell, Italian, *M to E*.
Lickskillet Farm, Southern, *M*.
Maggie Mae's, Continental, *M*.
The Public House, Continental, *M*.
River House, American, *I*.
The Steeplehouse Restaurant, American, *I to M*.

SANDY SPRINGS

Beef Cellar, Etcetera, *I*.
Cafe Intermezzo, Etcetera, *M*.
Cashin's Place, American, *I*.
elan, Continental, *M to E*.
El Azteca, International, *I*.
Embers Seafood Grille, Seafood, *M*.

Kobe Steaks, Oriental, *M*.
The Lark and Dove, Continental, *M*.
Ming Gardens, Oriental, *I*.
The Moorings, American, *M*.
My Friend's Place, Etcetera, *I*.
Papa Pirozki's, International, *M*.
Pizzeria Uno, Etcetera, *I*.
The Primavera Gelateria, Etcetera, *I*.
Raffles, American, *I*.
Round the Corner, Etcetera, *I*.
S & W Seafood, Seafood, *M*.

SOUTH ATLANTA

Captain's Roost, Seafood, *M*.
Davis Brothers, Cafeteria, *I*.
The Great Wall, Oriental, *I*.
Harold's, Southern, *I*.
Melears, American, *I*.
Pilgreen's, American, *M*.

RESTAURANTS

American

Atkins Park (C4), 794 N. Highland Ave. NE; 876-7249. *I*. Atkins Park is a restored jewel from Atlanta's 1920s past. First a deli, then a neighborhood beer and wine tavern, and later a dining room as well, Atkins Park has the oldest (1927) beer and wine license in Atlanta. Atkins Park serves American and continental fare in its cozy, fun, and eclectic environment. Lunch and dinner daily.

Baby Doe's (A2), 2239 Powers Ferry Rd., Marietta; 955-3637. *M*. Named after Baby Doe, the owner of the famous 19th-century silver mine in Colorado, this restaurant recreates the mine scene with scaffolding and tunnels, tin siding, mine rails, and Victorian stuffed chairs and bric-a-brac inside. Welcome yourself into another era for the evening; the view from the "mine" is super. Four levels of bars and dining rooms. Lunch Mon-Sat, dinner daily.

Bone's (B3), 3130 Piedmont Rd. NE; 237-2663. *E.* Bone's is synonymous with steak, some of the juiciest and thickest in town, and live lobster flown in daily. Highlighting the Victorian decor is the wonderful gallery of autographed photos of famous patrons. This is a place to enjoy both a congenial business meal and a family gathering. Lunch Mon-Fri, dinner daily.

Brandy House (B3), 4365 Roswell Rd. NE; 252-7784. *I.* Another W. D. Crowley restaurant, the Brandy House is popular with young singles looking for dapper environs, a cross section of foods from burgers to crabs, and each other. Lunch Mon-Fri, dinner Mon-Sat.

Brandywine Downs (H10), 689 Peachtree St. NE; 873-5361. *M.* Across from the Fox Theatre, dine and have an evening drink on the Downs patio. This small restaurant has a horse-racing motif throughout, even the menu is the Official Program. The wines are well selected and the atmosphere is both refined and friendly. Lunch Mon-Fri, dinner Mon-Sat.

Bucket Shop (B3), 3475 Lenox Rd. NE; 261-9244. *M.* Trimmed out in dark woods and brass fittings, the Bucket Shop sets the scene for the executive lunch and business dining. Steaks are the mainstay with fine offerings in seafood as well. The Dow Jones quotations are posted hourly on the chalkboard during the day. Lunch Mon-Fri, dinner Mon-Sat.

Cashin's Place (A4), Perimeter Mall, 393-3286; (B2), Cumberland Mall NW, 434-9434; (A1) Merchant's Walk Shopping Center NE, Marietta, 973-3756; and (I10), 675 W. Peachtree St. in the Southern Bell Building. *I.* Cashin's is a comfortable dining experience with the mood of a sidewalk cafe with real barnwood providing a soft, textured backdrop. The bar serves assorted concoctions and straight drinks; the restaurant has crepes, quiches, soups, salads, and sandwiches for lunch and a dinner menu including stuffed cornish hen and sweet and sour ribs. The menu is tongue-in-cheek Victoriana at Cashin's food-and-booze emporia. Lunch and dinner Mon-Sat.

The Coach and Six (C3), 1776 Peachtree St. NW; 872-6666. *E.* This classy New York-style restaurant serves thick prime and juicy steaks, two- to four-pound Maine lobsters, and triple-cut lamp chops with cosmopolitan pizazz. The waiters are pros, the proportions are extravagant, and the atmosphere is charged with conversation and bustle. The Coach and Six is a favorite for both lunch and dinner. Atlantans patronize this fine restaurant because consistency is one of its secrets. Lunch Mon-Fri, dinner daily.

Dante's Down the Hatch in Buckhead (B3), 3380 Peachtree Rd. NE; 266-1600. *M.* Dante's is both nightclub and specialty restaurant in an incredible nautical setting featuring a recreated wharf and restored sailing ship, infused with the authenticity of the sea, its ships, and creatures. Dante's specializes in fondue — cheese and beef and chocolate — all designed for the comradeship of eating from the same pot. Take a cheese tour and a wine tour of the world with Dante's broad selection of cheeses and wines. The restaurant is open for cocktails and dinner Mon-Sat. See the Music section of the NIGHTLIFE Chapter.

The Derby, 7716 Spalding Dr.; 448-2833. *I to M.* In the Spalding Corners Shopping Center, the Derby is a popular luncheon and dinner spot for business people and area residents. The mood is friendly and jovial; the fare is All-American. Lunch and dinner daily, brunch Sun.

The Diplomat (J9), 230 Spring St. NW; 525-6375. *M to E.* The historic building of The Diplomat restaurant is located in the heart of the convention district next to the Apparel and Merchandise Marts. American and continental cuisine are presented in an atmosphere of cosmopolitan professionalism. Orchestra and dancing each evening. Lunch Mon-Fri, dinner daily.

e.j.'s (B3), 128 E. Andrews Dr. NW; 262-1377. *M.* e.j.'s is perfect for many moods, serving comfortable American-fare dinner in greenhouse surroundings. It is a solid drawing card in the Buckhead area for good food and good friends. This is a favorite luncheon and dinner choice for business groups and residents in the area. Lunch Mon-Fri, dinner daily, brunch Sat-Sun.

57th Fighter Group (B4), 3829 Clairmont Rd.; 457-7757. *M.* This "environmental" restaurant will take you back in time to an officer's club in North Africa, World War II. The entrance is sandbagged, the bar and some of the restaurant seats overlook the landing strip of the DeKalb-Peachtree airport. The front desk is manned by waitresses in WWII Red Cross uniforms and WWII memorabilia is everywhere. Lunch and dinner daily, brunch Sun.

Good Ol' Days (C3), 3013 Peachtree Rd. NE, 266-2597; and (A3), 5841 Roswell Rd., 257-9183. *I.* Every now and then someone comes up with a new twist in restauranteering — like the owner of Good Ol' Days. Named one of 10 Top Women of the Year by *Glamour* Magazine, she patented her famous flowerpot-baked bread and opened up a sidewalk café and then another restaurant. It works so well that the outdoor tables and the cheery inside are filled with happy customers sampling cool drinks and everything homemade including flowerpot sandwiches, nachos, spinach salad, and full meals. Live entertainment sparks the evening crowd. Lunch and dinner and late night daily. Also at 231 Ivy St., in the Downtowner Hotel; 577-1132.

Herren's (J9), 84 Luckie St. NW; 524-4709. *M.* Atlanta's oldest restaurant, which opened in the depression years in 1934, is going strong in the 1980s. Atlanta bankers, stockbrokers, retailers, shoppers, lawyers, salespeople all come together in the Williamsburg dining rooms of Herren's at lunchtime, the most popular meal of the day. Join them for hot shrimp Arnaud, planked seafood, and steak. Lunch Mon-Fri, dinner Mon-Sat.

Houston's (B3), Lenox Rd. across from Lenox Square; 237-7534. 3539 Northside Parkway; 262-7130. *I to M.* Houston's is where you'll find some of Atlanta's finest preppies and young career types. The restaurant has the sophisticated dark-green and beige treatment popular in the last few years, and the fare includes light meals such as quiches, salads, burgers, and soups. Lunch and dinner daily.

Houlihan's Old Place (B3), Lenox Square, 261-5323; Park Place, 4505 Ashford-Dunwoody Rd., 394-8921. *I to M.* Dark walls, Tiffany lamps, Victorian memorabilia, and fluffy green plants provide a warm club-like restaurant and bar, where the twenties to forties set mingles over drinks and a menu from quiches to steaks, burgers to seafood. Lunch and dinner and late night daily, brunch Sun.

Hennessey's, (A3), 1033 Franklin Rd., Marietta; 953-1886. *I.* Marietta singles and young professionals gather at Hennessey's for drinks, camaraderie, and diversified American cuisine. Lunch Mon-Fri, dinner Mon-Sat.

Ivy Street Library and Pub (J9), 22 Ivy St. NE; 521-2584. *I.* Part of the W. D. Crowley chain this is a great meeting ground for downtown business people with a sophisticated pub atmosphere. After work hours are popular. Lunch Mon-Fri. Dinner Mon-Sat.

JAS Gourmet Steak House, (C3), 3129 Piedmont Rd. NE, 266-0040. *E.* The counterpoint restaurant to Jim White's Half Shell, JAS takes Jim's formal nickname and presents the tops in beef in a charming house restaurant in Buckhead. Dinner Mon-Sat.

Jilly's The Place for Ribs (B3), 4420 Roswell Rd. NE, 256-2803; (A2) 2647 Cobb Pkwy. NE, Marietta, 952-7437; (C6) 4933 Memorial Dr., Stone Mountain, 296-3302. *I to M.* This is a casual and popular place for those times when you crave mouth-watering ribs and barbeque. Entertainment is featured nightly. No reservations. Lunch and dinner daily.

Joe Dale's Cajun House (B3), 3209 Maple Dr.; 261-2741. *M.* Cajun specialties from Louisiana remain the strong favorites at Joe Dale's. Sample the gumbo, jambalaya, red beans, court bouillon, and have a bayou feast. Servings are large, the waitresses are fun-loving, and the piano bar adjoining the dining room is filled with regulars and rollicking music. Dinner Mon-Sat.

Lennox's at Lindbergh (C3), 660 Lindbergh Dr., NE, 233-5450. M.Cajun and Creole cooking from Louisiana is served up in this small cafe just off Piedmont. Expect tasty gumbos, crawfish etouffee, and blackened redfish plus other favorites. Lunch Tue-Sat, dinner daily.

Longhorn Steaks (C3), 2151 Peachtree Rd. NE; 351-6086; (A3), 4721 Lower Roswell Rd.; Marietta, 977-3045. *M.* Choice steaks at choice prices in the atmosphere of a Texas saloon and steakhouse — that's Longhorn Steaks. Rustic wood stalls, beer signs and cheerful waitresses accompany the savoring of good beef steaks. Lunch Mon-Fri, dinner daily.

The Lullwater Tavern (C4), 1545 N. Decatur Rd.; 377-6598. *I.* A very friendly place to go, right near Emory University. Local intown residents come for burgers and chicken and nachos and quiche. Or you can while away the time at the large and comfortable bar. Open for lunch Mon-Fri, dinner daily.

McKinnon's Louisiane (C4), 2100 Cheshire Bridge Rd. NE; 325-4141. *M.* McKinnon's is special, a small restaurant, gentle in manner, waiters in tuxedos, an aristocratic private dining room. The cuisine is traditional creole. On Thursdays McKinnon's will treat you to a sister food from that bayou area — Cajun Cuisine, a heartier, more robust fare with pungent spices. Dinner Mon-Sat.

McNeeley's (C3), 1900 Peachtree St. NW; 351-1957. *I.* At the intersection of Peachtree and Collier, McNeeley's pink stucco restaurant welcomes everyone to a mixed bag of goodies. For those who like to fraternize McNeeley's offers birds and burgers, neons and nachos, shooters and salads, cappuccinos and chickadees. Lunch and dinner daily.

Melears (F1), US 29, Union City; 964-9933. *I.* Melears is a barbecue pit, plain and simple with pig decorations on the walls and well-respected barbecue for south Atlantans for many, many years. Dinner daily.

The Moorings (A3), 6700 Powers Ferry Rd. NW; 955-1187. *M.* The Chattahoochee River was the site of Atlanta's first Indian settlements. Have a spectacular view of this beautiful river at Powers Ferry Crossing while you dine on steak and seafood. The lounge features live entertainment and dancing. Lunch Mon-Fri, dinner daily, brunch Sat-Sun.

Paschal's (D3), 830 Martin Luther King, Jr. Dr. NW; 577-3150. *M.* Paschal's is a landmark in Atlanta's black heritage, a thriving restaurant in the Atlanta University section of the city. Frequented by politicians, businessmen and businesswomen, and visiting entertainers, Paschal's introduces you to the pleasures of southern fare and to the traditional meeting place and forum for the black community. The restaurant, which is part of Paschal's Motor Inn is open for breakfast, lunch, and dinner daily.

Peachtree Cafe & Catering Co. (B3), 268 E. Paces Ferry Rd. NE; 233-4402. *I.* This extremely popular eatery, one block off Peachtree in Buckhead, combines light fare of burgers, pocket sandwiches, baked potatoes, soups, salads and desserts with 24 imported beers and a good selection of wines. Lunch and dinner Mon-Sat.

Penrod's (B5), Northlake II across from Northlake Mall, 939-9399; (B2), Akers Mill Square on US 41, 955-9599; and (C3), 3402 Piedmont Rd. NE; 266-9913. *I to M.* Penrod's serves good American fare featuring prime rib, oysters, great burgers, and chili. The place singles find each other in Atlanta. Lunch and dinner daily, brunch Sat-Sun.

Pilgreen's (D3), 1081 Lee St. SW; 758-4669. *M.* The house specialty in this long-time favorite of south Atlantans is the T-bone steak, but all steaks are recommended and big steak lovers can special-order a three-pounder. Lounge accompanies restaurant. Lunch and dinner Tue-Sat.

Polaris (J9), Hyatt Regency Atlanta, 265 Peachtree St. NE; 577-1234. *M.* Under the blue-glass dome of this landmark hotel dining is a moving experience. The Polaris restaurant revolves 360° during your lunch or dinner hour affording you a bird's-eye view of downtown and metro Atlanta on the horizon. Recently redecorated in contemporary pinks and mauves, you can now relax in comfortable wing chairs. American fare features the prime rib specialty. Dinner daily.

Quinn's Mill (B5), 3300 Northlake Pkwy.; 934-9180. *M.* Judging from the many streets named after mills, Atlanta and environs had a large share of mills in operation in the 19th century. The Victoria Station national chain has taken advantage of an authentic grist mill near Northlake Mall, turning it into a charming restaurant and restoring it to the rustic beauty of an earlier era. The American fare focuses on steak and seafood. Lunch Mon-Fri, dinner daily, brunch Sat-Sun.

Raffles (A4), 4400 Ashford-Dunwoody Rd., Perimeter Mall; 391-9648. *I.* Raffles is a fun place with a central platformed bar, interior brick walls, flower pots, and a dining area with carpet walls and bright contemporary posters. White square tiles join the design for trendy casual dining and an assortment of snacks, salads, and Raffles' favorites. Entertainment starts in the evening. Lunch and dinner daily, brunch Sat-Sun.

The Red Barn Inn (B3), 4300 Powers Ferry Rd.; 255-7277. *M.* For many years the Red Barn has been a landmark in dining for Atlantans. The space is divided into handsome barn stalls with a comprehensive equestrian theme throughout — thoroughbred prints on the walls, horse blankets, saddles, and polished chrome and leather riding gear. The effect is warm and clubby. Enjoy excellent Colorado prime beef, fresh seafood, veal, lamb, and cheesecake for dessert. Dinner Mon-Sat.

The River House (A3), 8849 Roswell Rd., Roswell; 993-5039. *I.* W. D. Crowley's restaurant in Roswell features the easy good cheer for singles and young working people as well as residents of the area of North Atlanta. The mood is sophisticated. So is the clientele. Lunch and dinner daily, brunch Sat-Sun.

The Sandpiper (C3), 2960 Piedmont Rd. NE; 266-1706. M. Maintaining an admirable reputation for its American cuisine of steaks and seafood, the restaurant has two levels, the "Downstairs" still the original restaurant with small dining rooms and a lounge with upholstered chairs and low lights. Some of the dining rooms look onto the garden greenhouse extensions. "Upstairs" the Young Americans Song and Dance Company stars at the Sandpiper's Musical Dinner Theatre. See NIGHTLIFE Chapter. Lunch Mon-Fri, dinner daily.

The Steeplehouse Restaurant (A3), on the corner of Johnson Ferry and Paper Mill Road in Roswell; 951-9585. *I to M.* Owned by the former chef of The Abbey, this Williamsburg-style breakfast house serves unusual breakfast and lunch fares from kippers to stuffed quail. Enjoy the deck overlooking a lake. Open early.

Sunday House (C6), 5885 Memorial Dr.; 292-3061. *M.* Sunday House brings back memories of large Sunday dinners at the family farmhouse. The building is new, painted in fresh white and blue trim and clapboard. Families come in droves for the hamburger pot pies, roast chicken, ham, and vegetables. No beer, wine or liquor. Lunch and dinner daily.

Swan Coach House (B3), Atlanta Historical Society, 3130 Slaton Dr. NW; 261-0636. *M.* This charming coach house for the elegant 1920s Swan House on the Atlanta Historical Society grounds is a perfect luncheon spot in Buckhead. The food is delectable; the atmosphere genteel. Lunch Mon-Sat.

Vickery's (G11), 1106 Crescent Ave. NE; 881-1106. *I to M.* Mrs. Vickery's turn-of-the-century house and antique store has been given a soft art deco interior treatment and presto, one of the friendliest bars and eateries in Midtown. In fair weather have your meal on the brick patio under the spreading oak. Lunch, dinner and late night Tue-Sun.

Walter Mitty's (C4), 816 N. Highland Ave. NE; 876-7115. *M.* Walter Mitty's has cut a dashing figure in the Atlanta restaurant and jazz scene. In the culturally booming Virginia-Highland neighborhood, it serves moderately priced fare in a restored early twentieth-century store. Everybody loves Walter Mitty's Chicago ambience. Eat well and then follow the crowd downstairs to the jazz room. No reservations. Dinner and jazz daily until 2 am.

Continental

The Abbey (I11), 163 Ponce de Leon Ave.; 876-8532. *E.* Housed in a landmark downtown church with vaulted ceilings and stained-glass windows, the Abbey restaurant brings you continental cuisine and a wine list considered one of the best in the city. The staff serves in monks' habits and your candlelit dinner is accompanied by the delicate sounds of the Abbey harpist. The lounge is open every evening. Dinner daily.

Anthony's (B3), 3109 Piedmont Rd. NE; 262-7379. *E.* Dine at Anthony's in the gracious setting of an antebellum plantation home. The house was carefully removed brick by brick and plank by plank from nearby Washington, Georgia in the 1970s and relocated at the present four-acre site on Piedmont Road. It is handsomely decorated with period antiques and reproductions in both art and furnishings. Dinner Mon-Sat.

Brass Key Restaurant (C3), 2355 Peachtree Rd. NE, in the Peachtree Battle Shopping Center; 233-3202. *M to E.* The owner-chef at the Brass Key presents one of the most delicious menus in town. The local following attests to his success. The excellent cuisine is complemented by elegant and courteous service. The wine cellar is extensive. Lunch Mon-Fri, and dinner Mon-Sat.

Cafe de la Paix (J10), Atlanta Hilton Hotel, Courtland and Harris Sts.; 659-2000. *M to E.* Country French decor, greenery, rattan, and prints turn this corner of Atlanta's modern Hilton Hotel into a welcome dining arena for visitors and Atlantans alike. The sumptuous International buffet for breakfast, lunch, and dinner will rival any worldwide. Sunday brunch is particularly breathtaking. Breakfast, lunch, and dinner daily.

Cafe des Amis (C3), 1428 Peachtree St. NE; 874-9188. *I to M.* The name suits this cafe on the first floor of a Pershing Point apartment house. Midtowners and out-of-towners mingle over a glass of wine or the continental fare. The balcony adjoining the tiny dining room is a fine place to watch passersby on Peachtree. Lunch and dinner daily, Sun brunch.

Café Milan (B2), 25 Galleria Pkwy.; 953-1121. *M.* Enter Café Milan through the doors and long vertical windows opening onto the enclosed promenade of the Galleria Mall. Ceilings are high, walls are mirrored, floors are tiled and carpeted, tablecloths are pink, and the brass cappucino machine shines behind the bar. At your right is the Café's collection of fresh coffees, which you can purchase, along with assorted continental coffee-makers, for home brewing. Lunch and dinner Mon-Sat, brunch Sun.

Cafe Plaza (B3), in Phipps Plaza on Peachtree; 262-1801. *I to M*. Eighteen tables on the open floor of Phipps second level provide an intimate cafe setting. The pleasant atmosphere is enhanced by a variety of salads, veal, duck, and seafood. The Cafe may have the best baked brie in town. Lunch Mon-Sat, dinner Tue-Sat.

Cafe Versailles (A4), 5486 Chamblee-Dunwoody Rd.; 393-9256. *I to M*. The chef at this sophisticated cafe prepares a delectable almond ginger chicken salad. A variety of fish and veal dishes are great, too. The Cafe boasts the largest cappucino machine in the state. Lunch and dinner daily, brunch Sat and Sun.

Carbo's Cafe (B3), 3717 Roswell Rd.; 231-4433. *E*. This eighty-seat restaurant is a jewel — intimate and elegant with the distinctive personal touch of the owner's art collection, a fresh rose on each table, and sparkling cut crystal and silver. Continental fare includes fresh seafood, veal, fowl, and steaks. Complete a superb meal at the cappucino and espresso bar. A visit to the piano bar is an after-dinner favorite with regular patrons. Piano bar and dinner daily.

Conversations, 515 N. McDonough St., Decatur; 373-1671. *I to M*. Conversations is indeed a place for informal gathering and conversation. The decor is eclectic and inviting with wall-hung oriental rugs, mellow oak furniture, a Victorian bar, and a cheerful forest-green awning at the entrance. You are two steps from the county courthouse and the MARTA rapid-rail station, an easy trip from downtown Atlanta. The menu follows the same eclectic drummer, imaginative quiches, soups, American and continental fare. Lunch Mon-Fri and dinner Mon-Sat.

The Country Place (G12), Colony Square, 14th St. and Peachtree St. NE; 881-0144. *M*. Portuguese tiles, large terra-cotta pots of greenery, and European country furniture transform this space in the Colony Square mall into clear Mediterranean ambience. The creative continental fare is presented orally by the waiter as well as written on a small chalkboard. Unusual selections include duck roasted in bourbon-plum sauce, vegetarian lasagna, fried bread, and the flowerpot dessert. Enjoy piano music in the lounge, a popular after-work spot for Colony Square tenants and residents. And finally, enjoy the superior Sunday brunch at the Country Place. No reservations. Lunch Mon-Fri, dinner daily, brunch Sun.

DINING

Dailey's (J9), 17 International Blvd.; 681-3303. *M.* The downtown link in the Peasant restaurant chain is next to Peachtree Center in a warehouse restored to turn-of-the-century character with brick walls, skylights, wide floorboards, antique carousel horses, and baskets of plants. The fare is creative continental in the upstairs restaurant. Street level is Dailey's bar and grill with piano entertainment and grill food service until 1 am. Sunday brunch is a special feature. Upstairs or downstairs Dailey's is a great place to be. Lunch Mon-Sat, dinner daily, brunch Sun.

Darcy's (B3), 3081 E. Shadowlawn Ave.; 237-9929. M *to* E. A sophisticated house restaurant in Buckhead, Darcy's features creative continental dishes served in intimate dining style. Fresh flowers on the tables, handsome prints on the wall, and pleasant service add up to a rewarding evening out. Lunch Mon-Fri, dinner Tue-Sat.

élan (A4), Park Place, 4505 Ashford-Dunwoody Rd.; 393-1333. *M to E.* The élan image is "now" chic, with tall upholstered seats, tiered spaces, and elegant trappings. The scene is set for fine continental food and social electricity. Lunch has a lavish salad and soup bar, the cocktail hour includes a complimentary buffet equally lavish, and dinner is followed by disco dancing. Lunch Mon-Fri, dinner Mon-Sat. See the Music section of the NIGHTLIFE Chapter.

Gregory's (I10), 857 W. Peachtree; 892-2289. M. Gregory's is clean, cool, and casual in decor, continental in cuisine. The food is imaginative with specialties such as Bahamian conch chowder, poached baby silver salmon, sweetbreads Madeira, and chicken livers Ginart. The late night menu is especially appetizing with multiple egg dishes for night-owls. Lunch Mon-Fri, dinner and late night daily until 3 am.

Hedgerose Heights Inn (B3), 490 E. Paces Ferry Rd. NE; 233-7673. *E.* The Hedgerose Heights Inn is an inviting, polished place for gourmet dining in the European tradition. This small, intimate restaurant will charm you with its peach and white decor, courteous service, and brilliant continental menu. Pheasant with a velvety morel sauce and medallions of venison from northeastern Italy exemplify the range of delights in selecting an entree. Hors d'oeuvres include piroschki topped with sauce béarnaise. For a return to elegant, expert, and beautiful wining and dining, reserve your table at the Hedgerose Heights Inn. Dinner Mon-Sat.

Hugo's (J9), Hyatt Regency Hotel, 265 Peachtree St.; 577-1234. *E.* Hugo's is the Hyatt Regency's elegant, quiet dinner restaurant right on Peachtree but far from the hustle and bustle of Atlanta's famous main street. Be soothed by the melodious sounds of the harp and by the continental culinary arts of Hugo's fine chefs. Add the glow of candlelight, a rose on your table, and muted contemporary decor for dining enchantment at one of Atlanta's premier downtown hotels. Dinner daily.

Jax (C2), 2116 DeFoors Ferry Rd.; 352-2724. *M.* Jax is a no-frills, good continental restaurant with French specialties and a favorite in northwest Atlanta. Dinner Mon-Sat.

Jonathan's (J9), 240 Peachtree St. NW; 688-8650. *M.* Atop the Merchandise Mart Jonathan's provides an indoor atrium garden setting for dining. The cuisine is continental, the atmosphere and location fine for business lunches and dinners. From the rooftop promenade enjoy a panoramic view of downtown Atlanta. Lunch Mon-Fri, dinner Mon-Sat.

The Lark and Dove (A3), at Roswell Rd. and I-285; 256-2922. A classy restaurant in Sandy Springs well known for its prime rib and other continental dishes. Enjoy live jazz Monday through Saturday as you eat and drink. Lunch Mon-Fri, dinner Mon-Sun.

The Lion and Unicorn (C5), 1850 Lawrenceville Hwy., Decatur; 329-1477. *M.* Behind etched art glass, this lovely small restaurant will host you to a varied menu from Carolina quail to Salmon Nordique. Flowered wallpaper, an 18th-century confessional, an antique sideboard for wine, and a balcony bar create a warm ambience for dining. Lunch Mon-Fri, dinner Mon-Sat.

Maggie Mae's 1090 Alpharetta St., Roswell; 993-4719. *M.* Charming, comfortable, delightful, and delicious. This small restaurant lends itself to quiet conversation. Located in an old home in Roswell, you will find both business people and northside Atlanta women lunching; at dinner couples of all ages make Maggie Mae's hum. Specializing in continental cuisine and original recipes. Lunch Mon-Fri, dinner Tue-Sat.

Maison Gourmet (C3), 2581 Piedmont Rd. NE; 231-8552. *M.* Maison Gourmet La Patisserie is a unique restaurant in Atlanta. The Dutch chef/proprietor has a pastry shop as the heart of the restaurant. Maison Gourmet offers special international Gourmet Nights in addition to its regular menu. Monday: Indonesian Rice table. Tuesday: Russian Night. Wednesday: Holland Food Night. These Special Dinners require reservations and are at a modest fixed price. This small European cafe is intimate, utterly charming. Lunch and dinner daily.

Ma Maison (B3), 2974 Grandview Ave.; 266-1799. *M.* This cozy house restaurant sparkles with green and white decor, a skylit dining room, and fine continental presentations. Lunch Mon-Fri, dinner Mon-Sat.

The Mansion (I11), 179 Ponce de Leon Ave. NE; 876-0727. *M to E.* The Mansion is the former estate house of one of Atlanta's oldest families. This Queen Anne-style residence of Edward C. Peters was built in 1885 and is listed in the National Register of Historic Places. Now visitors and Atlantans "come to dinner" at The Mansion, a Victorian delight of red brick, stone and half-timbered gables with the interior restored to the style of Atlanta's gilded age. Continental fare is served in the first-floor rooms with their ornate crown mouldings, Tiffany lamps, and crystal chandeliers, and also on the greenhouse veranda. Lunch Mon-Fri, dinner Mon-Sat, brunch Sat-Sun.

Maximillians (A2), 1857 Airport Industrial Dr., Marietta; 955-4286. *M to E.* Spacious countryside grounds and an early 20th-century historical home provide the setting for fine continental dining at Maximillians. Built in the Great Depression by a prominent Marietta lawyer, the former residence was the first to be lighted by electricity in Cobb County. Dine by candlelight, have a cocktail in winter by the roaring fire, and enjoy the sophisticated fare at Maximillians. Lunch Tue-Fri, dinner Mon-Sat.

The Midnight Sun (J9), in Peachtree Center Shopping Gallery (in the evenings valet parking on International Blvd.); 577-5050. *E.* This contemporary restaurant is considered to be among Atlanta's top in every way. The interior is built around a fountain with the sculpture *The Big One* by Willie Gutmann. The European menu is delicately seasoned, the service is outstanding, and the wine list is extensive. Cocktails at five are a pleasure with an accomplished pianist and complimentary hot hors d'oeuvres in elegant surroundings. Lunch Mon-Fri, dinner daily. Reservations suggested.

Milo's (C4), 1026 B North Highland Ave. NE; 876-6616. *M.* Milo's is a captivating little restaurant in Virginia-Highlands. Expect imaginative dishes from appetizer to dessert and enjoy the friendly atmosphere of blond oak and posters and the soft live guitar music. Dinner Tue-Sat, brunch Sun.

Old Vinings Inn (B2), 3020 Paces Mill Rd., Vinings; 434-5270. *M to E.* This is one of Atlanta's superior restaurants. The French cuisine is exemplary with light delicate sauces. The Old Vinings Inn is a wood frame structure in the historic village of Vinings, a perfect rendezvous for relaxed dining inside and on the porch, always under the attentive and friendly eye of the owner/chef. She greets you warmly at the door, during your meal, and at your departure, a gentle personal courtesy. Lunch and dinner Tue-Sat.

103 West (B3), 103 W. Paces Ferry Rd. NW; 233-5993. *E.* This fine restaurant is owned and run by two of Atlanta's reknowned restaurateurs. It joins Pano's and Paul's and The Fish Market with the same creative continental cuisine and excellent service. Marble and mirrors, floral prints and the gray and mauve decor add sensuous flare to the interior. The wines are superior. The menu is exciting, from venison to hot amaretto souffle. Servings are beautifully presented for each course. Dinner Mon-Sat.

Pano's and Paul's (B3), 1232 W. Paces Ferry Rd. NW; 261-3662. *E.* Pano's and Paul's is a restaurant in vogue with the residents of northside Atlanta and for good reason. The Victorian elegance of print-draped booths and brass and glass Edwardian appointments is a plush setting for the wide selection of continental and American cuisine. Pano's and Paul's has a proven and comprehensive menu with such varying delights as South African lobster tails, veal sweetbreads, white asparagus, crispy onions, Mississippi mud pie, and beignet of brie cheese. Pano's and Paul's is a place to dine well with Atlanta's social elite. Dinner Mon-Sat.

Le Papillon (D3), 785 Edgewood Ave.; 688-2172. *M.* For dining in Atlanta's first suburb try Le Papillon in Inman Park. The restaurant is a restored Victorian house, one of many lovely structures from the late 1900s. Continental is the cuisine accompanied by an excellent wine list at reasonable prices. Dinner daily.

The Patio (B3), 3349 Piedmont Rd.; 237-5878. *M to E.* The Patio is a local favorite for intimate dining with a provincial European cuisine of distinction. Specialties include roast leg of lamb, with spinach-mushroom stuffing, herbed oysters, pâtés, north Georgia rainbow trout, quail, sweetbreads, and frogs legs. The Patio decor is a subtle balance of Regency French antiques and classic contemporary, with art on the walls, lace napkins at the table — visual statements as harmonious as the superb fare. Lunch Mon-Fri, dinner daily.

Patrick's (C4), 484 Moreland Ave.; 525-0103. *I to M.* Patrick's is located in an Inman Park storefront, a popular restaurant with intowners. Expect a creative menu from Pasta Gary to Plantains with pistachios. Ceiling fans and paisley table cloths add a homey touch. Outside seating when it's warm. Lunch and dinner daily.

The Peasant Uptown (B3), Phipps Plaza, 3500 Peachtree Rd. NE; 261-6341. *M.* Part of the Peasant chain, the Peasant Uptown is on the upper level of Phipps Plaza. With a courtyard featuring a 100-foot greenhouse the ambience is casual and spatial elegance. The continental cuisine is creative and cool, and hot piano is featured in the lounge. While at Phipps don't miss dining at this excellent restaurant. Lunch and dinner daily.

The Planter's (B1), 780 S. Cobb Dr., Smyrna; 427-4646. *M.* This antebellum mansion built in 1848 by the first Mayor of Marietta is an impressive and original setting for fine southern dining. Authenticity on the exterior and interior mark this beautiful southern plantation that is on the National Register of Historic Places, with Greek revival architecture à la *Gone with the Wind* and restored period rooms with antiques and reproduction Victorian wallpaper and fabrics. For a taste of exquisite continental and American cuisine in the grand manner of the antebellum South, enter The Planter's white columned portico. Dinner Mon-Sat.

The Pleasant Peasant (H11), 555 Peachtree St.; 874-3223. *M.* This small wonderful restaurant in an old drugstore storefront on Peachtree was a trendsetter and tastemaker for Atlantans in the last decade. The Pleasant Peasant, a favorite for the local residents, is one of the Peasant group chain, which continues to expand into other sections of the city. The interiors are charming and cheerful, the management is meritorious, and the continental fare is deliciously inviting and consistent. Dinner daily.

The Public House, on Roswell Town Square; 992-4646. *M.* The Peasant restaurant group restored an antebellum brick structure on Roswell Square, just north of Atlanta, and called it The Public House. Nearby residents and vistors come in droves for the quality continental fare, to see each other, and to listen to the pianist in the loft. No reservations. Lunch Tue-Sat, dinner Mon-Sat.

Rousseau (C3), 227 10th St. NE; 874-1159. *I to M.* Rousseau is a small storefront restaurant in Midtown. The terra cotta-colored walls and the patterned tablecloths, combined with the use of copper pillars and bar make Rousseau a soothing environment. Have a candelit dinner, choosing from an imaginative menu. Dinner Sun-Sat.

Seasons, the Steak Club (C3), Lanier's Ramada Inn Central, 418 Armour Dr. NE; 873-5213. *E.* Seasons provides distinctive international cuisine in the rich, refined setting of the Lanier's Ramada Inn. Deep oak furnishings, handsome fabrics, and selective seating make the Seasons for all occasions, for business and pleasure. Lunch and dinner daily.

Sidney's Just South (B3), 4225 Roswell Rd.; 256-2339. *M to E.* Sidney's is not old South or new South, Just South, a liberty that the owner takes to cover an eccentric menu from all over the world with a pinch of Jewish culinary love in every dish. Sidney's is extremely popular; on the weekends it appears that the cozy frame house will split its seams. The wines are so good, the food is so good, the service is not so good; but nobody minds. Dinner daily.

Sun Dial Restaurant (J9), Westin Peachtree Plaza Hotel, Peachtree at International Blvd.; 659-1400. *E.* Dine at the peak of the world's tallest hotel. For a breathtaking view ascend the 73 stories in the hotel's exterior glass elevator. Then you are ready for feasting at the Sun Dial on American and continental specialties, overseeing Atlanta at high noon or as dusk brings the night. Cocktails are served in the revolving lounge. You have come full circle concluding a day of business or shopping in Atlanta. Lunch and dinner Mon-Sat, brunch Sun.

The Wedgewood of Atlanta (B4), 3355 Lenox Rd. NE, Lenox Center, Lower Level; 231-2345. *M.* Across from Lenox Square the Wedgewood of Atlanta presents gourmet dining without gourmet prices. Selections include fresh fish with dill sauce, bouillabaise, veal with watercress. End a pleasant meal with fresh desserts and coffees. Lunch Mon-Fri, dinner Mon-Sat.

Winfield's (B2), 100 Galleria Pkwy.; 955-5300. *M.* Winfield's anchors the west end of the Galleria shopping center with its bright red-orange awnings and handsome deep green interior. The bar and lounge to the left feature some of Atlanta's finest talent. The restaurant is the latest of the Atlanta-based Peasant chain, a sterling addition to Cobb County dining. Lunch Mon-Sat, dinner daily, brunch Sun.

Zasu's (C3), 1923 Peachtree St.; 352-3052. *M.* Zasu's is one of a cluster of restaurants within the one-block Brookwood Hills shopping village. It distinguishes itself with a versatile rotating weekly menu plus a late night breakfast to 3 am. The decorative effect of Zasu's is dapper, suave, and cool — an Art Deco environment of mirrors and scalloped design. Dining is, as they say, "chic to chic." Piano is featured in the lounge. Dinner and late night breakfast Mon-Sat.

Zelda's (I10), 654 Peachtree St. NE; 875-2080. *I to M.* Next to the Fox Theater, Zelda's is the perfect dining spot before or after the show. As the name implies the mood is a la Scott Fitzgerald and the roaring twenties, with brass fixtures and green and mauve decor. Dinner daily.

French

Anne Marie's (B3), 3340 Peachtree Rd.; 237-8686. *M to E.* Anne Marie's is a slice of France in the middle of Atlanta. In this small restaurant in elegant Tower Place, where locals and visitors mingle, it's conversation, it's conviviality, it's enchantment. Succulent French Provincial cooking includes seafood, veal, duck, and steaks. Outside an attractive café, brightened with fresh flowers, will encourage you to linger for lunch or cocktails. Friday and Saturday are especially popular; we recommend weekdays. Lunch Mon-Fri, dinner Mon-Sat.

Bernard's (C3), 1193 Collier Rd.; 352-2778. *E.* Bernard's is a small, French café, fun and friendly. Striped awnings on the interior, print tablecloths, and white lattice booths create a charming ambience. The staff is European. French, German, and Spanish mix with English and American accents. The menu features seafood, duck, sweetbreads, lamb, and beef but Bernard's will also serve "your" choice with advance notice. Dinner Mon-Sat.

Claudette De Lyon, 8815 Roswell Rd.; 587-3995. *M.* Claudette's is a small French restaurant in the neighboring Dunwoody suburb. The inside is attractive country French, with French prints warming the walls and occasionally a strolling minstrel complementing Claudette's classic French cuisine. Lunch Mon-Fri, dinner Mon-Sat.

Michelle's (J9), 133 Peachtree St. NE, Georgia-Pacific Center; 529-9400. *E.* Expect the height of modern elegance at Michelle's. The vaulted glass enclosure overlooking Margaret Mitchell Square will give you a breathtaking view of the setting sun and the urban core of Atlanta. Soothing mauve colors and soft furniture à la art-deco combine with lighted glass, brick, art, and a brass bar to offer you a lounge area for refreshments and nightly entertainment. The cuisine at Michelle's is predominantly French, masterfully prepared and served. Lunch Mon-Fri, dinner Mon-Sat.

Petite Auberge (C4), 2935 N. Druid Hills Rd. in Toco Hills Shopping Center; 634-6268. *M.* This "little inn" restaurant sits incongruously in a suburban shopping mall attracting a loyal clientele and offering the visitor a superior dining experience in French cuisine with German specials on Friday nights. The dining rooms are handsome and elegantly appointed, the service is winning, and the food is infallibly good. Entrees range from pink salmon with sauce sorrel to such delicacies as braised sweetbreads in cognac sauce and rack of lamb. Lunch Mon-Fri, dinner Mon-Sat.

Rue de Paris-La Chaumière (B3), 315 E. Paces Ferry Rd. NE; 261-9600. *M to E.* Rue de Paris is an established Parisian restaurant in the center of Buckhead with the sensitive French intuition for your level of dining comfort and complete satisfaction of taste. The theme of an elegant French inn is enhanced by the waiter's finesse and propriety. The gourmet specialties include Dover sole Waleska, lamb loin Catalane, mussels poulette, and mushroom salad. The wine cellar is extensive. Enjoy a piece of France in the heart of Atlanta. Dinner daily.

South of France (C4), 2345 Cheshire Bridge Rd. NE, in the square; 325-6963. *M.* The decor is unmistakably country French, stucco walls, half-timbers, and a marvelous stone double fireplace. The three French owners are brothers who bring to Atlanta a southern French cuisine of excellence and extend a warm welcome as you enter. For a casual evening of relaxed and friendly dining go to the South of France. Dinner by the fire in the winter months is a lovely seasonal garnishment. Lunch Mon-Fri, dinner daily.

Toulouse (G12), Colony Square Hotel, Peachtree at 14th St. NE; 892-6000. *E.* Named after Atlanta's sister city in France, this restaurant offers a remarkable five-course fixed-price dinner. Special touches such as chilled bottled water for your water glass, a table setting radiant with Wedgewood china, crystal, silver, and fresh flowers, a menu with an original serigraph by one of Atlanta's prominent printmakers, and matches with your name in gold all add to the dining pleasure. The superb cuisine is French, the entree course preceded by an intermezzo of sherbet served in beautiful ice swans. Service is attentive and individualized. Dinner Mon-Sat.

International

Anarkali (C4), 2115 W. Decatur Rd.; 321-0251. *M.* For an evening of Indian cuisine par excellence, Anarkali serves spicy and delicate dishes calibrated to delight the discriminating palate. The waiter will happily assist you in selecting a multi-course meal filled with the rhythms of many tastes. The dining space is adorned with a rich Indian tent motif and filled with soft sitar music. Lunch Mon-Fri, dinner Mon-Sat.

Blue Nile (C4), 810 N. Highland Ave. NE; 872-6483. *I.* Ethiopian food has come to Atlanta in this pleasing neighborhood restaurant in Midtown. White and blue tablecloths, Ethiopian pictures and artifacts adorning the walls, and soft native music set the mood for eating by hand in the Ethiopian tradition. Beef, chicken, and vegetable dishes have the tang of hot pepper and are served with spongy Ethiopian bread. Lunch and dinner daily.

Don Juan's (C3), 1927 Piedmont Cir. NE; 874-4285. *M.* Dishes from all of Spain are featured in this small house restaurant. Five-course dinners are available at reasonable rates along with excellent Spanish wines. Paella and roast suckling pig are favorites. Dinner daily.

Dos Amigos (3), 8 King's Cir. NE; 233-2438, 5444 Memorial Dr., Stone Mountain; 299-2400. *I.* This casual neighborhood eatery in the Peachtree Hills section features Texan-Mexican dishes of healthy proportions. The crowd is Atlanta's young professionals.

El Azteca, 2257 Peachtree Rd.; 355-9489; 6078 Roswell Rd.; 255-9807; 880 Atlanta St. in Roswell; 998-9253; 3424 Piedmont Rd.; 266-3787. *I.* These fun Mexican restaurants are simple, fast, and good. Outdoor tables make a good place to sit, sip, and watch the traffic go by. The one on Piedmont Road between Peachtree and Roswell has an especially large and shady outdoor cafe.

Jalisco (C3), 2337 Peachtree Rd. NE; 233-9244. *I.* Tucked near the elbow of the Peachtree Battle Shopping Center, Jalisco is a cheerful Mexican restaurant with a very reasonable price range and tasty south-of-the-border specialties. Dinner 5 - 10:30 pm daily.

Light of India (B3), 3861 Roswell Rd. NE; 233-9802. *M.* For excellent curry prepared to any taste, try the Light of India. To the strains of the sitar, sample chicken Tikka, delectable bite-size pieces of chicken cooked in a tandoori or baked-clay oven or Samosas, deep-fried vegetables dipped in a pineapple and mango sauce. Then progress to your curry, lamb, beef, chicken, or vegetable, served as you like it — mild, or medium (Madras), or hot (Vindaloo), or very, very hot (Phela). Lunch and dinner daily.

Nikolai's Roof (J10), the Atlanta Hilton Hotel, Courtland and Harris Sts.; 659-2000. *E.* At Nikolai's Roof you will usually need reservations in advance, sometimes weeks and months in advance. Atop the Atlanta Hilton Hotel, Nikolai's Roof brings you a five-course dinner fit for a Czar, a verbal menu, which rotates every ten days, recited by your waiter in an opulent environment reminiscent of Czarist Russia.

Flavored Russian vodka, rare wines, and a splendid series of culinary offerings — have it all at Nikolai's Roof. Prix fixe. Two dinner seatings nightly.

Niko's (C4), 1803 Cheshire Bridge Rd.; 872-1254. *I.* This charming, small family-operated restaurant offers excellent Greek dishes such as moussaka, pastitsio, dolmades, beef Stifado, melitzanes Parayenistes, and kalamadakios, all with Greek salad. Painted murals of the Greek seacoast and soft Greek music recreate the warmth and friendliness of a Mediterranean cafe. Greek beer and wines. Lunch and dinner Mon-Sat.

Papa Pirozki's (A3), 4953 Roswell Rd.; 252-1118. *M.* Small, intimate rooms in this authentic Russian café offer a romantic setting for homemade pirozkis and traditional Russian cuisine. Add Russian music and vodka and enjoy. Lunch and dinner Mon-Sat.

U.S. Bar & Grill (C3), 2002 Howell Mill Rd. NW; 352-0033. *I to M.* Cross the border into Mexico, name your beer, and be seated in the dining room with its slow-moving ceiling fans and wooden booths. Cabridos, goat, is being barbecued and every wonderful Mexican dish is on the menu. The U.S. Bar & Grill is a "must" for lovers of Mexican fare. Lunch and dinner daily.

Italian

Avanti Italian Restaurant (B3), 3689 Roswell Rd. NE; 266-1094. *M.* Avanti's has become a neighborhood restaurant, extremely popular with locals and also those from further afield, who all flock here for superb pastas. Dinner Mon-Sat.

Bugatti (J8), Omni International Hotel, One Omni International; 659-0000. *E.* Northern Italian fare is the specialty at Bugatti's plum elegant and quiet niche in the Omni Hotel. Bugatti offers you a dining place of stylish modernity and the quintessence of northern Italian cuisine, accenting delicate seafoods and veal entrees. Sunday brunch is a feast for the eyes as well as the palate. Lunch Mon-Fri, dinner and buffet daily.

Capo's Cafe (C4), 992 Virginia Ave. NE; 876-5655. *I to M.* Located in the Virginia-Highlands area, Capo's caters to this neighborhood of young professionals, writers and entrepreneurs. Pasta and other

Italian and continental specialties are lovingly prepared. Capo's is small and usually crowded so we suggest an early arrival. This restaurant maintains the reputation as one of Atlanta's finest. From downtown take a ten-minute cab ride to the intersection of Virginia Avenue and North Highland. Dinner Tue-Sat.

Cognito's Italian Restaurant (C3), 1928 Piedmont Circle NE; 876-4272. *M to E.* This restaurant is in a small, charming white brick house and takes full advantage of the individual rooms. It is comfortable and intimate. The menu is creative and extensive enough for all tastes. Valet parking is a plus, as is the excellent and friendly service. Dinner Mon-Sun.

Gene and Gabe's (C3), 1578 Piedmont Rd. NE; 874-6145. *M.* Gene and Gabe have been serving northern Italian fare to Atlantans for over a decade and a half. Veal dishes are the specialties. Gene and Gabe's is cozy Italian, a small dining space, with art works and low light, and adjoining bar with pianist and singer. After dining take in a cabaret show at the "Upstairs at Gene and Gabe's," another choice Atlanta act. See the Cabaret section in the NIGHTLIFE Chapter. Dinner daily.

Gene and Gabe's Lodge, 936 Canton St., Roswell; 993-7588. *M.* Both locals and visitors enjoy this popular establishment located in a restored 1800s Masonic lodge. The specialty here is northern Italian, but you will find other choices on the menu. Expect the same delicious consistency as in the original Gene and Gabe's. Join the rest of the crowd at the piano bar after dinner. Lunch Mon-Fri, dinner Mon-Sat.

La Grotta (C3), 2637 Peachtree Rd. NE; 231-1368. *E.* La Grotta is a pleasant surprise in the terrace level of a Peachtree condominium complex. A small sign points the way to some of Atlanta's finest in northern Italian cuisine. La Grotta offers a five-course testimonial to its superb reputation. Savor the evening starting with the antipasto, continuing to the homemade pasta, the fish and veal specialties and, on reaching the sweet, end with Italian ice cream and espresso, cappucino, or an assortment of after-dinner coffees. The courtyard setting is intimate and soft with candlelight. Valet parking. Dinner Tue-Sat.

DINING

La Grotta of Roswell, 647 Atlanta Street, Roswell; 998-0645. *E.* On the square in Roswell, a beautiful restored house is the setting for the suburban La Grotta. The excellent quality is illustrated with their unsurpassed pasta and the specialty entrees. Dinner Tue-Sat.

Nino's (C4), 1931 Cheshire Bridge Rd. NE; 874-6505. *M.* Looking for that little Italian restaurant for an intimate evening for conversation, unsurpassed Italian cuisine, and friendly service? Nino's is your place with veal saltimbocca the chef's specialty. Dinner daily.

Provino's (B3), 4387 Roswell Rd.; 256-4300. 5231 Memorial Dr. Stone Mountain; 292-3617, 1255 Grimes Bridge Rd. Roswell; 993-5839. *I.* Provino's has southern Italian fare for the budget-minded traveler, for families, and for those who have a penchant for pasta and rich sauces. Dinner Mon-Sat.

Joe Rigatoni's (A2), 2640 Windy Hill Rd., 952-5888; *I.* The exterior of Joe Rigatoni's is glassy and glossy in neonscript, a modern Italianesque design. This popular shop includes a drinking bar and spaghetti bar with 28 flavors of sauce. Joe's is an easy going place to go singly, doubly or with the family. Lunch and dinner daily.

1019 (C4), 1019 Virginia Ave. NE; 874-1019. *M.* This sophisticated dining experience in the Virginia-Highlands area focuses on delicate northern Italian dishes. The name is taken from the street number, the ambience of the storefront location is enhanced by the chocolate and rose decor, Victorian lamps, and spirited waiters. Make reservations in advance. Dinner Mon-Sat.

Trotter's (B3), 3215 Peachtree Rd. NE; 237-5988. *E.* Trotter's lines Peachtree Road with its creamy carriage-house architecture serving a fine northern Italian cuisine inside. The theme is harness racing; Currier and Ives prints and photographs of famous United States trotters line the walls. The Brunswick bar decor features authentic jockey silks and lamps from the Orient Express. Lunch Mon-Fri, dinner daily, brunch Sun.

Vittorio's (C3), 2263 Peachtree Rd. NE; 355-0874. *M.* Vittorio's is old Italy revisited. For twenty years this restaurant has attracted sports folks and politicos on the Atlanta scene with a mixture of Roman and American fare and a lively piano bar. Dinner Mon-Sat.

Oriental

Bangkok (C3), 1492-A Piedmont Rd. NE; 874-2514. *I*. Atlanta's first Thai restaurant, Bangkok has a fine choice of authentic foods from this oriental section of the world. The fare is spicy and generally hot. If you are a hot food or mild food person, check with your waiter with each selection. Service is friendly; the decor is modest as well as the price. No reservations. Closed Tue, lunch Mon, Wed-Sat, dinner Mon, Wed-Sun.

Benihana of Tokyo (J9), Peachtree Center, 522-9627; and (C3), 2143 Peachtree Rd. NE; 355-8565. *M*. For downtowners with a lust for raw seafood and for those who want the opportunity to try this exotic fare, the Sushi bar at Benihana's at Peachtree Center is a special treat from Japan. The first Benihana in Atlanta, at 2143 Peachtree Rd., is a recreated, 17th-century Japanese palace, hand-built by Japanese craftsmen with materials made in Japan. This restaurant and the newest location at Peachtree Center feature tabletop teppan-yaki cooking at your table with an expert flourish of the knives. Lunch Mon-Sat, dinner daily.

Cha Gio (H11), 998 Peachtree St. NE; 876-1817. *I*. The modest Cha Gio store-front restaurant is one of the nicest additions to Atlanta's international foods. Authentic Vietnamese fare includes a generous buffet lunch with fresh vegetables and four main dishes and a four-course dinner. Lunch and dinner Mon-Sat.

Golden Buddha (C4), 1905 Clairmont Rd. NE; 633-5252. *I*. The Chinese community in Atlanta patronizes the Golden Buddha with its plentiful cast of Chinese Mandarin foods. This restaurant is also a familiar family dining place for Emory University faculty, students, and neighbors. Combination dinners are a popular choice for two to eight persons, and the Imperial Mandarin Banquet is a must for a large group. This feast requires one day's notice but guarantees an evening of communal enjoyment for Chinese food fanciers. Lunch and dinner Tue-Sun.

Grand China (B3), 2975 Peachtree Rd. NE; 231-8690. *I*. In the heart of Buckhead, Grand China offers a triple treat, Szechuan, Mandarin, and Hunan cuisine. Take your pick in this restaurant of bone-white decor and smiling service. Grand China, with the dragon in its logo, serves lots and lots of good Chinese food at a reasonable price. Lunch Tue-Fri, dinner Mon-Sat.

Great Wall (J8), Omni International, 522-8213; and 3861 Washington Rd. near Hartsfield Airport, 767-8850. *I.* The Great Wall opens into the wonderful skylighted world of the Omni International mall. This restaurant with a flair for China-red decor features Mandarin Chinese food with Imperial dinners. Have an oriental feast before attending a sporting event or a concert at the Omni Coliseum next door. Omni location, lunch Mon-Sat; Washington Road location, lunch and dinner daily.

Ichiban Steak House (J9), 151 Ellis St. NE; 659-7607. *M.* Ichiban, conveniently located in downtown Atlanta, specializes in authentic Japanese teppan-yaki and hibachi table-cooking by your personal chef in the quiet sensuality of oriental surroundings. From prime sirloin steaks to the final fortune cookie, Ichiban has been a long time favorite with visitors. Dinner daily.

Kobe Steaks (A3), the Prado Shopping Center, 5600 Roswell Rd. NE; 256-0810. *M.* Kobe Steaks is in the tower plaza of the Prado Center, a few blocks from the perimeter I-285, and therefore convenient to the northside of town. The milieu is authentic Japanese designed by one of Japan's leading architects. Enjoy a gracious display of teppan-yaki table-cooking, oriental decor, and polished service from the kimono-clad waitresses. Kobe steak is the specialty, the ultimate in the choicest beef, as the name says, but seafood and chicken dishes are also offered. Dinner daily.

Ming Garden (B3), 5006 Roswell Rd.; 255-4515. *I.* Chef's specialties cover all geographical regions of China. Try family dinners, the Emperor's Feast, and Banquet Royale for parties. Lunch Mon-Fri, dinner daily.

Nakato (C3), 1893 Piedmont Rd. NE; 873-6582. *M.* Nakato has three dining rooms for three different Japanese cuisines. Teppan-yaki cooking features steel tables where the food is prepared, cooked, and individually served by the chef. Sukiyaki dinners include thin strips of beef simmered in special Nakato sauces with vegetables, shirataki noodles, and mushrooms cooked at your table. Tempura features shrimp, seafood, and vegetables deep fried with a crispy thin golden batter at the tempura bar. Choose one of Nakato's dining experiences and come back for another. Dinner daily.

A Taste of China (J9), Peachtree Center, Harris Tower; 659-6333. *M.* Authentic oriental cuisine from China's five provinces is served in the Taste of China's elegant two-story dining hall, adorned with colorful masks, dragons, kites, and calligraphy. The Peachtree Center location is ideal for downtown business, shoppers and conventioneers. Lunch Mon-Fri, dinner Mon-Sat.

Seafood

The Captain's Roost (E2), 2873 Main St., East Point; 761-9468. *M.* For south Atlanta, the Captain's Roost provides an attractive nautical setting for fresh fish. This restaurant has a long-standing reputation as "the" choice for south Atlantans. Lunch Tue-Fri, dinner Tue-Sat.

Caravan's Crab Shack (C5), 4761 Memorial Dr.; 292-1305. *I to M.* The main dish is the crab, served Maryland-style boiled with spices and red pepper. There is plenty of fruit from the sea in addition to the crab, drinks plain and fancy and good camaraderie. Lunch and dinner Mon-Sat.

Chequers (A4), 236 Perimeter Center Pkwy., 391-9383. *M.* Mesquite-grilled seafood and daily specials are served in a dining atmosphere reminiscent of an Old English Sea Coast House. Lunch and dinner daily. Jazz brunch Sun.

The Cross Roads (C3), 1556 Peachtree St. NE; 875-2288, 875-6375. *I to M.* This restaurant dates from 1948, one of Atlanta's oldest. Family atmosphere, a children's menu, amiable service, and "all you can eat" seafoods continue to make it a popular dining room. Lunch Sun-Fri, dinner daily.

Embers Seafood Grille (A3), 234 Hildebrand; 256-0977. *M.* Residents of Sandy Springs nightly patronize this small, select seafood restaurant. Grilled fish, mussels, conch chowder, and the taramasalata dip add up to a fine treat. Dinner daily.

The Fish Market (B3), Lenox Square in the new market section; 233-4469. *M to E.* The list of seafood is extensive. The restaurant is a piece of Adriatic fantasia, with an aromatic fish market display counter and a mauve-gray color theme accented with brass rails, green plants, marbleized urns and walls, and Victorian lace curtains and prints. Lounge, lunch and dinner Mon-Sat.

Jim White's Half Shell (C3), Peachtree Battle Shopping Center, 2349 Peachtree Rd. NE; 237-9924. *I to M.* The Half Shell is an informal neighborhood restaurant, a pioneer in seafood establishments in

Atlanta. Its location in the Peachtree Battle Shopping Center is convenient to downtown and the suburbs. For an evening of solid seafood satisfaction and atmosphere have dinner at the Half Shell. Dinner Mon-Sat.

Marra's (C3), 1782 Cheshire Bridge Rd. NE; 874-7347. *M.* Seafood at Marra's is charcoal-grilled with an Italian accent. Pasta accompanies fish. Mako shark, mussels, antipasto and cioppino complement the regular menu of seafood. Seating is on two levels in this attractive, small house-restaurant. Dinner Mon-Sat.

Rusty Scupper (B3), 3285 Peachtree Rd. NE, 266-0944; and (A2), Windy Hill Rd. at I-75, 952-6111. *M.* These uniquely contemporary restaurants are a maze of plants, wood, and balconies filled with local clientele as well as visitors. The bar and restaurant cater to the young business group, but there are customers of all ages. The specialty is seafood, with 23-ounce crab legs one of their offerings. There is a large friendly bar with live music Tuesday through Saturday. Lunch Mon-Sat and dinner every day.

S & W Seafood (A3), 6125 Roswell Rd.; 255-8218. *M.* You know the seafood is fresh when the S & W fish market adjoins the restaurant. To whet your appetite take a look at the beautiful bounty of the sea in the market counters before eating. Then settle in for a delicious meal in the dining area, trimmed with ships, lanterns, and nautical garb. Great for groups and families. No reservations. Lunch and dinner Mon-Sat.

Savannah the Cafe (B4), 2042 Johnson Ferry Rd., Cambridge Shopping Center; 452-1212. *M.* This charming small restaurant has the feel of dining in one of the fine homes of Savannah, Georgia. The peach and white decor is as relaxing as the classical music. Seafood is presented with attention to esthetics, and the dozen entrees afford ample pleasure for the discriminating seafood lover. The Cafe Bar is in the front, the separate dining room beyond. Lunch Mon-Fri, dinner Mon-Sat.

Savannah Fish Company, (J9), Westin Peachtree Plaza Hotel, Peachtree at International Blvd.; 523-2500. M. Named after Georgia's famous seacoast city of Savannah. Fish entrees may be broiled or pan-fried in butter — take your choice. In addition try the California wine bar and oyster bar, all this in John Portman's dramatic hotel setting. Lunch and dinner daily.

Simon's (B2), 2950 Cobb Parkway; 952-6042. *M.* This restaurant, gleaming with brass, wood, and dark green decor, offers exclusively charbroiled fish. The six fresh fish steaks or fillets of the day are presented by the waitress on a bed of lettuce for your choice and edification. Oyster bar, jazz quartet, dancing. Lunch and dinner daily, brunch Sun.

William's Seafood of Savannah (C4), 2922 Clairmont Rd.; 633-1088. *I to M.* The respected William's Seafood House of Savannah is now on the Atlanta scene, serving the freshest seafood available. William's is informal, family-oriented, and within everyone's seafood budget. Lunch and dinner daily.

Southern

Aunt Fanny's Cabin (B1), 2155 Campbell Rd., Smyrna; 436-5218. *M.* This restaurant will serve you "real Southern cooking" in the 130-year-old former slave cabin of Aunt Fanny Williams. Family-style dinners include regional foods such as fried chicken, Smithfield ham, home-cooked greens, and the house specialty, baked squash. Waiters and waitresses add impromptu nightly singing and piano playing. Dinner daily, lunch Sun.

Feedmill Restaurant (B3), 35-A W. Paces Ferry Rd. NW; 233-0134. *I.* For down-home Southern cooking, in the heart of Buckhead, visit the Feedmill Restaurant. Meat, two vegetables and delicious cornbread are favorites. Open all day Mon-Sat until 8 pm.

Harold's (D2), 171 McDonough Blvd. SE; 627-9268. *I.* This barbecue restaurant in south Atlanta brings in the faithful from Atlanta and surrounding counties. Lunch and dinner Mon-Sat.

Lickskillet Farm, Old Roswell Rd. and Buckmill Rd.; 475-6484. *M.* This pre-Civil War farmhouse is rural eloquence. Enjoy cocktails in the gazebo overlooking Foekiller Creek before stepping back to the restaurant for a select country menu of chicken, steaks, and seafood. A roaring fire in winter and piano entertainment in the evening make

Lickskillet Farm a special place. Dinner Tue-Sat, Champagne brunch Sun.

Mary Mac's (I11), 224 Ponce de Leon Ave. NE; 875-4337. *I.* If you've never been to the South, Mary Mac's will thrill you, and if you're from the South, especially any small town that has its local restaurant, you'll be right at home at Mary Mac's. The food is country southern — vegetables that will melt in your mouth, okra and tomatoes, collard greens, black-eyed peas, cornbread and biscuits, fried chicken, pies, and other gooey sweets. While you are enjoying writing your own order, look around for some politically famous faces. Everyone loves Mary Mac's; it's three minutes from downtown hotels. No reservations. Lunch and dinner until 8:00 pm Mon-Fri.

Old Hickory House (C3), 265 Pharr Rd. NE; 266-9353. *I.* Call for 18 other locations throughout metro Atlanta. Old Hickory House is an Atlanta barbecue institution, family-owned and operated, with some of the best secret barbecue recipes in the South. Try pork, beef, or chicken with or without jalapeno peppers, special slaw, and the famous Old Hickory House brunswick stew. Breakfast, lunch, and dinner daily.

Pittypat's Porch (J9), 25 International Blvd.; 525-8228. *M to E.* The tone is antebellum "Old South" at Pittypat's Porch with original southern antiques, period memorabilia, rocking chairs, and the staff in full costume. Traditional southern cooking is the main attraction although American and continental dishes are also on the menu. The extravagant cocktail buffet has a special "endless appetizer" ticket for those who can't get past the raw oysters, fresh shrimp, and other pre-dinner delectables. Dinner Mon-Sat.

The Silver Skillet (G10), 200 14th St. NW; 874-1388. *I.* Down home southern food — come and get it at the Silver Skillet, where grits and redeye gravy, buttermilk biscuits and country ham are for breakfast, and fried steak, fried chicken and succotash are for lunch. Breakfast beginning at 6 am and lunch Mon-Fri, open 6 - 11 am Sat.

Texas State Line Barbecue (B3), 25 Irby Ave.; 233-3909. *I to M.* Put on your jeans and boots and pull up a seat to the best barbecue from the Lone Star state. Lunch and dinner Mon-Sat.

ETCETERA

Here is a grab bag of interesting but difficult-to-define items in the Atlanta restaurant scene. Take your pick. Some gourmet fast foods, coffee houses, natural-food eateries, dessert places, and hamburger joints.

The Art of Conversation (G11), 1144 Crescent Ave.; 881-8865. From cappuccino and desserts to fine wines by the glass, the Art of Conversation is a cafe after the European tradition. A renovated turn-of-the-century home provides an inviting coffee house ambiance. Open 11 am - 1 am Tue-Sun.

Atlantis Natural Foods Restaurant (A4), 5475 Chamblee-Dunwoody Rd.; 393-1297. *I.* Juicy apples, avocado salads, guacamole galore and pita sandwiches, yogurts, and herb teas are served for lunch only at Atlantis in suburban Dunwoody Village Shopping Center where "beautiful women in the world come to shop." Lunch Mon-Sat.

B.K.'s Greenhouse Restaurant (C3), 1700 Monroe Dr. NE; 872-4428. *I.* Second location in Toco Hills Shopping Center (C4). *I.* Housed in the deluxe Kroger grocery stores in the above shopping centers, the Greenhouse Restaurants provide one-stop service for both shopping and dining. The restaurants sport the "greenhouse" look with plants, brass, and deep-green patterns. The prices are very modest, some of the lowest in town, the food is first class, and the atmosphere is for families, partners, or singles. Full bar also. Breakfast beginning at 6 am, lunch and dinner daily.

The Baker's Deli (D3), 1134 Euclid Ave., NE; 223-5039. *I.* It's a deli with delicious desserts, great sandwiches, and dinner pasta, chicken, and beef specialties. This is a regular haunt for the neighborhoods of Inman and Candler Park in the Little Five Points intersection. Bring your own beer or wine. Lunch and dinner Mon-Sat. Brunch Sun.

Beef Cellar (A3), 215 Copeland Rd. NE; 252-1256. *I.* A popular place for night-owls, who come here for delicious breakfasts, served until 5 am.

Brother Juniper's (G12), 1037 Peachtree St. NE; 881-6225. *I.* This bright breakfast and lunch spot in midtown is run by a Catholic brother offering good cheer, deli sandwiches with homemade bread in two sizes, whole and half, desserts such as poppy-seed cake, and beverages that include fresh lemonade, hot, spiced cider, and red zinger tea. Eggs, waffles, and omelets are for breakfast. Breakfast and lunch Mon-Fri.

Cafe Intermezzo (A4), Park Place, 4505 Ashford-Dunwoody Rd.; 396-1344. *M.* Cafe Intermezzo is a European sophisticate, a small, super-charming coffeehouse with the largest brass Italian espresso machine in the world as the center of attraction. Enjoy delicate and intricate pastries, flans, sandwiches, imported beer and wine, and wonderful coffee. Open Mon-Sat 10 am - 11 pm, Sun 4 - 10.

Chicago's (A3), Parkaire Mall, Johnson Ferry Rd.; 977-0990. *I.* For wonderful deep-dish pizza and mouth-watering baby back ribs, visit Chicago's. Open daily from 5 pm. P.S. Don't forget to sample their stunning mushrooms.

The Dessert Place (C4), 1000 Virginia Ave. NE; 892-8921; (B3), 279 E. Paces Ferry Rd., 233-2331. *I.* This small specialty eatery will soothe your sweet tooth with its regalia of desserts. Two Atlanta women opened the first Dessert Place in the Virginia-Highlands neighborhood, and they now have a second restaurant in Buckhead. Pop in after anything. Virginia Avenue open Tue-Thur 5 pm - 11:30 pm, Fri 5 pm - 12:30 am, and Sat 1 pm - 12:30 am. Buckhead location open Tue-Thur 12 noon - 11:30 pm, Fri 12 noon - 12:30 am, and Sat 1 pm - 12:30 am. Both locations are closed Sun and Mon.

D'Lites (C3), 1861 Peachtree Rd. NE; 448-0654. *I.* This lite, fast-food restaurant has drive-through service and a charming blonde oak, brass and glass restaurant catering to the calorie-conscious-but-hamburger-lovers. The menu contains a calorie count. Other locations in metro Atlanta. An unusual chain, lite beer and wine are served also. Lunch and dinner daily.

Eat Your Vegetables Cafe (C4), 438 Moreland Ave. NE; 523-2671. *I.* Stay and eat seafood and vegetables in this little exposed-brick-wall cafe or take them home or to a park in fair weather. Vegetable tempura, quiches, and vegetables with a difference make this place in Inman Park intriguing. No smoking. Lunch Mon - Sat 11:30 am - 2 pm; dinner Mon-Thu 6 pm - 10 pm, and Fri-Sat 6 pm - 11 pm.

Gabriel's (C3), 112 10th St. NE; 885-1502. *I to M*. Gabriel's is a storefront restaurant in Midtown, a neighborhood eatery, charming and relaxing. This is the perfect spot for late Sunday breakfast and reading the Sunday paper. Breakfast and lunch daily.

The Garden Room (K9), Georgia Plaza Park, Central Ave. and Mitchell St., across from the State Capitol. 656-6648. *I*. This delightful luncheon spot awaits the visitor touring Capitol Hill and the many hungry government employees and politicians in the area. Weigh your salad at the salad bar and eat in the park at umbrella-shaded picnic tables. Finish your lunch with an ice-cream cone from the stand. The ambience is Atlanta's finest in sidewalk cafes. Lunch only.

Gelateria (B3), Abernathy Square, 2½ miles north of I-285 and Roswell Rd.; 252-7718. *I*. Serving a variety of popular gelato and yogurt desserts, this small cafe also serves sandwiches. Call ahead if you're in a hurry.

Halperns' Seafood Bar (B3), Lenox Square, 3393 Peachtree Rd. NE; 231-5050. *M*. Pink shrimp, rosy lobsters, and plump shellfish are wondrously displayed on ice, tempting you to pull up a chair to the bar for light seafood fare. Open Mon-Sat 10 am - 9 pm, Sun 12 - 5 pm.

International Food Works (J9), 133 Peachtree St. NE; 529-9411. *I to M*. The "Works" is in the Georgia-Pacific Tower, second floor, a colorful marriage of eight pavillions of foods, open market-style. Take your pick: The New York Deli, Just Sweets, Bailey's Broiler, On Ice (salad bar), Chows (Chinese), Garcia's (Mexican), The Skillet (International) and "1896" (the year ice cream made its debut). Have the Works! Breakfast and lunch Mon-Fri.

Le Gourmet (C3), 2334 Peachtree Rd. NE; 266-8477. *M*. In the Peachtree Battle Shopping Center enjoy the delectables from this small bakery and deli. Mon-Sat 10 - 6.

Maison Robert Bakery (B4), 3867 Peachtree Rd. NE in Cherokee Plaza; 237-3675. *M*. This charming tearoom-bakery serves luncheon daily including special entrees, salads, and delicate confections. Eat in or take home some homemade pastries, candies, and genuine French croissants. Opened Tue-Fri 8:30 am - 5:30 pm; Sat 8 am - 6 pm.

Meat 'n Three's. *M*. For an unusual down-to-earth meal in a modest house or small restaurant/grill, try the Meat 'n Three's. . . . that's short for meat and three vegetables. Prices are low, the folks are nice, and you can still experience a small town atmosphere in urban

Atlanta. Try the following for breakfast or lunch. Melvin's and the Silver Grill are also open for dinner.

Burton's Grill (D3), 1029 Edgewood Ave. NE; 525-9439. **Melvin's** (C3), 1330 Northside Dr. NW; 352-2124. **Mr. B's** (C3), 1430 W. Peachtree St. NW; 892-3667. **Silver Grill** (C3), 900 Monroe Dr. NE; 876-8145.

My Friend's Place (A3), Hammond Square in Sandy Springs, half mile north of I-285 and Roswell Rd.; 252-6280. *I.* A small, family-run restaurant, My Friend's Place specializes in "healthy" food such as pita-bread sandwiches, quiches, and homemade soups. Opened Mon-Fri 9 am - 7:30 pm; Sat 9 am - 5 pm.

The Park (G12), Colony Square, 14th and Peachtree Sts. NE; 881-6449. *I.* Homemade gourmet fast foods with a flair include soups, salads, sandwiches, and desserts. The Park is a restful green and white sidewalk cafe. Mon-Sat 8 - 8.

Pizzeria Uno (A3), 5600 Roswell Rd. NE in the Prado; 256-0047. *I.* Delicious, deep-dish pizza smothered with homemade sausage and fresh vegetables is the specialty in this handsomely decorated pizza restaurant. The attractive bar, which serves a good selection of beer, is a favorite of the singles crowd and the pizza is to everybody's liking. Sun-Thu 11:30 am - 12 pm; Fri and Sat 11:30 am - 1:30 am.

The Primavera Gelateria (A3), Chastain Square in Sandy Springs; 843-3334. *I.* Atlanta's first gelateria is also a cafe decorated Italian-style and offering espresso, beer and wine, meat and cheese plates, and the popular Italian ice-cream, gelato. Open daily.

Rainbow Grocery and Cafe (C4), 2118 N. Decatur Rd. NE; 633-3538. *I.* Natural foods, fresh produce, cosmetics, and vitamins are sold in the grocery. The cafe at the back has wonderful hot entrees, soups, salads, sandwiches, and desserts, naturally. Lunch daily.

Round the Corner (B2), 2977 Cobb Pkwy., Smyrna, 952-5395; and (A3), 6317 Roswell Rd., in Sandy Springs, 252-6668. *I.* A most extraordinary hamburger place. Make your selection from more than 26 burger variants, pick up the phone at your table and place your order. When the buzzer sounds your order is ready. Meanwhile enjoy a mug of beer or a glass of wine. The atmosphere is friendly, family-oriented with green plants, wood baskets, and quilts. Open seven days a week.

The Varsity (I10), 61 North Ave. NW; 881-1706. *I.* The Varsity is an Atlanta landmark next to Georgia Tech. The shiny red enamel art-deco exterior, the jazzy curb service, and the TV rooms are part of Atlanta's fast-food history. Chili dogs are a must before Georgia Tech football games. Service is 24 hours.

CAFETERIAS

Cafeterias have many selections of meats, seafood, vegetables, and desserts at inexpensive prices. Many older Atlantans still have the habit of eating regularly at their favorite cafeteria. Below are our choices.

Davis Bros. (F3), State Farmers Market, Forest Park; 366-7414. Five other locations. The vegetables and fruits are fresh off the farmer's trucks. Try their southern cooking after a visit to this great Farmers Market.

International Food Works — See Etcetera above.

Morrison's (C3), Ansley Mall, 1544 Piedmont Ave. NE, 872-8091; and 2964 Peachtree Rd. NW, 237-1131. Six other locations. Morrison's is convenient to neighborhoods and is famous for its fried shrimp.

Picadilly Cafeteria (B2), Cumberland Mall; 432-3322. These cafeterias are popular with shoppers and families at Cumberland and the following malls: Greenbriar, Northlake, South DeKalb, and Southlake.

Terrace Cafeteria (J10), Atlanta Center, 250 Piedmont Ave. NE; 659-5243. The downtown Atlanta Center next to the Atlanta Hilton Hotel houses this fine cafeteria serving a variety of foods.

BRUNCH

Sunday brunch — that wonderful contraction of breakfast and lunch in a midday meal — has become a fashionable leisure activity for après-church or following a morning of rest. For the traveler, brunch can be a welcome shift in dining, leaving the morning and evening free. Remember that liquor cannot be served in Atlanta until after 12:30 on Sunday. We list below some selected brunch spots in the city. Call to check specific times and refer to restaurant listings for further information.

DINING

Brickworks (A1), 1 Depot St. NW, on the square in Marietta; 426-0544. For railroad buffs and friends have brunch "on the rails" in this old and elegantly refurbished warehouse.

Bugatti's (J8), in the Omni International Hotel; 659-0000. One of the most famous spreads in town.

Cafe de la Paix (J10), in the Atlanta Hilton Hotel, Courtland and Harris Sts.; 659-2000. The variety is overwhelming and delicious.

Café Milan (B2), 25 Galleria Pkwy.; 953-1121. Brunch in the Galleria is lovely.

Cashin's. Numerous locations. See above under American. Casual brunches in mall locations.

Clarence Foster's (C3), 1915 Peachtree Rd. NE; 351-0002. Soothing jazz tunes accompany your meal.

Clock of Five's (J9), Hyatt Regency Atlanta, 265 Peachtree St. NE; 577-1234. If you've brunched in a Hyatt before, you know to expect a delicious buffet.

W. D. Crowley restaurants. Numerous listings. See above under American. Upbeat brunch for the suburban set.

The Country Place (G12), Colony Square, 14th St. and Peachtree St. NE; 881-0144. Extra-popular midtown brunch.

The Crown Room (S12), Colony Square Hotel, 14th and Peachtree Sts. NE; 892-6000. Atlanta's famous "blue-jean brunch."

57th Fighter Group (B4), 3829 Clairmont Rd.; 457-7757. The officer's club is open for an all-American brunch.

T.G.I. Friday's (A3), 5600 Roswell Rd. in the Prado; 256-2482. Champagne brunch from the menu, balloons, and fun.

Houlihan's Old Place (B3), Lenox Square; 261-5323 and Park Place; 394-8921. All-you-can-drink Bloody Mary's accompany selections from the regular menu. Finish up with a visit to the tempting sweets' table.

Lickskillet Farm, Old Roswell Rd. and Buckmill Rd.; 475-6484. A popular brunch with a delicious fruit bar, homemade biscuits, and plenty more.

Penrod's (B5), Northlake II, 939-9399; (A2), Akers Mill Square on US 41, 955-9599. Special Saturday and Sunday brunches with free champagne popular with the singles' crowd.

Simons (B2), 2950 Cobb Pkwy.; 952-6042. Jazzy bruncheon at Simon's Seafood Bar.

The Sun Dial (J9), in the Westin Peachtree Plaza Hotel, 659-1400. Begin your week right with brunch seventy-three stories high.

Tower Rib Room (B3), in the Tower Place Hotel, Piedmont and Peachtree Sts.; 231-1234. Superb brunch beautifully served.

Trotters (B3), 3215 Peachtree Rd. NE; 237-5988. Elite, elegant brunch in the carriage house.

The Waverly (B2), The Galleria, 2450 Galleria Pkwy.; 953-4500. The Waverly, a Stouffer Hotel, serves brunch in the elegant tradition.

Winfield's (B2), 100 Galleria Pkwy.; 955-5300. A handsome magnet for East Cobb county for brunch.

PERFORMING ARTS

The performing arts match the economic surges in Atlanta with equally vigorous expressions in music, the dance, and theater. From jazz to symphony, from ballet to street mime, from storefront drama to the proscenium stage, Atlantans turn out to see and hear classical and cyclical performances as well as those on the cutting edge of change in cultural expressions. Turn one of our listings into an evening of special meaning and enrichment; let Atlanta perform for you.

Dance

The Atlanta Dance Festival is the highlight of the year in July. All the city's dance groups come together to present a varied and exciting city-sponsored event.

Atlanta Ballet, 477 Peachtree St. NE; 873-5811. This fine regional ballet company holds the honor of being the oldest continually performing ballet company in the United States. Born in 1929, the Atlanta Ballet repertory company, under the direction of Robert Barnett, has regularly scheduled performances in Atlanta and on tour. Expect innovation in presenting traditional and original programs at the Atlanta Civic Center (I11).

Callanwolde Dance Ensemble (C4), Callanwolde Fine Arts Center, 980 Briarcliff Rd. NE; 872-5338. This small young dance group specializes in ballet, both contemporary and classical.

Carl Ratcliff Dance Theater (B3), Phipps Plaza, 3500 Peachtree Rd. NE; 266-0010. This modern dance team headed by Carl Ratcliff specializes in modern dance, with public performances at the Peachtree Playhouse and other locations from September to June. The chamber-size company is in its second decade of dance in Atlanta.

Company Kaye (C4), 1060 St. Charles Ave. NE; 876-6998. Director Meli Kaye leads this company of ten in mime and modern dance, bringing speechless magic and humor to Atlanta audiences for over five years. Performances are held at schools, parks, festivals, and universities.

The Dance Coalition of Metro Atlanta, P.O. Box 13694, Atlanta 30324; 636-8106. This association of dance companies and individual dancers publishes a calendar of quarterly events.

Dancer's Collective Theater (C4), 1105 Euclid Ave.; 659-3267. Dance South, the resident professional company, performs 4 to 5 times a year and also tours. There is also a resident school. The theater is available to local artists on many weekends. A dance series with selected other companies is offered in the fall.

Lee Harper and Dancers, 3110 Roswell Rd.; 261-7416. This dance school and group performs modern dance with the Young People's Concerts of the Atlanta Symphony and at various other times during the year.

Ruth Mitchell Dance Company, 3509 Northside Pkwy. NW; 237-8829. The Ruth Mitchell Dance Company was founded over 20 years ago and performs originally choreographed ballet and jazz dancing. The Peachtree Playhouse at Peachtree and 13th Street (G12) is usually the setting for about 20 performances a year.

Music

The Atlanta Symphony Orchestra (G11), the Robert W. Woodruff Arts Center, 1280 Peachtree St. NE; 892-3600. Tickets 892-2414. Home for the Atlanta Symphony Orchestra is the Robert W. Woodruff Arts Center, built in the 1960s as a memorial to 122 members of the Atlanta Arts Association who were killed in a plane crash at Orly Airport, near Paris, France. The orchestra is under the magnificent direction of Robert Shaw. The season is full to overflowing with regular and special concerts, choral, and dance joint events, with guest conductors and musicians enriching a powerful Atlanta Symphony Orchestra entering its fourth decade. The Atlanta Symphony Orchestra, one of the keystones of cultural strength in the city, will bring you to your feet with its outstanding music.

Master Concerts. The Master Concert season begins in September and lasts to May, the Symphony performing in Symphony Hall on Thursday, Friday, and Saturday each week.

PERFORMING ARTS 97

The Callanwolde Fine Arts Center

Courtesy Callanwolde

Winter Pops Series. At the grand Fox Theatre (I10) downtown four Pops Concerts feature the Symphony and guest musicians and entertainers between October and April, a delightful setting and experience during the winter months.

Christmas Concerts. In Symphony Hall Handel's *Messiah* is performed throughout December with a special sing-along concert. Four family Christmas concerts are offered during this same festive month.

Atlanta Primavera. This Spring Festival of music features six special concerts in Symphony Hall to celebrate the earth's cyclical return to new life.

Atlanta Symphony Orchestra Chorus. The chorus is featured periodically during the Master Concert season and has its own annual special choral concert in April. With Robert Shaw's reputation as one of the world's great choral directors, we recommend these exhilarating combination concerts.

Chastain Concerts (B3). In the outdoor amphitheater in Atlanta's Chastain Park, the Symphony offers a 20-concert summer season under the stars, featuring a classical first act followed by a pops concert with such entertaining lights as Nancy Wilson, Peter Nero, The Fifth Dimension, and Judy Collins. Rent a table or bring your own, open up a gourmet or down-home picnic in the amphitheater, and then settle back for a balmy evening of splendid music. Concerts are held on Wednesday and Friday evenings.

Piedmont Park Free Concerts (C3). Another summer special is the Symphony's free Sunday night series in Piedmont Park. For six evenings Atlanta residents and visitors congregate on the rolling former golf course of Piedmont Park to listen to the classical choices of the Atlanta Symphony. Blankets are spread, picnic dinners are shared, candles are lit, and the city and its people allow the Symphony's sounds to fill the hush of the summer nights.

Children's Concerts. During the school year the Atlanta Symphony holds Young People's Concerts for the youngsters and Symphony Street concerts for small children.

The Atlanta Civic Opera, 2300 Gaslight Tower; 688-7195. This is a professional opera company which presents three productions each year; in the fall, at Christmastime, and in the spring. If they are performing during your stay in Atlanta, be sure to attend their performances at Symphony Hall.

Other organizations performing regularly in Atlanta include the **Atlanta Boy's Choir,** the **Atlanta Chamber Orchestra,** the **Atlanta Chamber Players, Atlanta Virtuosi** and the **Choral Guild of Atlanta.** Also, check the local churches and the colleges and universities for special music programs by faculty, students, and visiting musicians. See Students in the SPECIAL PEOPLE Chapter.

In May the **Metropolitan Opera Company** comes to Atlanta for a week of performances. Opera buffs and connoisseurs arrive from all points in the southeast to join Atlantans in this triumphant rite of spring music. See SPECIAL EVENTS.

Theater

Regional theater has grown from the early roots of the Alliance Theatre, Academy Theatre, and Theatre of the Stars to clusters of small companies, some spin offs, some specialists, all building a solid Atlanta theater community aware of its interdependence and dedicated to dramatic excellence. There is fire and sensitivity in this sector of Atlanta Resurgens.

Midtown from North Avenue to 14th Street has become the "Theater District" in Atlanta, convenient to downtown visitors and to residents throughout the metro area. Original plays take main stage at the local theaters during the annual New Play Project in June. This has become a stirring time for growth in regional theater.

Along with the recommended following companies check the weekly programs at the Fox Theatre, the Atlanta Civic Center, the Omni, and the Atlanta-Fulton County Stadium. Touring concerts, road companies, and other special shows are booked throughout the year. Call SEATS, the central ticket office, at 577-2626 for current programs, times, and locations.

Academy Theatre (I10), 1137 Peachtree St. NE; 892-0880. The Academy Theatre, which began in a Buckhead church, is now permanently located on Peachtree Street in Midtown Atlanta. This repertory company, one of Atlanta's oldest and most respected, presents a season of traditional, contemporary, and new plays with fresh intensity, verve, and improvisation. This is a remarkable Atlanta theater institution, which also includes a Children's Theatre and acting school.

Alliance Theatre (G11), the Robert W. Woodruff Arts Center, 1280 Peachtree St. NE; 892-2414. The Alliance is Atlanta's most prestigious theater company. The full season primarily consists of established and current plays, musicals, Shakespeare, and occasional new works. Each play runs for about a month from October to May, generally to a full house. The proscenium theater with balcony and orchestra has a very large stage and a scenic design facility. You will enjoy the high standard of the Alliance Theatre.

Atlanta Children's Theatre (G11), the Robert W. Woodruff Arts Center, 1280 Peachtree St. NE; 892-7607. Adult actors and actresses present classic and contemporary drama for children.

Callanwolde (C4), 980 Briarcliff Rd. NE; 872-5338. Provocative contemporary, classic, and new plays are all part of the theater at Callanwolde Fine Arts Center in the restored Charles Howard Candler mansion.

The Center for Puppetry Arts, (C3), 1404 Spring St. NW, (at 18th St.); 873-3089 or 873-3391. The center has become in over 15 years the most comprehensive puppetry center in the nation. It offers a museum of the South's largest permanent collection of international puppets, a puppetry school, and the resident troupe, the Vagabond Marionettes. International puppeteers give regularly scheduled performances. Call Box Office, 873-3391, for show times and museum times.

Fox Theatre, (I10), 660 Peachtree St. NE; 881-1977. Don't miss an opportunity to visit the Fox Theatre and the Fox district as a banner experience. The Fox is a 1920s movie palace complete with Moorish and Egyptian-revival decor, a majestic original period organ, and stars a-twinkling on its interior ceilings. Across the street is the Georgian Terrace Hotel where Clark Gable, Vivien Leigh, and the rest of the *Gone with the Wind* cast stayed for the 1939 premier showing. The management of the Fox looked on with envy as they left for the Loew's theater — now the location of the Georgia Pacific building — where the premier took place.

Horizon Theater (C3), 918 Highland View NE; 874-6506. This new company's focus is on plays by internationally renowned playwrights whose works are seldom performed in the Southeast, with an emphasis on works by and/or about women.

PERFORMING ARTS 101

Jomandi Productions (D3), 818 Washington St. SW; 344-3946. Four productions a year are presented by the innovative Jomandi troupe. New works are company-developed and innovative. The stage is the Sullivan Hall in south Atlanta.

Nexus Theatre (C4), 360 Fortune St. NE; 688-2500. New plays with contemporary themes are the heart of the Nexus Theatre, which is within an arts complex, formerly an Atlanta public school building.

Onstage Atlanta (I10), 420 Courtland St. NE; 897-1802. This small company produces fine contemporary drama in its new ex-warehouse location next to St. Luke's Church downtown. Its productions are acclaimed by the critics and enjoyed by the public.

People's Survival Theatre, 799-1597. This majority black theater company specializes in experimental drama, often with political messages.

Seven Stages (D4), 430 Moreland Ave. NE; 523-7647. Near Little Five Points in Inman Park, this theater does original and avant-garde works as well as readings.

The Studio Theatre (G11), the Robert W. Woodruff Arts Center, 1280 Peachtree St. NE; 957-4444. The Studio Theatre is noted for its exciting schedule of new plays, experimental production, and avant-garde material.

Theater in the Square (A1), 31 Mill St., Marietta; 422-8369. A small, 60-seat theater that has recently opened, with a surprisingly high standard of performance.

Theater of the Stars (I11), Civic Center, 395 Piedmont Ave. NE; 252-8960. This Atlanta company has faithfully brought stars of the theater, film, and television to Atlanta audiences for many years. The summer season is in the Civic Center, the winter season is at the Peachtree Playhouse, 1150 Peachtree St. NE.

The Theatrical Outfit (G11), 1012 Peachtree St. NE; 872-0665. Located in the old Kress five and dime building in Midtown, the Theatrical Outfit takes contemporary and experimental theater to a confronting pitch.

NIGHTLIFE

Atlanta has a swelling population of "night people," who shift the urban tempo to many beats after the sun sets. Atlanta "at night" is as exhilarating as the sparkling daytime city. Jazz clubs, neighborhood taverns, disco palaces, rock-music halls, corrals for country music and urban cowboys, big-band tea-dances, class hotel lounges, tasteful wine bars, mellow music, the crowded scene to be seen at, and the intimate corner to be alone and together — Atlanta nightlife is a wide spectrum of nocturnal delights.

Bars and Lounges

There are hundreds of bars in the Atlanta area. We list a few of the most popular that are convenient to visitors. Refer to the following Music for Listening and Dancing section for other bars specializing in music as well as spirits.

Ampersand (J9), in the lobby of the Hyatt Regency downtown; 577-1234. This is a cozy nook off the lobby level of the Hyatt. Conveniently located on Peachtree Street, this piano bar offers cocktails and music and conversation and . . .

Atkins Park (C4), 794 N. Highland Ave.; 876-7249. This is a friendly, neighborhood bar, with a beer garden that welcomes you during the warm season.

Bennigans (B3), Around Lenox and three other locations; 262-7142. Mainly a restaurant, but also a popular bar decked-out in green awnings, dark wood and brass rails — the Victorian tavern par excellence.

Casablanca (J10), in the lobby of the Atlanta Hilton Hotel; 659-2000. When you think of Casablanca, you think of wicker, overhead fans, palm trees (and Bogie!). A popular place to talk, play pool, or watch sporting events on their big-screen TV.

NIGHTLIFE 103

Churchill Arms (B3), 3223 Cains Hill Pl. NW; 233-5633. Drink English beer, play darts, and sing-along to the piano in this English-style pub near the "Buckhead Strip."

Clarence Foster's (C3), 1915 Peachtree St. NE; 351-0002. Singles gravitate to Clarence Foster's at lunch and at dusk for live music, camaraderie, and jazz at Sunday brunch. This New York-style bar is in the Brookwood Hills section of North Atlanta.

The Clubhouse (B3), 3300 Piedmont Rd. NE; 266-0948. This bar displays its allegiance clearly. Football lovers flock here for the congenial atmosphere. Pictures and momentos hang from the walls.

Courtyard (T10), Marriott Hotel Downtown; 659-6500. A splash of Southern tradition brings the past to the present. It has a wonderful atmosphere for relaxation with the feeling of outdoors and sunshine even on the most dreary of days. Your favorite beverage is served poolside; a retractable roof brings the outside in during summer and when closed creates summer in winter. It's perfect for Bloody Mary's with continental breakfast, at lunch, or for a cocktail in the evening.

T.G.I. Friday's (A3), 5600 Roswell Rd. NE in the Prado; 256-2482. *I to M.* Catering to the singles' crowd, Friday's offers juicy hamburgers served as you like, omelets, nachos, and delicious stuffed potato skins. Crazy waiters and wonderful drinks add to the fun-loving atmosphere. The place to be for Happy Hour, Sunday brunch, and late night drinks. Daily 11:30 am - 1 am.

Harrison's on Peachtree (C3), 2110 Peachtree Rd. NW; 351-7596. Harrison's is an attractive uptown bar a la Victoria and a regular meeting place for the smart single set, especially between 6 and 8 pm on Friday. Harrison's is now also at the Galleria (B2), on two levels with an oyster bar below and restaurant and bar above.

P.J. Haley's (C4), 1799 Briarcliff Rd. NE; 874-3116. From the college crowd to the 30s set P.J. Haley's is a casual place to stop in, see friends, and have a drink.

Little Five Points Pub (D4), 1174 Euclid Ave. NE; 577-7767. In the thriving Inman Park area, this pub caters to neighborhood customers in their early 30s who come mainly for conversation, a few drinks, and a lot of great jazz.

McNeeley's (C3), 1900 Peachtree St. NW; 351-1957. McNeeley's is a fun place to be, and is popular with neighborhood residents. See DINING Chapter.

Manuel's Tavern (C4), 602 N. Highland Ave. NE; 525-3447. For 24 years Manuel's has been a watering hole for writers, politicians, students, and those curious about the above. Catch sports on TV, darts, and the inside word on what's happening in Atlanta.

O'Henry's (J9), 230 Peachtree St. NE; 524-5175. This Victorian bar in Peachtree Center East is a perfect resting place for the Atlanta downtown crowd and visitors at lunch and after work.

Pewter Mug (J9), 25 Auburn Ave. NE; 577-6161. Just behind Central City Park, the Pewter Mug attracts more than it can hold for lunch from the central business district. Go early.

Piper's Roost (B3), 375 Pharr Rd. NW; 239-0650. Complete with outdoor cafe, this Buckhead pub features Scottish fare and 23 different imported beers for lunch and dinner. Bag-pipes, Irish folk music, jazz piano and more offered. Closed Sunday.

The Pods (J9), in the Peachtree Plaza Hotel; 659-1400. These islands of comfort jut out into the lake located in the lobby of the Peachtree Plaza. A relaxing place to people-watch as you have a cocktail.

Portner's on Piedmont (B3), 3402 Piedmont Rd.; 266-2855. Come for "unwind time" after work in this fashionable watering hole for the business world. Popular in the evenings and all day Saturday, too.

Raffle's Bar & Grill (A4), Perimeter Mall; 391-9648. Dine and dance to the Top 40 in an art-deco setting, nightly.

Reflections Lounge (C3), Lanier's Ramada Inn Central, 418 Armour Drive NE; 873-4661. Intimate atmosphere, elegant and tasteful with lush plantings, rich oak furnishings, and with top notch entertainment Mon thru Sat.

Reggie's British Pub (J8), Omni International; 525-1437. Loyalty to the crown and the British traditions of the public drinking house characterize this marvelous pub. Reggie will recite Kipling to you and delight you with stories of his stint in India. Great selection of British ale. Lunch and dinner is inexpensive.

The Stein Club (H11), 929 Peachtree St. NE; 876-3707. This tavern has been a long-term resident of Peachtree in midtown, drawing local artists and writers. A jukebox full of old favorites, backroom chess and backgammon, and an open-air beer garden are bonus features.

Taco Mac (C4), 1006 N. Highland Ave. NE; 873-6529. The name suggests Mexican food, which is readily available, but the real specialty is beer, foreign beer in cartons from floor to ceiling. The Taco Mac encyclopedia of beer includes 122 selections, Atlanta's largest. If you love beer, how can you resist?

Timothy John's Restaurant and Tavern (A4), 270 Carpenter Dr., Roswell Rd. at I-285; 252-4695. Beer nights, big screen football nights, and radio station sponsor nights, all attract a young crowd, college and otherwise all week.

The Veranda (G12), in the Colony Square Hotel on Peachtree and 14th Sts.; 892-6000. Enjoy a cocktail while overlooking the tree-studded mall at Colony Square in this meeting place for the sophisticated. Hot hors d'oeuvres served at cocktail hour are an added treat.

Cabarets and Supper Clubs

The Plush Room Cabaret (H10), Hotel York, 683 Peachtree St. NE; 874-9200. Located in the restored Hotel York in Midtown the neon, art-deco sign points the way to the new hot spot for showing Atlanta's talented singers as well as the nation's best. Tue-Sun.

The Punch Line (A3), 280 Hildebrand; 252-5233. Very live and lively comedy that fills the bill. Amateur nights for budding comedians. Tue-Sun.

Saso's (H11), Ansley Mall; 875-8242. This new dinner club features original musical revues and the option of a five-course meal before the show. An outdoor cafe for lunch as well as the late night Berlin Hour featuring local performers and a lot of fun are in the works. Shows Tue-Sat 8:30 pm.

Tom Foolery (B3), 3166 Peachtree Rd. NE, on the strip in Buckhead; 231-8666. This is hard-to-categorize entertainment, a one-man cabaret act or stand-up comedian or magic show. The small bar features the antics, pranks and jokes of 26-year old Tom who delights his full audience each evening, except Sunday. Come enjoy this modern-day jester and trickster.

Upstairs at Gene and Gabe's (C3), 1582 1/2 Piedmont Ave. NE; 892-2261. All seats are excellent in Atlanta's classy New York-style cabaret. Upstairs boasts Atlanta's top performers in satire and musical comedy. The shows are usually original. For an exciting evening of entertainment, head Upstairs. Shows Tue-Thu 8:30 pm; Fri-Sat 8:30 pm and 11 pm.

Upstairs at the Sandpiper (C3), 2960 Piedmont Rd. NE; 266-1706. The Young Americans Song and Dance Company plays a dual role of entertainer as well as waiter or waitress. The versatile performers serve delicious three-course dinners while singing and dancing, with an after-dinner musical revue featuring hits from American music. Showtimes 6 and 8:30 pm, Tue-Sun.

Film

Atlanta has a number of theaters offering vintage and foreign films. Check the newspaper for showings, and also for other theaters with current releases.

Garden Hills (B3), 2835 Peachtree Rd. in Buckhead; 266-2202.

LeFont Ansley (C3), 1544 Piedmont Rd. NE in Ansley Mall; 881-9955.

LeFont Tara (C4), Cheshire Bridge Rd. at I-85; 634-6288.

Rhodes (C3), 1500 Peachtree St. NE; 876-7919. Repertory film program.

The Screening Room (C3), 2581 Piedmont Rd. in Broadview Plaza; 231-1924.

Special films are shown at the following centers. Call for information.

Atlanta Historical Society (B3), 3101 Andrews Dr. NW; 261-1837. With the South as its theme, this summer film series features a movie every Wednesday night from June through August.

Atlanta Public Library (J9), 1 Margaret Mitchell Square NE; 688-4636, ext. 262. These are generally classics and educational films. Also at the Branch Libraries. Free.

Goethe Institute (G12), 400 Colony Square NE, 14th and Peachtree Sts.; 892-2388. This is the German cultural center offering current and classic German films as well as lectures and special programs. Free.

High Museum of Art (G11), 1280 Peachtree St. NE in Walter Hill Auditorium; 892-3600. Many of these films are shown free.

There are also a number of theaters in Atlanta which show current and re-released films at surprisingly low prices, often as little as $1. Also check local colleges and universities. See Students in the SPECIAL PEOPLE Chapter.

Buckhead Cinema 'n Drafthouse (B3), 3110 Roswell Rd. NE in Buckhead; 231-5811. Waitresses serve beer, wine, and sandwiches during the showing.

Cobb Cinema (A1), 2542 S. Cobb Dr. in Marietta; 435-8749.

Franklin Three (A2), Franklin Rd. at Delk Rd. in Marietta; 952-1712.

North Springs Theatre (A3), 7270 Roswell Rd., just north of Sandy Springs; 394-6823.

Omni Six (J8), Omni International, 688-6766. Six separate theaters.

Toco Hills (C4), North Druid Hills Rd. at LaVista Rd.; 636-1858.

Music for Listening and Dancing

In our selected listings we include both music for listening and music for dancing. Atlanta is an aggregate of many strains of music — country music from the Appalachian region, rock from the cities, beach music from the past, disco from the record industry, big band from the 40s, and a large concentration of jazz from the South.

Atlanta's quality hotels have first-class music in their clubs, and we include some of the exceptional clubs in our listings.

The "Buckhead Strip" in Atlanta is located at the intersection of Peachtree and Roswell Roads between Pharr Road and E. Andrews Drive. The "Strip" offers music and fun for everyone from jazz at Carlos McGee's to beach music at Studebaker's. Some of these clubs cater to students, and some attract an older crowd, but they all appeal to the young at heart. Park your car and try a few of the dozen or so clubs.

Hours in Atlanta's clubs vary so check the individual listings and also the newspaper for current offerings. Expect a cover charge or minimum unless otherwise designated.

Another World (J10), Atlanta Hilton Hotel, 255 Courtland St.; 659-2000. Atop the downtown Hilton Hotel this chic discotheque will take you to its namesake, another world of strobing lights and rhythmic dreams.

Banks and Shane (A3), 5975 Roswell Rd., Sandy Springs; 255-0519. This popular neighborhood spot features entertainment nightly by the duo and their guests plus an array of good food.

The Buckboard (A2), 2080 Cobb Pkwy. SE, Smyrna; 955-7340. The Buckboard is where you'll find homesick Texans who come here for country-bar bands and the dancing.

Buckhead Saloon (B3), 3330 Piedmont Rd. NE; 231-2326. Two bars in one at the Buckhead Saloon. On the one side is a piano bar, and on the other a variety of music is served up.

Cafe Erewhon (H10), 60 5th St. NW; 892-6253. The place to hear unusual guitar and singing by Atlanta talent. Cy Timmons has been a regular performer for many years, bringing laughs to many Atlantans.

Carlos McGee's (B3), 3035 Peachtree Rd. NE, on the "Buckhead Strip", 231-7979; (A4), 3360 Chamblee-Tucker Rd., 452-8880. This club specializes in live jazz and reggae music, along with delicious margaritas served in pitchers and 'tex-mex' style food.

Charley Magruders (A3), 6300 Powers Ferry Rd. NW; 955-1157. Always packed, Magruders offers local bands and is popular with young professionals.

Chequer's Bar and Grill (A4), 236 Perimeter Center Pkwy; 391-9383. Fresh mesquite-grilled seafood flown in daily with live jazz Tuesday through Saturday. Also a Sunday brunch with Dixieland jazz. A new and fun place.

Colony Square (G12), Peachtree St. at 14th St. NE; 892-6000. The Ray Block orchestra offers tea dances on Friday evenings in the Colony Square Mall. Gather at Colony Square to dance because the Big Band is back. Free with cash bar available.

Confetti's (B3), 3906 Roswell Rd. NW; 237-4238. Confetti's is a great place to dance and fraternize; popular with the college and post-college crowd. The parties never stop at this colorful eatery on Roswell Rd. Complete with living room-bars.

Dante's Down the Hatch in Buckhead (B3), 3380 Peachtree Rd. NE; 266-1600. For over a decade, Dante's Down the Hatch has been an Atlanta showcase. His nautical nightclub is unique in manifold ways. The Paul Mitchell Trio, one of Atlanta's greats in jazz, plays on board "the sailing ship." Besides the reputation for terrific music, Dante prides himself on his fondue fare, service, wines, and whiskey, in surroundings that are thoroughly seaworthy. Jazz Mon-Sat from 9 pm. See DINING Chapter.

élan (A4), Park Place, 4505 Ashford-Dunwoody Rd. NE; 393-1333. elan has lunch, dinner, and a packed disco scene in the evenings. The mood and clientele is sexy and sophisticated or as the establishment says of itself "élan is electric."

Excelsior Mill (C4), 695 North Ave. NE; 577-6455. Take in a pizza first and then a concert at this restored Atlanta excelsior mill. Music ranges from jazz and rock to country and blues. The mill has a two-story skylighted beer garden, is open for lunch.

Harvest Moon Saloon (C3), 2423 Piedmont Rd. NE; 233-7826. Atlanta musicians and performers draw other Atlantans into their musical orbits, ranging from rock to jazz and folk. Admission is free.

Hemingway's (C4), 3910 N. Druid Hills Rd.; 325-3094. Country rock brought live to you nightly, Mon-Sat.

Jerry Farber's (B3), 54 Pharr Rd. NE; 237-5181. Jerry Farber provides a great combination in his comedy-jazz club. Featuring national and local jazz and comedy artists, it's also a great place for late-night breakfast.

Johnny's Hideaway (B3), 3771 Roswell Rd.; 233-8026. An Atlanta institution. Music from the 40s and a favorite of those over 40 — but you'll find just as many patrons in their 20s and 30s simply because they like the music and "that kind of ballroom dancing."

Joyful Noise Christian Supper Club (E2), 2669 Church St., East Point; 768-5100. For eight years this unusual supper club has attracted the big name Christian music groups. All you can eat buffet, no smoking, no alcohol and then a hearty evangelistic performance follows. Buffet starts at 6:30, music at 8:30. Children invited.

La Carousel in Paschal's Motor Hotel (D3), 830 Martin Luther King Jr. Dr. SW; 577-3150. Near Atlanta University, this black jazz club is one of the oldest in the city, a rendezvous for Atlanta's black leadership for over 20 years.

Lanier Land Music Park, Jotemdown Rd., just off GA 400 in Cumming; 681-1596. This music park is filled to its 5000 capacity with two shows every Friday and Saturday night from May to October. The setting is a pasture. The biggies in country music from Johnny Cash to Loretta Lynn and Charlie Pride pull in the crowds from every county around.

Limelight (B3), 3330 Piedmont Rd. NE; 231-3520. Limelight is a discotheque in all its glory with every technical stop pulled out and a decor charged with funky decadence. Open nightly 9 pm - 4 am.

Mr. V's Figure 8 Club (D2), 3131 Campbellton Rd. SW; 349-5215. Mr. V's is "the" club on the southside. Plush carpets, mirrors, and the vibrating sounds of disco. Add the Game Room, Gift Shop and Mr. V's II and you get the status nightspot for Black Atlanta. Make a night of it and hit Cisco's and other clubs on the Campbellton Road "strip."

Moonshadow Saloon (C4), 1880 Johnson Rd. NE; 881-6666. Spin off, but big brother in size, to the Harvest Moon, the Moonshadow is friendly and the jazz terrific, no cover for Atlanta bands.

The Point (C4), 420 Moreland Ave. SE; 577-6468. This new restaurant and bar in midtown features a house band playing classics from the 40s, 50s, and 60s.

The Purple Parrot (C4), 1040 N. Highland Ave. NE; 874-3082. The Purple Parrot in the Virginia-Highlands section offers shows at 10 and 11:30 pm Tue-Sat and late shows Fri-Sat. Atlanta's top vocalists perform.

Scooters Music and Dance Hall (A3), 6521 Roswell Rd., Sandy Springs; 255-7295. Scooters has lots of rock music and dancing to go with it — a popular place on the Roswell Strip. No cover. Mon-Fri 4 pm - 4 am, Sat 8 pm - 3 am.

Studebaker's (B3), 3227 Roswell Rd. NW; 266-9856. The sounds of the surf come rolling in at Studebaker's, the specialty club for 50s beach music on the "Buckhead Strip." Mon-Sat 8 pm - 2 am.

Walter Mitty's Jazz (C4), 816 N. Highland Ave. NE; 876-7115. This jazz spot is below Walter Mitty's restaurant in Virginia-Highlands. Intimate, with an art-deco touch, Walter Mitty's has made its mark on Atlanta's jazz scene with its excellent performances. Open daily until 2 am.

Winfield's (B2), 100 Galleria Pkwy.; 955-5300. A delightful piano bar features some of Atlanta's finest talent. See DINING Chapter.

Zasu's (C3), 1923 Peachtree St.; 352-3052. Join the regulars who crowd round the piano, particularly on the weekend. See DINING Chapter.

SIGHTS

Atlanta's major attractions reflect the pluralistic character of the city. A building boom is being balanced more and more with preservation awareness, interfacing a futuristic city with scattered samples of turn-of-the-century Atlanta.

Consider some of the sights to be seen, all intriguing in their own right and held together as a catalog of attractions by a city that thrives on contrast and competition. Here are megastructures for the sophisticated traveler and urbanite and a charming toy museum for the child in all of us. Here are an intown zoo too big for its surroundings and a botanical garden just beginning to grow. Here are recreational parks built on fun and fantasy and a historical society geared to keeping the traditions and artifacts. Consider a small Victorian cottage that housed the writer of the Uncle Remus tales — an earlier, more gentle way of explaining how things came to be, then reflect on the whizzing technological center of one of the newest broadcasting companies in the nation. Visit an observatory to chart the southern skies, and creek beds and battlefields to scour for arrowheads and Civil War relics. Visit the government, stately in its gold-domed splendor, and another district honoring civil rights — once again, for all Americans.

From the heady rush of the glass elevators up the outside of the Westin Peachtree Plaza Hotel to your viewing station at the top, to the lateral movement in the downtown business district, Atlanta, the city reaching for her destiny, is the greatest sight to see. Enjoy the many faces of this vibrant city.

Ante-Bellum Plantation. See Stone Mountain Memorial Park below.

Atlanta Botanical Garden (C3), Piedmont Park at The Prado NE; 876-5858. *NCH.* Situated on 60 acres in Piedmont Park, the botanical garden offers a conservatory with tropical plants and orchids, a vegetable garden for the urban gardener with displays of seasonal crops, a home-demonstration garden, and three specialized gardens

The Swan House

Courtesy R. Cotten Alston, Jr.

— the Fragrance Garden, the Japanese Garden, and the Rose Garden. The Botanical Garden is a key to enjoying and understanding the verdant beauty of Atlanta. The Garden has been completely re-landscaped; there is a visitors center with programs, speakers scheduled, woodland tours, and ongoing classes and workshops for members and non-members; cultural and social events are presented throughout the year in these carefully groomed and colorful gardens. The Atlanta Botanical Garden is impressive, a quiet resting place, only five minutes from downtown. Open Mon-Sat 9 am - 4 pm, Sun 12 - 4 pm.

Atlanta Historical Society (B3), 3101 Andrews Dr. NW (off W. Paces Ferry Rd. in Buckhead); 261-1837. *CH*. A half-day's visit to the historical society, with lunch at the Swan Coach House, is a delightful must for the visitor. The society maintains three buildings on the Andrews Drive property.

Walter McElreath Hall, the modern administration building, is named for the society's chief benefactor and houses the archives and library. Collections of photographs, manuscripts, and artifacts are on exhibit throughout the year and afford the visitor an important look into Atlanta's past. Films, seminars, and lectures are presented in the Woodruff Auditorium. Special programs and field trips are scheduled also. Call ahead for details.

The *Swan House* (233-2991), fronting on Andrews Drive, is an elegant neo-Palladian mansion built in the 1920s by Atlanta's classical architect Philip Schutze, for Edward H. Inman and is furnished with a spectacular collection of antiques from England and other parts of the world. This is one of the most beautiful residences in Atlanta and an excellent example of the Gatsby era in the South.

Swan Coach House, originally the servants quarters, houses your luncheon restaurant, an art gallery, and gift shop.

The *Tullie Smith House* (262-1067) was moved from DeKalb County to a site behind the Swan House in the late sixties and is an excellent example of a "plantation plain" Georgia farmhouse from 1835, with log barn, slave cabin, and double corn-crib outbuildings.

Tours of both houses are available on the half hours, and there is a trail through the grounds. Offices and library open Mon-Fri 9 am - 5 pm. Exhibits and houses open Tue-Sat 10:30 am - 4:30 pm, Sun 2 - 4:30 pm. Student, senior citizen, and group rates. No charge for McElreath Hall.

The **Atlanta Museum** (H10), 537 Peachtree St., NE; 872-8233. *CH.* Eight rooms in the old Rose Mansion on Peachtree are the setting for this museum of eclectic delights. The Queen Anne-style brick house is on the National Register of Historic Places, one of the few extant residences of Peachtree Street from the turn of the century. Eight rooms are filled with memorabilia from all over the world — antiques, porcelain, costumes, an abundant collection put together by the owner's father in the 1920s. Exhibits include the earliest Coca-Cola crate, Chinese teakwood from the Murphy home in Atlanta, Hitler's coat and hat, a section of the rope with which Tojo hung himself, flying propellers from 1919, early railroad items, Revolutionary guns, a crossbow, Indian and Civil War artifacts, in the attic a conestoga wagon, and in the backyard an intact Japanese Zero warplane. All these marvels await you Mon-Fri, 10 am - 5 pm or by appointment for groups.

Atlanta Public Library (J9), One Margaret Mitchell Sq. NW (one block northwest of Central City Park, downtown); 688-4636. *NCH.* Marcel Breuer designed the new library on the site of the old Carnegie Library. The building transforms one city block into an exciting consortium of Bauhaus geometrics, well worth a walk around the block. Inside the structure holds over a million volumes, the Margaret Mitchell collection of memorabilia, the Sam Williams collection of black history, a children's reading and program room, 1300 periodicals, a cafeteria, and a book and gift shop. For the traveler a special section offers a complete travel library with maps and information. A full program of films, lectures, and art exhibits Mon-Sat 9 am - 6 pm, Sun 2 - 6 pm.

Atlanta State Farmers Market (F3), 16 Forest Pkwy., Forest Park (just off I-75 south of the Perimeter, look for Farmers Market exit); 366-6910. *NCH.* With one hundred forty-six acres of produce sheds, the South's largest farmers market (and the second largest in the nation) is a colorful place to visit. Christmas trees in winter and giant gourds in fall are complemented by the seasonal selection of fresh vegetables and fruits, which you can then take to the do-it-yourself cannery. Stop by at the Welcome Center and, after a few hours browsing and buying, satisfy your appetite with a farm-fresh meal of southern cooking at the Farmers Market cafeteria. Sign up for a tour and take the "Fresh Express," pulled by a tractor. Market and cafeteria open 24 hours, seven days a week.

SIGHTS 115

Big Shanty Museum, US 41 in Kennesaw (30 miles northwest of Atlanta); 427-2117. *CH.* The town of Kennesaw was known in Civil War days as "Big Shanty." The museum here displays artifacts from the war period, the main attraction being the Confederate locomotive "The General." The Walt Disney film, *The Great Locomotive Chase,* popularized and dramatized the skirmishes and chase in the historical incident associated with this train. Mon-Sun 9:30 am - 6 pm.

Bulloch Hall. See Historic Roswell below.

Central City Park (J9), downtown park bounded by Peachtree and Pryor Sts., Edgewood and Auburn Aves., at Five Points. *NCH.* This is the breathing space for the Central Business District. Trees, grass, fountains, and a small amphitheater provide a place for downtown activities, such as concerts, political rallies, art exhibits, and festivals, as well as a daily pedestrian path for tourists, bankers, business people, and a complete cross-section of Atlantans.

Chattahoochee Nature Center, 9135 Willeo Rd. (in Roswell); 992-2055. *NCH.* The center is located in a rustic wood building beside a small pond and offers live exhibits of reptile and animal wildlife native to the area. The shop sells field guides and wildlife publications. Two short but charming nature trails adjoin the center. A refreshing visit for children and adults, ideal for a picnic lunch. Mon-Sat 9 am - 5 pm, Sun 1 - 5 pm.

Chattahoochee River National Recreational Area. See SPORTS Chapter, Hiking.

Civil War Relics. If you have the Civil War bug, Atlanta is a great place to concentrate. The sites of the battles of Atlanta and Peachtree Creek are nearby for starters. Contact Stone Mountain Relics Inc. at 968 Main St., Stone Mountain; 469-1425. They can set you up with metal detectors and loads of advice. This trail can lead you right up to the Tennessee border.

Confederate and National Cemeteries, Goss St. off Powder Springs St., and Washington St. in Marietta. These two cemeteries are the burial grounds of soldiers killed during the Civil War. Both contain monuments and grave markers of historical interest.

Cyclorama (D3), 800 Cherokee Ave. SE (in Grant Park); 658-6374. *CH*. The amazing 50-foot-high, 400-foot (15 x 122 meters) painting in the round, with three dimensional figures, sound and light effects, and narration, depicts the 1864 Civil War Battle of Atlanta. The restoration of the original painting of 1886, the largest painting in the round in the world, combined with the renovation of the facility in which it is installed, makes this sight one of Atlanta's most memorable. If weather permits visit the Cyclorama and then have a picnic lunch in Grant Park.

Dahlonega, Georgia, located in the North Georgia Mountains. Take Hwy. 400 to its end; turn left onto Hwy. 60 and follow it into Dahlonega. The site of the nation's first goldrush, this old Southern town has recently undergone a charming restoration and is a unique attraction that should not be missed. Park and stroll around the courthouse square which features a gold museum, bricked sidewalks lined with massive trees, antique shops, boutiques selling handmade clothing, and bakeries. There are several good places to eat, including *Martha's Tearoom* on the square and several other eateries where one will find quick service and seating on porches overlooking the square. Within walking distance is the *Worley Homestead Bed and Breakfast Inn* featuring seven rooms furnished in antiques. This 1840s home has also been recently restored and the staff dresses in period costumes. It is located at 410 W. Main Street, Dahlonega, GA 30533; 864-7002. There is also a wealth of antique stores in and around the town, including *Split Rail Antiques*, located at Highway 9 South. Its wares include furniture, crystal, china, linens, dolls, and other fine selections, mainly from estates. Call 864-6777 for information. Open Thu-Sun 10 am - 5 pm. For more information about Dahlonega, call the Chamber of Commerce at 864-3711.

Emory University Museum of Art and Archaeology (C4), Carlos Hall, Emory University, N. Decatur Rd. at Oxford Rd. (on southside of quad behind the Administration Building); 329-7522. *NCH*. A trip here will introduce you to the attractive Emory campus and the surrounding turn-of-the-century neighborhood of Druid Hills. The museum houses art and archaeology from the ancient Mediterranean and Middle East as well as Asian, pre-Columbian, and Indian artifacts. Also prints, photos, paintings, and sculpture from the Middle Ages to the present. Advanced reservation required for groups. Park in the 45-minute spaces in front of the Administration Building and have lunch in the college cafeteria or in Emory Village at Everybody's or Lullwater. Re-opening in January, 1985. Tue-Sat.

Etowah Indian Mounds, RFD 1, Cartersville, GA (north of I-75 forty miles to Cartersville, turn west on GA 61, and follow signs to Etowah Indian Mounds); 1-382-2704. *CH.* Just an hour's drive from Atlanta you will see the remains of the Etowah Indian culture that thrived on the banks of the Etowah River between A. D. 1000 and 1650. The three large mounds on a 50-acre plain were originally surrounded by a wooden palisade. The museum displays artifacts from this early north-American civilization. Tue-Sat 9 am - 5 pm, Sun 2 - 5:30 pm; closed Mon.

Federal Reserve Bank Monetary Museum (J8), 104 Marietta St. NW (near Spring St. in the Central Business District); 586-8747. *NCH.* The museum houses a historical collection of monetary artifacts, from early trade beads and hides to gold bars and sheets of gold certificates and other paper money. Mon, Wed, Fri, 9 am - 4:30 pm. Advance appointments required.

Fernbank Science Center (C4), 156 Heaton Park Dr. NE (Near Artwood Rd., Decatur); 378-4311. Another must-visit, for families especially, the center, operated by the DeKalb County Public School System, offers a variety of facilities and programs day and night. The 65-acre original *Fernbank Forest* has trails open Mon-Fri and Sun 2 - 5 pm, Sat 10 am - 5 pm. The *Observatory* has the Southeast's largest telescope, open Thu-Fri dark to 10:30 pm if sky is clear, 8 - 9:30 pm if sky is cloudy, closed during inclement weather. The *Planetarium's* 70-foot-diameter dome features excellent programs beginning at 8 pm Tue-Fri, 3 pm and 11 pm Sat, and 3 pm Sun. The *museum and science library* is open Mon, Fri, and Sat 9 am - 5 pm; Tue, Wed, and Thu 9 am - 10 pm. The *greenhouse,* 755 Clifton Rd., NE, is open 1 - 5 pm Sun only. Also included at the center are botanical gardens, a meteorological lab, and an electron-microscope lab. Free admission except for Planetarium.

Fort Peachtree (C2), 2630 Ridgewood Rd. NW (near Moores Mill Rd.); 355-8229. *NCH.* The reconstructed fort commemorates the first white settlement in the Atlanta area. The original fort was erected as a defense against the Creek Indians who were sympathetic to the English during the War of 1812, and it served as a trading post until the Indians' removal in the 1830s. Indian and pioneer artifacts are displayed in a reconstructed log cabin of the period. Mon-Fri 8 am - 4 pm.

Georgia Department of Archives (D3), 330 Capitol Ave. SW (near the Atlanta Stadium); 656-2393. *NCH.* The archives building is the resting place for all the state's historical and genealogical records and maps. Featured on the interior are the Victorian staircase and hand-painted windows depicting the fall of the Confederacy, which have been preserved from the original archives repository, the Rhodes Memorial Hall. The lobby houses changing exhibits, and original documents and artifacts. The archives collection includes gifts to the state of Georgia from other nations, such as France's gift to Georgia of historical French items as a token of appreciation following World War II and a statue of Confucius from the People's Republic of China given during the U. S. bicentennial celebration. Call for current exhibitions.

Georgia State Capitol (K9), Capitol Square SW; 656-2844. *NCH.* Georgia was the thirteenth and last of the original colonies of the United States. The present state capitol building was built in 1889 and is headquarters for the Georgia governor, legislature, and secretary of state. The gold leaf on the dome was mined near Dahlonega in North Georgia and first brought to Atlanta in 1958 in mule-drawn carts. The Georgia Assembly meets from January to March; you can see the legislative process in action during this time.

The building also includes the *Georgia State Museum of Science and Industry,* the *Georgia Hall of Fame,* and the *Hall of Flags* — all well worth the visual instruction in the state's history, as is the tour of the capitol buildings, gardens, and statuary. Mon-Fri 8 am - 5:30 pm, tours between 9 am and 4 pm.

Georgia World Congress Center (J8), Marietta St., NW at International Blvd. (next to Omni International Hotel); 656-7600. *NCH.* The center, officially named the George L. Smith II Georgia World Congress Center, is an enormous trade facility — 352,000 square feet on a single floor, the largest of its kind in the U. S. The *Georgia Hall* has displays on historical Georgia, industrial and agricultural products, Coca-Cola, Southern Bell, Lumus Industries, Georgia Pacific and Georgia Ports, and special Georgia attractions.

Governor's Mansion (B3), 391 W. Paces Ferry Rd. NW (in Buckhead); 261-1776. *NCH.* The present mansion, built in 1968 by Maddox, reflects the Greek Revival style of the antebellum South, with Federal period furnishings. The mansion has a featured location in one of Atlanta's most beautiful northside residential areas on West

Paces Ferry Road. Include the Governor's Mansion in your day of touring the historical society in this elegant section of the city. Tours Tue, Wed, and Thu 10 - 11:45 am.

Historic Roswell (25 miles north of Atlanta); 992-1665. Browse amongst the antique shops and boutiques bordering the square. The Roswell Historical Society will arrange, one week in advance, group tours (minimum of 10) of this charming, small antebellum town. The tour includes a visit to a private and occupied home in the area that is open to the public on a restricted schedule. CH. *Bulloch Hall*, the childhood home of President Teddy Roosevelt's mother, is open Wed 10 am -3 pm. Call for special programs and tours.

The Johnny Mercer Exhibit (J8), downtown in the Georgia State University Library, Decatur St.; 658-2376. *NCH*. This Georgia-born lyricist, composer, and entertainer is remembered through an excellent collection of manuscripts, photos, awards, and letters from the likes of Irving Berlin and Eubie Blake, all donated by Mrs. Johnny Mercer and the Mercer Foundation. Mon-Fri 10 am - 2 pm and 3 - 5 pm, Sat-Sun, 1 - 5 pm.

Kennesaw Mountain National Battlefield Park, GA 120 about 25 miles north of Atlanta; 427-4686. *NCH*. This was a major Civil War site in the Union movement from Chattanooga to Atlanta. Self-guided tours of the battlefield are available. We suggest starting at the visitors' center and museum where a slide presentation will acquaint you with the battle sequence. The park has two picnic areas, four hiking trails, and a free shuttle bus to the top of the mountain. Mon-Sun 8:30 am - 5 pm, during summer 8:30 am - 6 pm.

Martin Luther King, Jr. Memorial, Historic District, and Center for Social Change (K11), Auburn Ave. at Boulevard SE; 523-0606. *CH*. The five-block historic district is on the National Register of Historic Districts and includes new and old buildings of importance to the memory of one of Atlanta's renowned citizens, Nobel Prize winner and father of the Civil Rights Movement, Dr. Martin Luther King, Jr. Dr. King's birthplace at 501 Auburn Avenue is open Mon-Fri 9:30 am - 5:30 pm. The Ebenezer Baptist Church at 407 Auburn Ave., where Dr. King shared the pulpit with his father, is open Mon-Fri 10 am - 4 pm, Sat and Sun during summer. Dr. King's tomb is within the memorial park. The district also includes an Interfaith Peace Chapel, a community center, and the Center for Social Change, headed by Dr. King's widow, Coretta Scott King. Tours Mon-Fri, 11 am - 4 pm, Sat 12 - 5 pm.

Monastery of the Holy Spirit, Conyers (from downtown, take I-20 east for 27 miles to GA 138 exit, right 5 miles to GA 212, left 2 miles); 483-8705. *NCH.* The monastery was built by the Trappist monks and is a self-sufficient working, religious community open to the public. The abbey is clean white gothic architecture, radiating with colored lights from the stained-glass windows and filled with plain song during services. The grounds are immaculate — a picnic area by a small pond is ideal for lunch. The monastery welcomes visitors to its greenhouse and to its gift shop with pottery, handcrafts, and monastery bread available for purchase. Women are not allowed in the cloister, but are offered a slide presentation on the life of the Trappists. Open daily from dawn until dusk. Group tours must be prearranged. Call for tours and services open to the public. Leaving the city for a day trip to the Monastery will give you an appreciation for the spiritual and agricultural tradition still preserved in monastic life plus a side trip to the farm lands of north Georgia.

Oakland Cemetery (D3), 248 Oakland Ave. SE (at Martin Luther King, Jr. Dr.); 577-8163. *NCH.* Oakland is Atlanta's oldest cemetery, established in 1850 and the burial ground for eminent Atlantans including *Gone With the Wind* author Margaret Mitchell and Atlanta's first mayor, Moses Formwalt. The tombstones reflect the multiple funeral styles of the late nineteenth century, and the office building is from circa 1899. A bell tolls at sundown each day to alert visitors to closing time. Open dawn to dusk every day.

Omni Complex (J8), 40 Marietta St. NW (at International Blvd.). The complex is one of Atlanta's megastructures housing a large atrium mall with boutiques, shops, and offices. The mall is connected to the Omni International Hotel with its famous restaurant Bugatti, and to the World Congress Center and the Omni sports arena, where the NBA Atlanta Hawks perform. The Omni megastructure should not be missed — a perfect place to shop, dine, or meet before or after the special events.

Peachtree Center (J9), Peachtree St. between Harris St. and International Blvd. Atlanta's Peachtree Center is a showcase for the urban development and design concepts of Atlanta's international architect John Portman. This is a downtown center still expanding from its original core development at the Merchandise Mart and the Hyatt Regency Atlanta Hotel. The spectacular atrium hotel with its capsule elevators is the prototype and trademark for other Portman hotels. The center is located on the highest point of the Peachtree ridge, a few blocks north of Five Points. The complex includes office towers, a plaza for people-watching on Peachtree Street, a shopping mall, the Merchandise Mart, the Apparel Mart, the Peachtree Plaza Hotel and the Hyatt Regency Atlanta Hotel, and ample parking lots, all connected by pedestrian bridges. Peachtree Center is a hub of commercial and retail activity, a meeting place for Atlantans, a convention center, and an area for sophisticated dining and entertaining from Japanese to continental cuisine.

The Amos Giles Rhodes Memorial Hall (C3), 1516 Peachtree St. NE (1 block north of Pershing Pt.); 656-6576. *NCH.* This granite neo-Romanesque structure was the elegant home of one of Atlanta's wealthy families. Mr. Rhodes willed the property to the state archives, and from 1930 to 1965 the Rhodes Memorial Hall was the primary archives building. The house is maintained in its original state with period furnishings and an exhibit hall. The original staircase and stained-glass windows are now on display at the current archives building. See above. Mon-Fri 8 am - 4 pm. Reservations for group tours required one week in advance.

Shroud of Turin Exhibit (J8), presently housed in the Omni complex; 577-5990. Suggested donations. This permanent exhibit features photos, sculptures, and scientific displays of what many believe to be the cloth in which Jesus was buried. Hourly tours, Tue-Sat.

Six Flags (C1); 948-9290. (Off I-20 Six Flags exit, ten miles west of downtown.) *CH.* This recreational park is named for the six flags that have flown over Georgia — from Spain, France, England, Georgia, the Confederacy, and the U.S.A. The 31 acres of rolling hills and ponds are packed with breath-taking rides, spectacular shows, a mini-zoo, trainride, concessions, restaurants, and resting places.

The "Land of Screams and Dreams" lives up to its reputation with the world's only triple-loop roller coaster, appropriately named the "Mind Bender"; the "Great Gasp," a parachute that drops you 210 feet to the ground in about ten seconds; The "Thunder River" ride speaks for itself.

You will find Six Flags is a clean, well-managed, and cheerful place. The season runs from mid-March to mid-November, and is open Sun-Thu 10 am - 10 pm., Fri-Sat 10 am - 12 midnight during the summer; weekends only from mid-March to mid-May and from Labor Day to November. One-price ticket is good for all rides and shows, including repeats.

Stone Mountain Memorial Park (C6); 469-9831. (Seven miles east of I-285 on US 78, Stone Mountain Freeway.) *CH.* Stone Mountain, the largest granite outcropping in the world, can be seen from the city on the eastern horizon. The relief carving on its northside, only recently finished, depicts Jefferson Davis, the Confederate president, and Robert E. Lee and Stonewall Jackson, the two Confederate generals. A 3200-acre park surrounds this national phenomenon and massive sculpture, providing a full-day's entertainment out of doors.

The *Swiss skylift* will take you to the top of the mountain, however, if you are feeling energetic, walk the 1.3 miles up its side.

The *Ante-bellum Plantation* will bring alive those days before the Civil War, having 19 authentically-restored different buildings, including the manor home, overseers house, slave cabins, and more.

The *Heritage Museum* records Georgia's revolutionary past and should not be missed by the history buff.

The world's largest electronic *Carillon* is played Mon-Sat at 12, 4, and 7 pm; Sun 1, 3, 5, and 7 pm. It is a delightful experience to sit out and listen to it.

The *Laser Light and Sound Show* is displayed on the carved side of the mountain every night at 9:30 pm from May through Labor Day.

The *Scenic Railroad* takes you for a ride around the base of the mountain, whilst the *Riverboat* cruises around the 365-acre lake.

Clayton House Craft Shop features the largest pottery collection in the southeast, and works of over 150 Georgia craftspeople.

If you still haven't seen and done enough there are beaches, golf, tennis, roller-skating through the woods, waterslides, canoeing, and an Ice Chalet with full skating facilities. Rent a bike to get around and explore the healthy way.

Picnicking and camping are available, as well as more formal overnight accommodations at the Stone Mountain Inn.

Open year round Mon-Sun 6 am - 12 midnight. Attractions and rides open 10 am - 5:30 pm in winter, 10 am - 9 pm in summer. Special rates for groups over 25. Call for current admission and charges.

Stone Mountain Village (C6). Be sure to include a visit to Stone Mountain Village, restored small town at the base of the mountain, filled with wonderful shops, crafts, and antiques.

SIGHTS 123

Confederate Memorial Carving, Stone Mountain
Courtesy Stone Mountain Park

Swan Coach House. See Atlanta Historical Society above.

Swan House. See Atlanta Historical Society above.

Toy Museum of Atlanta (C3), 2800 Peachtree Rd. NE (in Buckhead); 266-8697. *CH.* The museum opens up the magic of toyland within a turn-of-the-century Peachtree mansion. Over 100,000 toys are in period settings and creative displays. Dolls, dollhouses, boats, trains, soldiers, circuses, and games delight the adult as much as the child. Mon-Sat 10 am - 5 pm, Sun 2 - 5 pm. Free parking in rear. Group rates available.

Tullie Smith House. See Atlanta Historical Society above.

White Water Park (A1), 250 North Cobb Pkwy, Marietta; 396-1090. *CH.* Located just off I-75 at Exit 113 this exciting Atlanta park offers a variety of water attractions, including a 40-foot Water Wheel, a wave pool (The Atlanta Ocean) that creates 4-foot waves, a continuous flowing river called "The Little Hooch," and thousands of feet of water flumes. The park also features a children's participation area with more than 25 activities with water guns, water slides, and tube rides. There are locker and shower facilities for your convenience as well as restaurants and picnic areas.

William Weinman Mineral Center and Museum, (A1), 30 minutes north of Atlanta in Cartersville at the corner of I-75 and U.S. 441; 386-0576. *CH.* Gems and minerals from all over the world in an impressive new marble building featuring a mock cavern and audiovisual room. Georgia gems and minerals are strongly represented. Tue-Sat 10 am - 4:30 pm, Sun 2-4:30 pm.

Wren's Nest (D3), 1050 Gordon St. SW (near Lawton St.); 753-8535. *CH.* The home of Joel Chandler Harris, Georgia author of the Uncle Remus stories, is preserved in its original Victorian cottage style with the addition of Uncle Remus memorabilia. The house is located in West End. Mon-Sat 9:30 - 4 pm, Sun 2 - 5 pm.

Yellow River Wildlife Game Ranch, Hwy 78, 3 miles east of Stone Mountain, across Yellow River bridge, Snellville; 972-6643. *CH.* This game ranch features wild animals such as deer, buffalo, bears, lions, and racoons as well as the farm animals, chickens, ducks, goats, sheep, and ponies. Bring a picnic lunch, and take the $1/2$-mile trail to see, pet, and feed the animals. A delight for kids of all ages. In the fall, there are hayrides and hot dog roasts. Open daily. Group rates available. Children under 4 free.

VISUAL ARTS

Atlanta's emergence as a regional visual arts center is evidenced by the increasing development of its major museum, the High Museum, by the expansion and depth of its gallery system, and its incorporation of the visual arts into the burgeoning urban landscape.

MUSEUMS

The **High Museum of Art,** Atlanta Memorial Arts Center (C3), 1280 Peachtree St. NE; 892-3600. *CH*.

The High Museum is Atlanta's major visual-arts museum and is the oldest member of the Atlanta Arts Alliance. The museum was first proposed in 1905 by the newborn Atlanta Art Association and became a reality in 1926 when Mrs. Joseph High donated her home as a museum. In 1968 the present Alliance building incorporated the former museum site, and now the museum, designed by architect Richard Meier, occupies a separate, new High Museum of Art next to the Alliance building.

The High Museum inaugurated in 1983 its new building, a gleaming post-modern asymmetrical structure sheathed in white enamel panels. Designed by Richard Meier, the new High Museum of Art is a unique architectural and cultural landmark for the city.

The museum collection includes works from early Renaissance to modern, with emphasis on European and American works from the late nineteenth and twentieth centuries. The museum is noted for its strong contemporary painting and print collection. The equally strong photography collection focuses on late nineteenth- and twentieth-century masters. The African Gallery offers theme-centered exhibitions from the African collection throughout the year. Also, the decorative arts are featured in the Decorative Arts Gallery in a continuing series of displays. The Junior Arts Center leases a permanent exhibition for children called *Sensation*. The High Museum program of regular events includes lectures, films, tours,

New High Museum of Art designed by Richard Meier

Courtesy Ezra Stoller; copyright ESTO

VISUAL ARTS

festivals, and special educational courses. Conclude your visit at the excellent Museum Shop. For the weekly schedule of events call the Public Information number, 892-4444. Museum hours, Tue-Sat 10 am - 5 pm, Sun 12 - 5 pm.

Catherine Waddell Gallery (D3), in Trevor Arnett Library, Atlanta University, 223 Chestnut St. SW; 681-0251, ext. 282. This permanent Afro-American art collection is the largest in the nation featuring paintings, sculpture, and graphics by black artists including Charles White, Elizabeth Catlett, John Wilson, Calvin Burnett, and Jacob Lawrence. Permanent historical African art collection and a contemporary European art collection. Also featured in the library is the Hale Woodruff Art of the Negro murals. Mon, Wed, Fri—call for hours.

GALLERIES

Atlanta's gallery scene has grown in size, sophistication, and substance in the last decade. Galleries are generally grouped in three areas of the city — downtown, midtown, and Buckhead.

Although the listing below is comprehensive we recommend to you, as a casual viewer or serious collector, the following galleries for their excellence in quality, uniqueness of concept, and established professionalism.

The finest studio gallery in Atlanta is the world-renowned Hans Frabel Gallery. Hans Frabel came to Atlanta from East Germany many years ago, having been trained at the Jena Glasswerks. He is accepted as the world's best flamework glass sculptor, with work in the Smithsonian and White House collections and numerous international collections. His exquisite glass sculptures are sold only in the Hans Frabel Galleries in Atlanta. For galleries featuring the work of national and international artists in all media we suggest the Ann Jacob Gallery and Aronson Gallery. The Fay Gold Gallery, Heath Gallery, and Stanley and Schenck Gallery exhibit exclusively American art. The work primarily of southeastern regional artists can be viewed at Gallery 515. If your special interest is photography we advise a visit to the Atlanta Gallery of Photography and Olympia Galleries. For the finest in a whole spectrum of the crafted arts we recommend the Signature Shop.

Abstein Gallery (G11), 1139 Spring St. NW (midtown); 872-8020. Original art in all media by Atlanta and Southeastern artists, Leila Kepert Yarborough, Betty Loehle, Michael Crouse, and others. Mon-Fri 8:30 am - 5:30 pm, Sat 10 am - 4 pm.

Alexander Gallery (B3), 442 E. Paces Ferry Rd. NE (Buckhead); 266-2311 or 266-2792. Specializes in painting and sculpture by folk artists including Ned Cartledge, Carleton Garrett, Nellie Mae Rowe, and Edwin Sammett. Contemporary prints and drawings by Johns, Stella, and others. Fri-Sat 12:30 - 5 pm.

Ann Jackson Gallery, 587 Atlanta St., (Roswell, on the Square); 993-4783. Mostly 20th-century traditional American art, oils, lithographs, prints. Custom framing. Mon-Fri 10 am - 5:30 pm, Sat 10 am - 5 pm.

Ann Jacob Gallery (B3), 3500 Peachtree Rd. NE; 262-3399. Contemporary sculpture featuring Pomodoro, Consagra, Calder, Berrocal. Paintings, tapestries, art glass, collectibles, antiquities, and African and Asian art collection. Mon-Sat 10 am - 6 pm.

Aronson Gallery, Ltd. (B3), 56 E. Andrews Dr. (Buckhead); 262-7331. Eighteenth- through twentieth-century European and American paintings, graphics sculpture, including works by Dine, Stella, Vasarely, Bellmer, Ronalt, Miro, Calder, Oldenberg, and Jean de Botton estate. Tue-Sat 10 am - 5 pm. Admission free.

Art in Atlanta/The Ten to Four (B3), 511 E. Paces Ferry Rd. NE (Buckhead); 237-1960. Large collection of affordable graphics by local, regional, national, and international artists. Mon-Sat 10 am - 4 pm.

Artists Associates Gallery (B3), 3261 Roswell Rd. NE (Buckhead); 261-4960. An association of thirty local artists exhibiting a wide variety of paintings, prints, drawings, sculpture, and pottery. Tue-Sat 10 am - 5 pm, Sun 1 - 5 pm.

Atlanta College of Art Gallery (C3), Colony Square Mall, Peachtree at 14th St. NE (midtown); 898-1168. Non-profit gallery specializing in painting, sculpture, photography, and crafts by regional, national artists, and students. Tue-Sat 10 am - 5 pm.

Atlanta Gallery of Photography (B3), 3205 Paces Ferry Pl. NW (Buckhead); 233-1462. Features twentieth-century master photographers such as Ansel Adams, Andre Kertesz, Henri Cartier-Bresson, Michael Siede, and Diane Arbus. Tue-Sat, 11 am 5:30 pm.

VISUAL ARTS

Atlanta Jewish Community Center (C3), 1745 Peachtree St. NE, 875-7881; Zaban Branch (A4), 5342 Tilly Mill Rd., Dunwoody, 396-3250. The rich variety of cultural arts programs at the Jewish Community Center is open to the general public. Programs include concerts, gallery exhibits, theater, lectures, dance. Classes are offered in crafts, photography, dance, and music. Mon-Thu 9 am - 10 pm, Fri and Sun 9 am - 5 pm.

Brass Rubbings by Martha Huey; 255-0498. Learn the fun, easy, and historical art of brass rubbing in Ms. Huey's basement studio. She also lectures to clubs and schools.

Callanwolde Fine Arts Center Gallery (C4), 980 Briarcliff Rd. NE (near Virginia Ave.); 872-5338. DeKalb County operates this center in the restored Candler mansion, offering classes and programs for the public in the visual, literary, and performing arts. The center is the headquarters for a dance group, concert band, theater group, the Callanwolde Young Singers, and small musical ensembles. Special events include the Callanwolde Fall Festival and Christmas at Callanwolde.

Chastain Arts Center Gallery (B3), 135 W. Wieuca Rd. NW (in Chastain Park); 252-2927. The Chastain Center is known for its extensive selection of classes in visual arts and handcrafts for adults and children. Sessions last eight weeks. Mon-Thu 9 am - 10 pm, Fri 9 am - 4 pm. The center houses the Chastain Gallery which shows local, regional, and national artists. Gallery open Mon-Fri 10 am - 4 pm, or by appointment. Come to the openings the first Friday of the month. Free admission.

Clay Work (C3), 1131 Euclid Ave.; 525-CLAY. Pottery by Rick Berman and Jennifer Ashcraft are featured along with other artists work. Call for hours.

Dalton Galleries (C4), Dana Fine Arts Building, Agnes Scott College, E. College Ave. (Decatur); 373-2571, ext. 256. Changing exhibits such as southeast fiber exhibits, black art, American art. Mon-Fri 9 am - 9 pm, Sat 9 am - 5 pm, Sun 2 - 5 pm.

David S. Ramus Ltd. (B3), 273 E. Paces Ferry Rd. NE; 266-0044. Ramus handles American and European nineteenth- and twentieth-century paintings, drawings, and watercolors. Tue-Fri 10 am - 6 pm, Sat 12 pm - 4 pm. Free admission.

Eve Mannes Gallery (B3), 288 E. Paces Ferry Rd. NE (Buckhead); 237-8477. Contemporary art by local and national artists in clay, fiber, glass, painting, and sculpture. Mon-Fri 10 am - 5 pm, Sat 11 am - 5 pm.

Fay Gold Gallery (B3), 3221 Cains Hill Pl. NW (Buckhead); 233-3843. Features paintings, prints, photography, and sculpture by contemporary American artists, including Robert Rauschenberg, Alex Katz, and George Segal. Tue-Sat 10 am - 5:30 pm.

The Frabel Gallery, Inc. (J9), Peachtree Center (downtown), 659-2832; and (B3) Lenox Square, Peachtree Rd. NE (Buckhead); 233-8129. Featuring the original and signed crystal sculptures of Hans Frabel and the Hans Frabel Studio of Atlanta. Mon-Sat 10 am - 6 pm, Thu 10 am - 9:30 pm.

Gallery 515 (B3), 515 E. Paces Ferry Rd. NE (Buckhead); 233-2911. Contemporary regional art. Mon-Sat 10 am - 6 pm.

Gallery Two Nine One (C3), 1 Rhodes Ctr. NE; 877-9718. Paintings, sculptures, and prints by local and regional artists. Tue-Fri 10 am-6 pm.

Georgia State University Gallery (K9), Art and Music Building, 10 Ivy St. (downtown); 658-2257. Changing exhibits of nationally known artists in all medias with accompanying lectures and workshops. The National Competitive Clay, Fiber, and Metal Exhibition hosted at Georgia State annually. Call for current exhibits and lectures.

Georgia Tech Student Center Gallery (H9), 350 Ferst Dr. NW (downtown); 894-2805. Contemporary American artists in photography, painting, sculpture, fiber arts, and prints. Gallery hosts the Annual Dogwood Festival International Art Show in the spring in conjunction with Atlanta Playhouse Theatre.

Gillette-Frutchey Gallery, Ltd. (C3), 1925 and 1931 Peachtree Rd. NE; 351-3179. In the Brookwood Hills area, this tasteful shop displays American crafts of excellence. Mon-Sat 10 am - 5 pm.

Goethe Institute (G12), 400 Colony Square, Peachtree at 14th St. (midtown); 892-2388. The German cultural center in Atlanta offers

VISUAL ARTS 131

an excellent regular schedule of German art exhibits, films, and programs. Mon-Fri 10 am - 5 pm, Wed 10 am - 7 pm.

Heath Gallery (B3), 416 E. Paces Ferry Rd. NE (Buckhead); 262-6407. American art of the 60s, 70s, and 80s. Tue-Sat 11 am - 5 pm.

Highland Art and Frame Shop (C4), 1038 N. Highland Ave. NE (midtown); 885-1815. Twentieth-century painting, prints, posters specializing in southeastern artists. Tue-Sat 9:45 am - 5:45 pm, Fri 9:45 am - 9 pm.

Knoke Galleries (A1), 93 Church St., Marietta; 428-1797. The Knoke houses the largest gallery of American paintings south of New York. Tue-Sat 11 am - 5 pm. Free admission.

Lagerquist Gallery (B3), 3235 Paces Ferry Pl. NW (Buckhead); 261-8273. American artists including Dale Rayburn, Burke, Winterle, Loehle, Carpenter, Ramsey. Tue-Sat 10:30 am - 5 pm.

Madison-Morgan Cultural Center, 434 S. Main St., Madison; 1-342-4743. This fine regional center is well worth a days visit in Madison for its reputable art shows, theater, and music programs. Call for hours.

The McIntosh Gallery (G11), 1122 Peachtree St. NE (midtown); 892-4023. Regional and national artists such as Romare Bearden are featured in this handsome midtown gallery. Tue-Sat 10 am - 5 pm.

Neighborhood Arts Center Gallery (D3), 252 Georgia Ave. SW (between Pryor and McDaniel Sts.); 523-6458. Located in one of Atlanta's black communities, this center sponsors regular classes in painting, drama, music, dance, and karate. The center's self-proclaimed goal is to "provide cultural activities for the black community and help black artists develop their skills." Monthly exhibits of local artists are held in the Romare Bearden Gallery. Mon-Fri 9 am - 6 pm, Sat 10 am - 2 pm.

Nexus, Inc. (C3), 360 Fortune St. NE (Glen Iris Dr. at Ralph McGill Blvd.); 688-1970. A consortium of arts organizations and independent artists are headquartered here. **Nexus,** the photographic gallery and the **Third Floor Gallery** share space, regular exhibits, and phone number, 588-1105. The **Nexus Press** publishes original books of southern artists, an excellent buying opportunity, 577-3579. For general information, space rental, and workshop hours for the **Sculpture Center** call 688-1970.

Odyssey Studio of Fine Art (B3), 546 E. Paces Ferry Rd. NE (Buckhead); 261-3060. Contemporary prints featuring etchings and collographs of Ann Dergara and R. F. Williams. Mon-Fri 8 am - 5 pm, Thu 8 am - 8 pm, Sat 10 am - 4 pm.

Olympia Galleries, Ltd. (B3), 267 E. Paces Ferry Rd. NE (Buckhead); 237-5660. European and American 19th-century photography as well as 18th-, 19th-, and 20th-century painting, drawings, sculpture, and prints. Tue-Sat 11 am - 5:30 pm.

Picture House, Inc. (G11), 1109 W. Peachtree St. NE (midtown); 875-9341. Old prints, graphics, watercolors, oil paintings, reproductions. Custom framing. Mon-Fri 8:30 am - 5:30 pm, Sat 10 am 4 pm.

Rockefeller Fine Arts Building (D3), Spelman College, 350 Spelman Lane SW (downtown); 681-3643. Spelman collection includes African, Caribbean, and contemporary American art. Mon-Fri 9 am - 5 pm.

Shirley Fox Galleries (G12), 1586-90 Piedmont Ave. NE (midtown); 874-7294. Contemporary graphics including Alvar, Boulanger, Calder, Dale, Folon, Nieman, and Walt Disney Studios. Mon-Wed 10 am - 6 pm, Thu-Sat 10 am - 10 pm. Free.

The Signature Shop (B3), 3267 Roswell Rd. NW (Buckhead); 237-4426. Premier contemporary American crafts in all metals, glass, fiber, ceramics, wood, weaving.

Southeastern Center for the Photographic Arts Gallery (B3), 470 E. Paces Ferry Rd. NE (Buckhead); 231-5323. This photography center offers a quarterly school program and a gallery with regular exhibits by national and regional photographers. Gallery open Tue-Wed 6 pm - 9 pm, Sat 12 - 6 pm, Sun 2 - 8 pm.

Stanley and Schenck (J9), 145 Ralph McGill Blvd.; 892-0595. Specializes in 20th-century American art, primarily southeastern artists working in painting, sculpture, and photography. Mon-Fri 10 am - 6 pm, Sat 12 - 4 pm.

Touch of Glass (C5), 1850 Lawrenceville Hwy. (Decatur); 329-1486. Atlanta's premier stained-glass studio for custom design also exhibits art by American artists.

Trail of Tears Gallery (B3), 271-B E. Paces Ferry Rd. NE; 231-5735. Native American art and crafts. Tue-Sat 11 am - 5 pm.

Unitarian Universalist Art Gallery (B4), 1911 Cliff Valley Way NE (off I-85); 634-5134. Monthly shows of local and regional artists, in all media. Mon-Fri 9 am - 5 pm, Sat and Sun 9 am - 1 pm.

SELECTED SCULPTOR STUDIOS

The following studios of some of Atlanta's most established and respected sculptors and artists are recommended to the visitor or resident with serious art interest, art collectors, and those in the professional arts.

Carley Craig Sculpture Garden. Carley Craig's large abstract sculptures (mostly metal) are companions with the wildlife on a wooded inner-city hillside. There are paths, a small bridge, and spaces to sit and enjoy. The sculpture "grows" out of the ground, trails in the stream, vibrates in the winds, a succinct union of the forces of nature and woman. The garden is open by appointment only; call 355-6058.

The studio of **Julian Harris,** N.A., F.A.I.A., F.N.S.S. Julian Harris is an architect and sculptor, a Fellow in both arts, with over fifty sculptures in public buildings in the southeast. His figures have graced government and commercial facades and plazas in Atlanta for many years as well as private homes and gardens. See his seventy-two-foot panel recently installed in the Omni MARTA station. The studio is open for individuals by appointment only; call 892-6513.

Steffen Thomas Studio. Steffen Thomas came to Atlanta in 1928 with the rigorous technical training of the German schools. He is accomplished in every aspect of artistic enterprise: metal, stone, clay, and wood sculpture; mosaics; painting; drawing; stained glass. His studio teams with figures and shapes of enormous energy, power, and complicity. His Trilon fountain can be seen at Peachtree and 15th Street across from Colony Square and the Robert W. Woodruff Arts Center. The home studio is open by appointment only; call 876-5374.

Studio 312. Five artists live and work in this large warehouse. The art is exciting, the inner look into an artist's life a unique and fascinating opportunity. The artistic accomplishments range from sculpture to wooden boat building, silk screens, clothes design, and painting. The artists are generous, lovely people. Open by appointment only; call 522-3300.

ART IN PUBLIC PLACES

The city has made public space a ground for creative expression. Urban art complements the vigorous transportation systems, the government building programs, and Atlanta's business ventures. Atlanta will greet you with visual art if you arrive by air or by interstate.

At the airport you will be presented with serial works by fourteen artists accompanying you on your passage from gate to baggage claim. Six of the MARTA stations, many of which were designed by Atlanta architectural firms, include murals, mosaics, and sculpture.

The ambitious urban walls program is visible from the downtown connectors, I-75 and I-85, as you enter the city. Nine urban walls entice and enchant as you walk or ride in the downtown business district. Themes range from Kudzu, film clips, cartoons, and balloonists to sparse and complicated abstractions — each wall designed for its particular location and social access. Remember to look up for a pleasant visual surprise as you turn the corners in downtown Atlanta.

The megacenters of Atlanta are another setting for art in public places: the Omni's atrium laser sculpture by Rockne Krebs, exterior light towers by Boyd Meffird, and hotel paintings by local and national artists; stainless steel sculpture by Carolyn Montague in front of the Equitable Building downtown; Peachtree Center's sidewalk and interior sculptures by Helsmoortel, Van de Bovencamp, Perry, Lamberechts, Gutmann, and Leeber; the bronze sculpture at the intersection of Spring and Carnegie Way titled **Emerging** by Atlanta sculptor Mark Smith; and Colony Square's Calder murals and plaza sculptures by Pomodoro and Burge.

One new and very special collection of art can be found at the Waverly Hotel next to the Galleria Mall. The hotel's permanent grouping of more than 75 works of art can be enjoyed by taking a stroll through the hotel's lobby and following it up the stairs to the mezzanine level. There is also a rare jade display owned by real estate magnate Trammel Crowe, developer of the Waverly.

The parks have introduced sculpture into their green spaces, most notably **Playscapes,** a sculptured playground in Piedmont Park by Isamu Noguchi.

Atlanta hospitals are treated with loving care and colorful art by Atlanta artist John Feight. Beginning at Northside Hospital sixteen years ago, Feight offered his time and talent to paint one of the hospital walls. Three hundred walls at Northside are now part of that healing environment. Feight's work is also at Atlanta's Scottish Rite Hospital, Georgia Baptist Hospital, Georgia Regional Hospital, and the Veterans Administration Hospital, in twenty-two hospitals in the United States and four in Europe, providing through his jungle landscapes, seascapes, and peoplescapes, a soft human touch for the sick.

Finally Atlanta offers art which is more an attraction than an architectural component, the **Cyclorama** and the Stone Mountain bas-relief carving. The Cyclorama executed in 1885 is the largest circular painting in the world, a trompe l'oeil reviewing of the Battle of Atlanta. The Stone Mountain carving of the heroes of the Confederacy measures 90 feet high by 190 feet wide, the world's largest sculpture carved on the north side of a mountain.

SHOPPING

You have come to *the* place to shop in the southeast, a retail wonderworld of everything from haute couture and antiquities to trendy camp and bargains galore. Atlanta's shopping trade is in full gear at all times with sales and incentives constantly enticing the spoiled natives, southern pilgrims, and domestic and international visitors.

Downtown, Buckhead, the metro malls, and mini-centers offer a wide variety of shopping experiences. A birthday or anniversary coming up in your family? Thinking about the next holiday season, a house gift, a business purchase, an addition to your private collection, a hard-to-find accessory for your home, a unique antique, or a spontaneous splurge on yourself? They are all here in Atlanta. We will help you match the Atlanta merchant to your shopping need.

SHOPPING DISTRICTS

Downtown

The downtown shopping area is historically the first shopping center of the city and is still in title the headquarters of the retail trade. The wholesale Apparel and Merchandise Marts draw buyers from all over the country. The suburban mall stores are still considered branches of the main stores downtown. Rich's and Davison's, two large and prominent department stores, have been downtown for decades, Rich's now being owned by Federated Department Stores and Davison's, the Atlanta division of Macy's of New York. Both stores are household words in Atlanta and are civic-minded enterprises devoted to a prosperous core city. Since the regional malls tend to be crowded, we especially recommend Rich's and Davison's downtown stores, as well as Muses, Zachry, H. Stockton, Brooks Brothers, and many other fine downtown shops for an unencumbered and friendly shopping spree. Two complexes in this area deserve your attention for their international boutiques and specialty offerings, the Omni near Rich's and Peachtree Center with its shopping gallery near Davison's.

Davison's (J9), 180 Peachtree St. NW; 221-7221.
Rich's (K8), 45 Broad St. SW; 586-4636.
Omni International (J8), Marietta Blvd. at Techwood Dr. NW; 681-2161.
Peachtree Center Shopping Gallery (J9), 230 Peachtree St. NE; 659-0800.

Buckhead

This district lies about eight miles north of downtown, straight out on Peachtree Street. The character of this village outside original Atlanta is still maintained in the old storefronts and street furniture. Buckhead is a center for antique and boutique shopping and services. Mini-centers such as Cates Plaza, Andrews Square, Peachtree Battle Shopping Center, plus East Paces Ferry Road from Peachtree to Piedmont are crammed with different and exciting stores.

Lenox Square and Phipps Plaza

About two miles beyond Buckhead proper, two well-established malls on Peachtree Street offer you some of the most fertile shopping grounds in the South and in the nation.

Lenox Square is a pioneer mall built in the early 1950s and is still exploring new shopping frontiers with its three-story redevelopment of the Plaza area. Lenox is a blend of Southern comfort and cosmopolitan flair. Rich's, Davison's, and Neiman-Marcus stake out three corners, and filling in between the finest shops in the United States and Europe, quality restaurants featuring continental fare, fast-food houses, movie theaters, and superb community programs draw the crowds through the greenhouse spaces at this remarkable shopping center.

Phipps Plaza is the New York of the south, a large center with New York's Saks Fifth Avenue and Lord and Taylor anchoring the wings and Tiffany's right in the middle. Points in between include first-class boutiques and specialty shops such as Abercrombie & Fitch, and Gucci's, movie theaters, and restaurants.

Lenox Square (B3), 3393 Peachtree Rd. NE; 233-6767.
Phipps Plaza (B3), 3500 Peachtree Rd. NE; 261-7910.
Generally open from 10 am to 9:30 pm Mon-Sat, afternoons on Sunday.

Suburban Malls

The Galleria Mall (B2), Galleria Parkway, US 41 and I-285. Atlanta's newest mall takes its lead from the Houston Galleria with vast retail space intermingled with restaurants under an airy skylight. The tempo is upscale in the specialty mall and the Waverly Hotel and office towers adjoining.

As Atlanta has expanded so have her shopping needs in the outlying communities. Most malls listed below have a similar covered skylight interior with a host of shops; Rich's, Davison's, J.C. Penney, and Sears represented, restaurants; and large parking lots encircling them. The following is a list of other major regional malls.

Cumberland Mall (B2), US 41 at I-285 NW.
Greenbriar (E2), 2841 Greenbriar Pkwy., SW (at GA 166).
Gwinnett Place, 2100 Pleasant Hill Rd., Duluth; 476-5160.
North DeKalb Mall (C5), 2050 Lawrenceville Hwy. (at N. Druid Hills).
Northlake Mall (B5), LaVista Rd. NE at I-285.
Perimeter Mall (A4), 4400 Ashford-Dunwoody Rd. (at I-285).
Shannon Mall (F1), at GA 138 and I-85 South.
South DeKalb Mall (D5), Candler Rd. at I-20.
Southlake Mall (F4), I-75 at Morrow-Jonesboro exit.
Hours generally 10 am to 9:30 pm Mon-Sat, afternoons on Sunday.

Mini-Centers

Atlanta's growth has also spawned a number of intriguing small shopping centers filling in between the major districts above, downtown, Buckhead, Lenox-Phipps, and the malls on the Perimeter.

Around Lenox, an independent center of variety shops, is next to Lenox Square.

Colony Square at Peachtree and Fourteenth Streets has a charming shopping and meeting area around its tree-studded mall.

Loehmann's shopping center is a mini-mall of discount high-fashion shops, a perfect spot for the well-off shopper with frugal instincts and the spartan shopper with champagne tastes.

Merchants Walk in Marietta will introduce you to a restored town square, its storefronts filled with attractive gifts.
Park Place across from Perimeter Mall is for chic, sophisticated clientele looking for the latest "in" things and "in" haunts of Atlanta's young professional class.
Stone Mountain Village is a historic district with its Main Street an irresistable row of antique shops, gift shops, and craft galleries.
Vinings is an old village on Paces Ferry Road, west across the Chattahoochee River, and north across the river is **Roswell Historic Square**. There is lots of good browsing and buying at both locations for the antique seeker, along with specialty shops, custom-made items, and fine eating.

Around Lenox (B3), adjacent to Lenox Square NE.
Colony Square (G12), Peachtree at 14th St. NE.
Loehmann's (B2), 2460 Cobb Pkwy. SE, Smyrna.
Merchants Walk (A1), 1325 Johnson Ferry Rd. NE, Marietta.
Park Place (A4), 4505 Ashford-Dunwoody Rd. NE.
Peachtree Market (B3), 3167 Peachtree Rd. NE.
Roswell Historic Square, Main Street, Route 19, Roswell.
Stone Mountain Village (C6), Stone Mountain Freeway into the village.
Vinings Village (B2), Paces Ferry Rd. NW at Vinings.

ANTIQUES

Connoisseurs of fine things and antique hounds will find their dream pieces and little surprises here in Atlanta. Since the antique-shopping areas define themselves we suggest the following districts and then a selected list of scattered independent shops. Flea markets, which have many fine antique shops, are listed under a separate section.

Buckhead

Beverly Bremer Silver Shop (B3), 3164-A Peachtree Rd. NE; 261-4009. This is a sterling shop for sterling silver offering matching flatware service.

Deanne D. Levison American Antiques (C3), 1933 Peachtree Rd. NE; 355-0106. This small shop specializes in period American antiques, with an early American selection, pure and exquisite.

Gerald R. Brown Antiques (B3), 520 E. Paces Ferry Rd. NE; 233-8249. Eighteenth- and nineteenth-century American, English, and continental furniture and accessories await your discriminating taste.

Kings and Queens Antiques (B3), 514 E. Paces Ferry Rd. NE; 237-7980. Period English furniture, art, and accessories.

Trosby Auction Galleries (C3), 81 Peachtree Park Dr. NE; 351-4400. This fine auctioneers and antique and fine-art house has an Atlanta branch offering estate sales, fine arts, antiques, oriental works of art, silver, and jewelry.

Downtown

W. E. Browne Decorating Co. (H10), 443 Peachtree St. NE; 874-4416. Browne's comprehensive collection of English and continental antiques, fine paintings, silver, and porcelain fill the period rooms of this old stucco building on Peachtree.

Davison's Corner Shop Antiques, Davison's Department Store (J9), 180 Peachtree St. NW; 221-7518. Prize antique gems are offered in the midst of this full-service department store.

J. H. Elliott Antiques (H10), 537 Peachtree St. NE; 872-8233. A National Register Queen Anne house, originally the home of Mr. Rose of Four Roses Whiskey fame, provides an incredible selection of choice antiques, both American and English from the eighteenth and nineteenth centuries. Mr. Elliott has a long-established reputation for appraisals. (See SIGHTS Chapter under Atlanta Museum.)

Howell Mill and 14th Street Area

Atlanta Antiques Exchange (C3), 1185 Howell Mill Rd. NW; 351-0727. This emporium sparkles with a vast collection of eighteenth- and nineteenth-century English and Chinese porcelains, furniture, and objets d'art.

Kennedy Antique Auction, Inc. (C2), 2050 Hills Ave. NW; 351-4464. This giant house is one of the southeast's largest importers, importing directly from England, with auctions every Monday evening.

SHOPPING

The Turnage Place, Ltd. (C3), 1001 Brady Ave. NW; 872-4100. The owner charmingly offers old world antiques — some *below* your means . . . you can bargain here.

Lenox

Rich's Connoisseur Gallery (B3), Lenox Square, 3393 Peachtree Rd. NE; 231-2913. This notable gallery, in the furniture department of Rich's, has English antiques from the eighteenth and nineteenth centuries.

Decatur Area

Hawthorne Village, 3032 N. Decatur Rd., Scottdale. A collection of eleven stores offering great collectibles and antiques, everything from vintage clothing to dolls, Victorian furniture, and books. We particularly enjoy the tags in "Mama's Memories."

Other Antique Shops

The Antique Store of Marietta (A1), 81 Church St., Marietta; 428-3376. Excellent collection of primitive furniture and accessories.

Atlanta Flea Market and Antique Center (A5), 5360 Peachtree Industrial Blvd., Chamblee. Exhibitors offer a large selection of real collectibles including furniture, glass, china, fabrics and more.

The Attic, 1028 Canton St., Roswell; 993-2900. Fine shops housed in an old Roswell residence bring back the magic of ransacking grandma's attic. Doll houses and miniatures, vintage clothing, lace and linens, oriental rugs, crystal, silver, and wonderful "things" from yesteryear are all part of the Attic collection.

Broad Street Antique Mall (A5), 3550 Broad St., Chamblee; 458-6316. Choices here are wide in areas from Primitives to fine dark wood furniture as well as in accessories.

Bygone Era (B4), 4783 Peachtree Rd.; 458-3016. Here you will find American architectural antiques from carved oak mantles to Victorian tubs and flying machines.

Chamblee Antique Row (A4), 5485 Peachtree Rd.; 455-4751. You can spend a full day in this conglomerate of antique stores sharing the same location.

Haygood House, Main St., Watkinsville, GA; 1-769-8129. The restoration studio is located six miles south of Athens and the gallery about a block from there. The studio offers a woodworking expertise to those who seek the finest. The Haygood House Gallery features

Primitives, fine furniture in oak, clocks, and miscellaneous items. Appointments are advised.

Split Rail Antiques, see SIGHTS Dahlonega.

Williams Antiques (B4), 4010 Peachtree Rd. NE; 233-4072. Since 1927 Williams has graced the antique scene in Atlanta, one of the south's largest dealers for mainly eighteenth- and nineteenth-century American and English antiques.

Wrecking Bar (C4), 292 Moreland Ave. NE; 525-0468. The Wrecking Bar's grand old estate house boasts four hundred years of architectural art from two continents.

ART SUPPLIES

Any and every art supply needed by the commercial and amateur artist can be found at the centers below.

Atlanta Art Supply (I10), 734 W. Peachtree NW, 881-1741; (B3), 3175 Peachtree Rd. NE, 222-7105.

Binders (B3), 3221 Peachtree Rd. NE; 233-5423.

Sam Flax (C3), 1515 Spring St. NW; 873-1515.

BOOKS

It is impossible to list all the excellent bookstores in Atlanta, even those carrying this book. We have chosen those that are unique for one reason or another. If you are a resident seek out your neighborhood bookstore. It's a pleasure to browse and pass the time.

B. Dalton, Coles, and **Walden books** are national chains with multiple stores in the Atlanta area malls. **Rich's** and **Davison's** have excellent book departments with author days year-round for meeting the public, promoting, and signing books. If you are in town at the same time an autographed copy of a favorite book is a superlative, personal gift. Old-book collectors will be pleased with the American Association of University Women's annual used-book sale, which fills Lenox Square from one end to the other in September.

American Institute of Architects (G12), Colony Square Retail Mall, 1197 Peachtree St. NE; 873-3207. A choice selection of quality art and architectural books is offered by the Atlanta Chapter bookstore.

Ansley Mall Bookstore (C3), 1544 Piedmont Ave. NE; 875-6492. An excellent store for all sorts of books with substantial sections in psychology, education, children's, and religion.

SHOPPING 143

Ardmore Book End (A3), 5964 Roswell Rd., Sandy Springs; 256-4203. This is the major bookstore in Sandy Springs.

Arnold's Archives (C4), 1579 N. Decatur Rd. NE; 377-2665. Across from Emory University, Arnold's Archives has first editions as well as general books.

Chapter One (C4), 133 Sycamore St., Decatur; 377-2373. Bookstore on the square in Decatur.

Charis Books (D4), 419 Moreland Ave. NE; 524-0304. The place to find any feminist publication, plus a solid small bookstore in the Inman Park neighborhood.

Children's Book and Gift Market (B3), 315-A Pharr Rd. NE; 261-3442. This is Atlanta's all-children's bookstore. Also has children's reading programs.

Cokesbury (C5), 2495 Lawrenceville Hwy., Decatur; 320-1034. This Methodist-owned bookstore has a new location and building in Decatur.

Coles The Book People (A4), Perimeter Mall, 4400 Ashford-Dunwoody Rd.; 394-6658. Three other mall locations. This Canadian-based chain has a full line of books plus office supplies and stationery.

Dunwoody Book Center (A4), 5552 Chamblee-Dunwoody Rd.; 393-0902. A fine bookstore in Dunwoody Hall Shopping Center.

Hale's Books (A3), 1315 Johnson Ferry Rd., Merchants Walk, Marietta; 977-9456. Hale's is a bibliophile's joy in Marietta.

Majors Scientific Book Store (C3), 141 North Ave.; 873-3229. While this store specializes in scientific books it offers a variety and is the favorite of the local and visiting members of the medical profession.

McGuire's Bookshop (C4), 1055 Ponce de Leon Ave.; 875-7323. Located in the Plaza Shopping Center, McGuire's is a new favorite of intowners.

Old New York Book Store (G12), 1069 Juniper St. NE; 881-1285. Scholarly and rare used books are the specialty here. Regular visitors include Atlanta's writers, journalists, and literati.

Oxford Book Store (C3), Peachtree Battle Shopping Center, 2345 Peachtree Rd. NE; 262-3332. The Oxford Book Store is Atlanta's largest bookstore with a spate of foreign magazines and newspapers.

A bonus offering is an out-of-print search department. The oblique interior-design patterns are an enjoyable change from usual bookstore organization of space, as is the coffee served in the upstairs gallery.

Roswell Bookstore, 100 Norcross St., Roswell; 992-8485. This store is located conveniently in Canterbury Plaza in Roswell.

The Science Fiction and Mystery Bookshop (C4), 752½ N. Highland Ave. NE; 875-7326. Very good selection of new works in hardback and paperback; also magazines and games.

Tall Tales Bookshop (C4), 2999 N. Druid Hills Rd. NE; 636-2498. Tall Tales can be found in the Toco Hills shopping center.

Williamsburg Bookstore (B4), 2777 Clairmont Rd. NE; 633-4151. The Williamsburg store is just east of I-85 on Clairmont.

Yesteryear Book Shop (B3), 256 E. Paces Ferry Rd. NE; 237-0163 This store is exclusively for old and rare books; appraisal service.

CLOTHING

Women, men, and children find Atlanta a mecca for clothes shopping. With the largest apparel mart in the southeast, Atlanta is a regional distribution center and fashion frontier, as well as a mecca for the well-dressed consumer.

Women's Clothing

Atlanta women have had two alternative sources for apparel shopping — the large, established clothing and department stores and the small, specialty clothiers. The first group includes Atlanta's favorites — **Rich's, Davison's,** and **Muses,** all located downtown, at Lenox Square, and other malls; **Neiman-Marcus** at Lenox Square; **Lord and Taylor, Saks Fifth Avenue,** and **Isaacsons** at Phipps Plaza; and **Regensteins*** in Buckhead and Decatur.

The apparel boutiques that carry fashions from the world's most lustrous designers include **Givenchy Nouvelle Boutique,** in the Omni International luxury row, and at Lenox Square are **Saint Laurent Rive Gauche, Courreges, Charles Jourdan Boutique,** and **Bonnie White.** Phipps Plaza showcases **Gucci, Abercrombie & Fitch, Lillie Rubin, Inc.,** and **Jonni L. Walker's Panache.**

Fine quality informal wear for day and night is offered at Lenox Square and other locations by **Casual Corner, Singer's Casual Shop,** and **Laura Ashley,** and in Buckhead at the **Snappy Turtle*.**

For maternity clothes we recommend **Lady Madonna,** in Lenox Square, for clothing exclusively for the large woman try **Added Dimensions** at Perimeter Mall, and for that all-American commodity, blue jeans, you'll find a mind-boggling selection from Levis to designer types at **The County Seat, The Gap,** and **The Limited** at most malls. Finally, for lovers of camp, vintage, and secondhand clothes see **Stefan's*** in Inman Park, **Annie's Hall***, or **Play It Again***, specialists in costuming companies filming in Georgia.

Atlanta's shopping districts have innumerable other stores to meet women's fashion needs and financial requirements. The business woman, the homemaker, the socialite, the retired woman, and the young teenager will each find the outfit of her choice in the bustling malls or in individual boutiques. Atlanta is a fashion-conscious, image-creating city, where women shop to look their very best.

Listed below are the shops starred in our text that are not located in designated shopping malls.

Annie's Hall (C3), 951 Peachtree St. NW; 881-9059.
Play It Again (B3), 273 Buckhead Ave.; 261-2135.
Regensteins (B3), 3187 Peachtree Rd. NE; 261-8520.
The Snappy Turtle (B3), 110 E. Andrews Dr. NW; 237-8341.
Stefan's (C4), 1160 Euclid Ave. NE; 688-4929.

Men's Clothing

Men's dress in Atlanta has traditionally been conservative, even during the 1960s-70s advent of new casual styles and leisure suits. The tassled loafer is said to have never been obsolete in Atlanta even during those former decades of changing fashions.

At Lenox Square you can shop at a large cluster of fine men's stores — **Rich's, Davison's, Neiman-Marcus, Muses,** and the smaller men's clothiers **Britches of Georgetowne, Gokey's, Brooks Brothers, H. Stockton,** and **Zachry.** Directly across from Lenox Square you will find **Joseph A. Bank***, and at Phipps Plaza the esteemed **Saks Fifth Avenue** and **Lord and Taylor** offer their fine lines as well as **Abercrombie & Fitch** and **Gucci's. Fishers Men's Shop*, Guffeys*, Spencer's*,** and **H. Stockton*,** Four small excellent Atlanta establishments, offer personal attention along with fine selections of traditional men's wear. For clothing for the great outdoors visit **Britches Great Outdoors, High Country,** and **Georgia Outdoors***. For large men **Hyroops** will combine fashion authority with a large physique.

Listed below are the shops starred in our text which are not located in shopping malls.

Joseph A. Bank Clothiers (B3), 3384 Peachtree Rd. NE; 262-7100.
Fishers Men's Shop (B3), 269 E. Paces Ferry Rd. NE; 237-4208.
Georgia Outdoors (A3), 6518 Roswell Rd. NE; 256-4040.
Guffey's of Atlanta (J9), 230 Peachtree St. NE; 522-0044. Two locations.
High Country (A3), 6300 Powers Ferry Rd. NW; 955-1866. Seven locations.
Spencer's Ltd. (H11), 693 Peachtree St. NE; 875-0267.
H. Stockton (J9), 80 Forsyth St. NW; 523-7741. Three locations.

Children's Clothing

The major department stores, **Rich's** and **Davison's,** have clothed Atlanta children for festive occasions and everyday wear since the 1920s. **Saks** and **Lord and Taylor** have children's departments of the first rank. Smaller children's shops with exceptional children's clothes include **Chocolate Soup** and **Toy Safari** at Phipps Plaza and **Lady Madonna** and **Petite Folie** at Lenox Square. The gift shop at the **Swan Coach House*** of the Atlanta Historical Society offers lovely handmade apparel for infants, and **Kiddie City*** is the southeast's answer to total shopping for your child — a large children's department store with four divisions of clothing, toys, infant furniture, and children's shoes, all premier quality offerings and in abundant quantity.

Kiddie City (A3), 6285 Roswell Rd. NE; 252-2214.
Swan Coach House (B3), 3130 Slaton Dr. NW; 261-0224.

COINS AND STAMPS

Trading, gift giving, collecting, investing? Atlanta is a superb market in which to do all four.

Al Adams Rare Coins (B3), 3525 Piedmont Rd. NE; 261-4601. Rare coins are bought and sold in this full-service establishment.

Georgia Stamp and Coin Company (J9), 141 Carnegie Way NW; 524-2676. Georgia's oldest, this stamp and coin company has been a tradition since 1947.

Rich's (K8), 45 Broad St. SW; 586-4798. Rich's department store offers complete satisfaction, or your money back (!) as well as the convenience of a Rich's charge account.

Stamps Unlimited of Georgia (D3), 133 Carnegie Way NW; 688-9161. One of the best stamp stores in Atlanta for visitors and residents is Tony Roozen's shop.

CRAFTS

Babyland General Hospital, 19 Underwood St., Cleveland, GA 30528; 865-2171. Soft-sculpture, life-size babies are delivered by skilled crafts people at this old city hospital. Signed and unsigned editions are available at many Atlanta "adoption centers." Visit the showroom in Cleveland, one and a half hours north of Atlanta, or call to find the adoption center closest to you. A unique craft product and fantasy experience.

Clayton House Craft Shop (C6), Stone Mountain Park; 469-9831, ext. 253. Georgia crafts in pottery, jewelry, quilts, leather, and baskets are on display in the reconstructed log Clayton house. Over 150 crafts people from the southeastern U. S. show their wares here also.

The Patch, Inc. (D3), 242 Blvd. at Memorial Dr. SE; 525-6383. Original designs of hand-painted tile.

The Signature Shop and Galleries, Inc. (B3), 3269 Roswell Rd. NE; 237-4426. The most sophisticated crafted works of art in the southeast. This long-established gallery includes the finest in ceramics, fiber, metals, and glass.

Terminus Gift Shop (J9), 230 Peachtree St. NE; 588-1580. In the center of the Peachtree Center shopping gallery, this intriguing gift shop features native Georgia mountain crafts.

FACTORY OUTLETS AND DISCOUNT STORES

Bargain-hunters can have a field day in metro Atlanta. Remember Georgia is a textile state; factory outlets abound as well as discount stores. If this is your first introduction to this form of shopping keep in mind the following tips. To cut costs outlets are usually very plain and unpretentious on the outside; the merchandise on the inside is your reason for shopping. Merchandise is received weekly, so come back if you miss your buy the first visit. Outlets offer a savings of 30% to 70%, so plan for your future needs as well as pick up a few surprises.

Outlets Square of Atlanta (B5), 4166 Buford Hwy. NE; 633-2566. This mall contains over 40 restaurants and outlets including Burlington's and Marshalls. Other stores feature shoes, books, linens, housewares, and much more.

The Promenade, Loehmann's Plaza (B2), 2460 Cobb Pkwy. SE, Smyrna. Designer outlets in one convenient location: Loehmann's, Men's Wear Outlet, Catherine's Stout Shoppe, Zee Shoes (women), Kid's Konnection, Michelle's (women), Textile Mill, Bennie's Shoes (men), Buyrite Beauty Supply, and the Gift Horse.

Women's Clothing Outlets

Banker's Note (C3), 2581 Piedmont Rd. NE; 233-5233. Four other locations.
The Clothes Bin (C3), 1950 Howell Mill Rd. NW; 351-5064.
Loehmann's Northeast (B4), 3299 Buford Hwy. NE; 633-4156.
R. A. Lyndon (B3), 3330 Piedmont Rd. NE; 262-7941.
Marshalls (A3), 6337 Roswell Rd. NE; 252-9679. Other locations.
Maternity Factory Outlet (B2), 2477 Cobb Pkwy., Smyrna; 952-7600.

Men's Clothing Outlets

Cluett Apparel Outlet (F3), 4847 Jonesboro Rd., Forest Park; 361-7727.
Men's Wear Outlet (B4), 3343 Buford Highway NE; 325-1923. Two other locations.
Outletter Super Store (A5), 5850 Peachtree Industrial Blvd., Norcross; 441-0791. Men's and women's clothing and shoes.
Walton Manufacturing Co., Inc. (B2), 2670 Cobb Pkwy., Smyrna; 952-1313. Other locations.
Zeeman Manufacturing Co., Inc. (B4), 5700 Peachtree Industrial Blvd., Chamblee; 451-5476.

Children's Clothing

Children's Outlet (A5), 4166 Buford Hwy.; 329-0008.

Shoes

Bennie's (C3), 2581 Piedmont Rd.; 262-1966. All major brand names men's shoes. Also in Loehmann's Plaza.
Friedman's Shoes (B3), 4340 Roswell Rd. NW; 843-2414. Men's and women's shoes. Also at 209 Mitchell St. SW; 524-1311. Men's shoes only.
Shoe Inn (B3), 3184 Peachtree Rd. NE; 231-0977. Men's shoes.
Shoe's Unlimited (C4), 2865 N. Druid Hills Rd. NE; 321-0631. Stores also in Sandy Springs, Decatur and Marietta. Women's and men's shoes.

FABRICS AND LINENS

Calico Corners Fabrics (B3), 4256 Roswell Rd. NW; 252-7443. Upholstery, drapery, slipcovers, and fine decorator seconds.

Gallery of Fabrics (B3), Phipps Plaza, 3500 Peachtree Rd. NE; 233-4484. A large selection of better fabrics — silks, cottens, linens, and wools.

Hancock Fabrics (C3), Broadview Shopping Center, Six other locations; 266-0517. For everyday fabric shopping Hancocks has it.

Linens Inc., 2179 Roswell Rd. Marietta; 977-1179. Quality linen for bed, bath, and table at reasonable prices.

Pierre Deux (B3), 111 W. Paces Ferry Rd. NW; 262-7790. French fabrics and accessories.

Textile Mill Store (B3), 3804 Roswell Rd. NE, 237-8740; (A2) 2454 Cobb Pkwy. NW, 955-5541. Other locations. Towels; sheets; bedspreads; comforters; bath and table accessories at discount prices; seconds.

FLEA MARKETS

Atlanta is a mecca for the flea-market aficionado. Whether you are searching for junk or jewels, check out one of these Atlanta area markets.

Aunties (F3), 7471 GA Highway 85 in Riverdale; 996-9967. Open Sat-Sun 7 am - 5 pm. Find everything in this outdoor market.

Bill's, Bankhead Hwy., Lithia Springs; 941-8258. Open Sat-Sun from 6:30 am until dark. Another outdoor market with up to 300 vendors.

Elco's Georgia Antique Fair (E3), 4150 I-75 South Expwy., Hapeville; 361-0726. Open the second weekend of each month. Sat 9 am - 6 pm, Sun 10 am - 6 pm. A large, high-quality market, in existence since 1973.

The Flea Market (C4), 209 E. Ponce de Leon Ave., Decatur; 377-8676. Open Mon-Sat 10 am - 6 pm, Sun 1 pm - 5 pm. This is a small indoor market featuring antiques, wicker, and handicrafts.

Flea Market at Forest Square (E3), 4855 Jonesboro Rd., Forest Park; 361-1221. Open Fri-Sat 10 am - 9 pm, Sun 12 pm - 6 pm. An indoor market with a little of everything.

Great Southeast Flea Market of Atlanta (A5), 4343 Northeast Expwy. Access Rd. in Doraville; 491-7246. This is a large indoor facility with over 450 merchants and some unusual restaurants. Fri-Sun 12 pm - 7 pm.

Gwinnett Drive-In (A6), 1225 Jimmy Carter Blvd., Norcross; 448-2281. Sat only 8 am - 5 pm. A drive-in theater becomes transformed into a flea market every Saturday.

North-85 Drive-In (A5), 3265 Northeast Expwy. Access Rd., Doraville; 451-4570. Open Sun 4 am - 5 pm. A large, outdoor market located in a drive-in lot.

FLORISTS

When the occasion calls for flowers or plants see the following selected florists in Atlanta. Most have FTD (Florist Telegraph Delivery) service and local delivery.

Botany Bay (B3), 2965 Peachtree Rd. NE; 231-9469. Cut flowers and floral arrangements are combined with house plants in this Buckhead location.

Colony Square Florist (G12), 1197 Peachtree St. NE; 881-1803. From a midtown location, Colony Square Florist creates exquisite arrangements.

Gresham's Flowers (J9), 159 Spring St. NW; 522-3215. Since 1913 Gresham's has brought flowers to Atlantans and sent flowers from Atlanta's homes and Atlanta's visitors.

Harpers Flowers (C3), 1300 Spring St. NW; 876-5766. Three generations have served Atlanta since 1921.

Holland Flower Boutique. Two convenient locations at (C4) 1000 1/2 Virginia Ave. NE, 874-3283; and 587 Atlanta St., Roswell, 498-0288. Fresh-cut flowers from Holland in a bucket. Pick a single stem or huge bouquet. Large variety. Arrangements and delivery.

The Potted Plant (B3), 3165 E. Shadowlawn Ave. NE; 233-7800. Atlanta's oldest horticultural shop, The Potted Plant also features cachepots, terra-cotta sculpture, and other related decorative accessories.

South Flower Market (B3), Lenox Square, 3393 Peachtree Rd.; 233-0081. The new spare look in florists with cut flowers arranged in modern cylinders, priced by the flower — more like a street market inside.

Weinstock's Flowers (B3), 4090 Roswell Rd. NW; 255-1611. Weinstock's began their florist business in 1917, another fine established Atlanta company.

FOODS

Shopping for foods can be a tasty addition to the total shopping experience. Here are some appetizing suggestions for gifts of food or immediate consumption.

Bakeries

Edelweiss Bakery (A4), 3575 Chamblee-Tucker Rd., Chamblee; 455-4847. Edelweiss Bakery specializes in German pastries, breads, and sweet delights.

Entenmann's Thrift Cake Bakery (C4), 1451 Scott Blvd.; 378-5546. This national bakery has a thrift outlet near the DeKalb Farmers Market, a lovely coincidence for fresh food and bread shoppers.

Henri's Bakery (B3), 61 Irby Ave. NE; 237-0202. A superior local bakery, a tradition in Atlanta for over fifty years, Henri's is also a fine delicatessen and meeting place in the heart of Buckhead.

Le Gourmet (C3), 2341 Peachtree Rd. NE; 266-8477. Le Gourmet is in the Peachtree Battle Shopping Center. Stop by for goodies from the bakery and deli.

Middle East Baking Co., Inc. (A6), 4000-B Pleasantdale Rd.; 448-9190. Fresh pita bread and a full range of middle-eastern products are ready for delicious picnics.

Midnight Sun Bakery (J9), Peachtree Center, Garden Mall; 577-7080. Here are the finest Danish pastries and delectables.

Pepperidge Farm Thrift Store (B3), 318 Pharr Rd. NE; 262-7580.

This national chain will sell you quality breads at considerable discounts, especially good for bulk buying.

Rich's Bake Shops (B3), 1228 W. Paces Ferry Rd. NW; 233-9892. At fourteen other locations, Rich's Bake Shops have had thousands of satisfied customers for many, many years.

The Royal Bagel (C3), 1544 Piedmont Ave. NE; 876-3512. Bagels come rolling off the pans with a variety of seeds and seasonings, but all with that marvelous aroma from the staff of life. A deli and snack bar also.

Vie de France Corp. (C1), 3940 Shirley Dr. SW; 696-5486. This bakery brings crusty French bread in all sizes to Atlanta's dinner tables.

Health Food Stores

Health food establishments have come into their own during the last two decades, offering a variety of products from grains and vitamins to equipment and cosmetics.

Ari's Health Market (C3), 1544 Piedmont Rd. NE; 876-4373. Also in Doraville and Stone Mountain.

Fields Health Foods, Deli and Bakery (C3), Colony Square, NE; 881-6734. Two other locations. Fields is a triple treat combining health foods, a delicious deli, and a bakery using exclusively natural foods.

The Good Earth (B3), 375 Pharr Rd. NE; 266-2919. Also in Marietta.

Stone Soup (C3), 1243 Virginia Ave. NE; 872-8991. A natural-food grocery store with a full line of fresh produce, dairy products, bulk dried goods. Stone Soup also offers aluminum, glass, and paper recycling as a community service.

Unity Natural Food Markets (B3), 2915 Peachtree Rd.; 261-0110. Four locations in Buckhead, Toco Hills, Sandy Springs, and Roswell.

International and Gourmet Foods

Treasures of specialty foods are hidden in Atlanta's neighborhood pockets, shopping centers, and along the commuter highways. Follow us to an assortment of international foods, fish, meats, and cheese, an offering which expands with Atlanta's increasingly international population.

Arthur's Kosher Meat Market (C4), 2166 Briarcliff Rd. NE; 634-6881. Kosher meats in a friendly atmosphere mark this small butcher shop.

Asian Trading Company (C3), 2581 Piedmont Rd. NE; 266-0362. This is a comprehensive oriental market filled with dried foods, fresh produce, meats and fish, and a myriad of oriental products and gifts.

Callaway Gardens Country Store (E2), Atlanta Airport, 767-3820 and (J8) World Congress Center, 588-1545. This famous mid-Georgia resort also produces a lengthy selection of canned goods and preserves, hams and slab bacon, grits and grains, and country folk crafts. Try the muscadine sauce made from one of Georgia's varietal grapes.

Castleberry's Prepared Meats (C3), 532 10th St. NW; 892-7706. Prime cuts and prime meats have defined Castleberry's reputation for years.

The Cheese Shop (B3), 320 Pharr Rd. NE; 261-4422. The Cheese Shop offers a cheese for every taste, every wine, and every occasion. Also **St. Charles Wine and Cheese** at 1062 St. Charles Ave. (C3).

Dak-Tung Trading Company (C3), 659 Ethel St. NW (off Northside Dr.); 873-2066. Dak-Tung provides oriental foods to Atlanta's restaurateurs and retail customers. Noodles are made fresh each day, and other oriental fare will delight.

Halperns (B3), Lenox Square, Market Level; 231-5050. Halperns sells not only the best and most exotic in fresh produce, meats, and fish but presents it all with theatrical flare. Specialty meats, such as sweetbreads, kidneys, and brains, which are hard to find in the Atlanta area, are reliably part of Halperns eloquent and standard gourmet delights. Also stop by for some fresh oysters and a glass of beer at Halperns seafood bar.

Happy Herman's (C3), 2297 Cheshire Bridge Rd. NE; 321-6385. Also in Perimeter Mall and Sandy Springs. One of Atlanta's most reputable delicatessens, Happy Herman's stocks everything from soup to nuts, lox to tenderloin, and wines and beer from the world over.

SHOPPING

Harold's Butcher Shop and Seafood (B3), 322 Pharr Rd. NE; 262-1730. Harold's serves the northside clientele with excellent meats and fresh, fresh seafood right in the core of Buckhead.

Honey Baked Ham Company (A3), 6500 Roswell Rd. NW.; 252-5556. For easy serving and delicious sweet ham, try this company's spiral-sliced honey-baked ham. Five locations.

Lim's Oriental Food and Gifts (C5), 4887 Memorial Dr., Stone Mountain; 296-6106. Lim's brings you the exotic sauces, pickled fruit, teas, vegetables, and dried seafood from Thailand and the Philippines.

Maison Gourmet (C3), 2581 Piedmont Rd. NE, Broadview Plaza; 231-8552. The Dutch proprietor sells gourmet foods and a complete selection of Dutch and Indonesian foods, as well as running a charming, small cafe serving continental pastries, cheeses, lunch, and dinner.

Mira Enterprises (B4), 2376 Shallowford Terrace, Chamblee; 455-8856. For Indian curries, rice, pickles, chutneys, herbs, spices, pastas, and fresh produce plus Indian bread come to this shop in a small house off Buford Highway.

Pasta & Cheese (B3), Lenox Square, Market Level; 266-1582. The name says it all, for pastas and cheese in every beautiful shape and texture and for every palate.

Proof of the Pudding. (H12), 980 Piedmont Ave. NE; 892-2359. Gourmet meals to go, jars of spices, coffees and teas, and shelves filled with gourmet delectables make this attractive shop and catering company, a constant stopping-off place for Atlantans.

Quality Meats and Kosher Delicatessan (B4), 2161 Briarcliff Rd. NE; 636-1114. This small friendly deli specializes in everything from A to Z in kosher foods and products.

Rinconcito Latino (C3), 2581 Piedmont Rd. NE; Broadview Plaza; 231-2329. A full scope of Spanish and Latin American foods are offered from every type of chili to fresh papayas and tortillas.

S & W Seafood Company (A3), 6125 Roswell Rd., Sandy Springs; 255-8218. For forty plus years in the seafood business S & W has been offering forty varieties of fresh fish in its market and now has a new oyster bar and restaurant.

Markets

Atlanta State Farmers Market (F3), 16 Forest Pkwy., Forest Park; 366-6910. See SIGHTS Chapter.

DeKalb Farmers Market (C4), 640 Medlock Rd., Decatur (one block northwest of Decatur Rd. and Scott Blvd.); 325-8730. A bustling farmers market in Atlanta. Fresh produce is complemented by a superior seafood and cheese section, all at beautiful prices. A shopping place for international communities, suburbanites, and urbanites. Tue-Fri 10 am - 8 pm, Sat 9 am - 8 pm, Sun 12 - 8 pm. Closed Mon.

The Municipal Market of Atlanta (K10), 209 Edgewood Ave. SE; 659-1665. Situated in the Sweet Auburn historic district, the municipal market will introduce you to the "soul food" of southern greens, chitlins, tripe, and pork. Enjoy the colorful signs, succulent food, and social life especially on Friday and Saturday when folks come to market.

FURNITURE MAKERS

If you are furniture shopping take advantage of the varied selections below.

The Chattahoochee Makers Company (B3), 517 E. Paces Ferry Rd. NE; 266-9423. These crafters of distinctive garden furnishings offer outdoor adaptations of classical chair and bench designs from colonial to contemporary styling. Coordinating tables and planters can also be seen in the garden showroom.

Furniture Craftsmen (A1), 1700 White Circle, Marietta; 427-4205. This large shop carries traditional furniture, colonial and eighteenth-century, including their own reproductions.

Furniture to Finish (B1), 3244 South Cobb Dr.; 432-4208. Unusual selections of unfinished furniture such as nineteenth-century design oak-pattern back chairs, and oak and wrought iron park benches can be yours for the finishing.

Georgia Maple Block Co., McDonough. Local tel. 957-5272. Custom-made butcher-block furniture in maple or oak is offered by this McDonough company. Design your own — the price is right.

Allow 4-6 weeks delivery, and pick up in McDonough. Take I-75 south for 45 minutes, exit 70.

Matthews' (B2), 1240 W. Paces Ferry Rd. NW; 237-8271. Matthews' offers fine eighteenth-century reproductions in mahogany and cherry in their elegant northside showroom.

The Rocker Shop (A1), 1421 White Circle NW, Marietta; 427-2618. The Brumby rockers were first designed and constructed by the Brumby family of Marietta in the 1870s with cane seats and backs and extra large arms, and were as sturdy as the red oak from northern Appalachia from which they were made. These rockers are still crafted for rocking on the porch in the summer and by the hearth in the winter and are now part of the White House collection of American furniture.

GIFT SHOPS AND GREETING CARDS

There are many fun-filled gift shops in the city, many in the suburban malls. Our selections highlight some of the best.

The Brookstone Company (B3), Lenox Square; 231-1439. Perimeter Mall also. This store will warm the hearts of the whole family with its happy combination of tools, household gifts, and personal items.

Fragments (A4), Park Place; 396-9200. This is a very uptown gift shop in one of Atlanta's most chic places to shop.

The Golden Rooster (A4), Perimeter Mall; 394-2415. The Golden Rooster is your entry into the world of Colonial Williamsburg. Pewter and brass, glass and china, plus gifts and decorative accessories are available.

High Museum of Art Gift Shop (G11), Atlanta Memorial Arts Center, 1280 Peachtree St. NE; 898-1155. Unusual and interesting greeting cards and notes are sold as well as local and international crafts, gifts and clothing, art magazines, and books.

Hoffritz Gifts and Cutlery (B3), Lenox Square; 231-1300. Hoffritz gifts are a super-sophisticated class of their own, the cutlery especially attractive to men.

John Simmons (B3), Phipps Plaza; 233-5479, and Cumberland Mall. John Simmons carries a broad range of delightful gifts in china, brass, and glass along with sophisticated household items and paper goods.

The Lemon Tree (B3), 34 E. Andrews Dr. NW; 233-2300. Enjoy the potpourri of charming gifts at this sunny shop.

Norway House of Vinings (B2), 2099 Paces Ferry Rd. NW; 435-1502. This marvelous Norwegian collection ranges from ski sweaters to jewelry, pewter to fine cheeses.

Silver Moon (B2), Akers Mill Square; 955-7244. Also in Emory Village. Silver Moon has gifts of whimsey, humor, and class — an unusual selection.

UNICEF Greeting Cards (B3), US Committee for UNICEF, 3384 Peachtree Rd. NE; 233-9429. These cards are sold to help meet the needs of the world's children. World-renowned artists offer designs for business or personal use.

JEWELRY

Atlanta's established jewelers are joined by a group of relative newcomers to assure you a comprehensive jewelry selection. The downtown and Lenox areas are emerging as the diamond and gem center of the city.

Bailey Banks & Biddle Jewelers (B3), Lenox Square; 237-9247. The Atlanta branch of BB&B continues the tradition of fine jewelry since 1832.

Claude S. Bennett (B3), Lenox Square; 233-8201. From the early 1920s Bennetts has been selling and designing jewelry for Atlantans.

Cains Hill Ltd. (B3), 56 E. Andrews Dr. NW; 233-9489. Antique estate jewelry is beautifully displayed in this exquisite shop.

Eighteen K (B3), 99 W. Paces Ferry Rd. NW; 261-0969. This shop offers exclusive custom-designed jewelry by Martin Dubler.

Geode Ltd. Jewelry Designs (B3), Lenox Square; 261-9346. For gold and silver jewelry designed by local and national craftspeople come to Geode's for chic care and service in Lenox.

Knox Jewelers' (C3), 180 Allen Rd. NE; 252-2256. Knox Jewelers' specialize in custom design, pure and simple.

Maier and Berkele (B3), 3225 Peachtree Rd. NE; 261-4911. Founded in 1887, this Atlanta house has six locations now in the metro area.

Skippy Musket (B3), Phipps Plaza; 233-3462. Looking for antique and estate jewelry? Here is another source of pleasure for your treasure hunt.

Tiffany and Company (B3), Phipps Plaza; 261-0074. One of the world's greatest jewelers with over one hundred forty years experience, Tiffany's has swiftly become an Atlanta tradition, too.

LEATHER

Gucci (B3), Phipps Plaza; 233-4899. The Italian designer's premier works are on display for Atlantans to purchase, from soft leather goods to silken scarves.

Mark Cross (B3), Phipps Plaza; 237-2417. Mark Cross has carried fine luggage, briefcases, ladies' and gentlemen's accessories since 1845.

Mori Luggage and Gifts (B3), Lenox Square; 231-2146. This shop has a very wide spectrum of leather accessories in an equally wide price range.

Seriously Western Company (B3), Lenox Square; 233-2045. For would-be cowboys and cowgirls try this outfitter for western wear.

Tannery West (B3), Lenox Square; 233-5397. Handsome, contemporary and traditional leather clothing are featured at Tannery West.

OFFICE SUPPLIES

Anderson Office Supply (C3), 1184 W. Peachtree St. NW; 875-8042. This is a complete office outfitter, with printing and prompt delivery. Second store in Executive Park, 633-6415.

Artlite Office Supply Co. (C3), 1851 Piedmont Rd. NE; 875-7271. Artlite is a full-service supplier, including furniture, free delivery, and copy service. See the historic Artlite pen collection. Open Saturday.

Carithers-Wallace-Courtnay (J10), 223 Courtland St. NE; 659-5900. Office planning, design, topline furniture, and office supplies.

Ivan Allen (J9), 221 Ivy St. NE; 521-0800. Other locations. Complete office service from design to supplies.

Pen and Paper Supply, Inc. (B3), Piedmont & Marion Sts., Broadview Plaza; 266-2512. Pen and Paper offers 10% off cash and carry.

PHOTOGRAPHIC SUPPLIES

The following retail stores provide full customer service including equipment sales, repairs, and developing for both shutterbugs and professional photographers.

Alan's Photography (A5), 3700 Oakcliff Rd., Doraville; 448-4036. Sixteen locations.
Crown Camera (C3), 1000 Piedmont Ave. NE; 873-2102.
Wolf Camera (C3), 150 14th St. NW; 892-1707. Nine locations.

For quick, guaranteed, one-day film development see the following.

Carson's (C3), 562 Dutch Valley Rd. NE; 872-2241. For black and white film.
Fox Photo (C3), 580 Dutch Valley Rd. NE; 873-3663. For color film.

RECORDS AND TAPES

Franklin Music (B3), Lenox Square; 261-7422. Three other locations. Records, tapes, video discs and games, sales and rental of video movies.

Turtle's Records and Tapes (B4), 3337 Buford Hwy. NE; 633-2539. There are 26 Turtle's stores in Atlanta surrounding the Perimeter, so no matter where you are, you're always close to a Turtle's store.

SHOES

Atlanta has many shoe stores of excellence for men, women, and children. We list a few below because of their unusual appeal.

Bally of Switzerland (B3), Lenox Square; 231-0327. This men's shop filled with Bally's elegant continental footwear, leather briefcases, and wallets is one of Atlanta's most exclusive stores.

Shop for Pappagallo (B3), 3201 Peachtree Rd. NE; 233-4544. Those cute Pappagallo shoes for women are just waiting for you at the Pappagallo shop in Buckhead.

SKIN CARE

I Natural Cosmetics (J9), 233 Peachtree St. NE, 586-4806; (B3), Lenox Square, 233-3500. For the natural approach to skin care, I Natural offers skin analysis and make-up sessions using organic products.

Judith Sans Internationale (B3), 56 E. Andrews Dr. NE; 237-5583. Other locations in Sandy Springs, Smyrna, Stone Mountain, Northlake Mall, and College Park. Judith Sans skin care centers offer men and women revitalizing treatments, cleaning, and conditioning to keep face and body looking their best.

SPORTS EQUIPMENT

With Atlanta's temperate climate, outdoor sports activity maintains a year-long momentum. If your tennis racket breaks while visiting the city or you have a sudden urge to buy some new camping equipment, scan the list below for some of the best places to shop.

Abercrombie & Fitch (B3), Phipps Plaza; 233-8522. This nationally known name in sporting goods opened in Atlanta in 1982.

Anglers Afield (B3), 3271 Roswell Rd.; 262-1772. This small store specializes in fine fishing and hunting supplies exclusively.

Bair's Ski Shop (B3), 3228 Roswell Rd. NE; 261-8978. This ski shop offers sales, repair, and a service shop for adults and children.

Deercliff Archery Supplies (C4), 2852 LaVista Rd., Decatur; 633-3080. Deercliff is a specialty shop featuring archery equipment, fencing supplies, and darts.

The Fish Hawk (B3), 283 Buckhead Ave. NE; 237-3473. This is a special place for anglers who seriously fish the fresh and salt waters of Georgia and beyond.

Georgia Outdoors (A3), 6518 Roswell Rd.; 256-4040. Two other locations in Stone Mountain and Decatur. A full-service sporting-goods store emphasizing camping, fishing, hunting and canoeing equipment.

Golf Tennis Specialty Centers (B4), 2965 N. Druid Hills Rd. NE; 321-3572. Excellent equipment selections for these two popular sports can be found at the center's three locations.

High Country (B2), 6300 Powers Ferry Rd. NW; 955-1866. Four locations. Camping equipment, backpacks, canoes, kayaks, and outdoor clothing are High Country's major offerings.

Old Sarge Army-Navy Surplus Store (A5), 5316 Buford Hwy., Doraville; 451-6031. Old Sarge defines the Army-Navy store where you can wander endlessly through surplus military equipment to find a rugged Eisenhower jacket, boots to last a lifetime, or a heavy-duty duffle bag for your tent.

Oshman's Sporting Goods (B3), 3157 Peachtree Rd. NE; 266-2391. Six locations. A general sporting-goods store, Oshman's brings you a complete line of sports equipment and clothing for men and women.

Phidippides Sports Center (C3), 1544 Piedmont Ave. NE; 875-4268. Three locations. Phidippides, the great Greek marathon runner, is honored in this specialist running center. For running shoes and clothes, expert advice, and up-to-date data on Atlanta's running courses, clinics, and programs, come to Phidippides.

TOBACCO

Alfred Dunhill of London (B3), Lenox Square; 231-2142. All the accoutrements for the smoker in the most traditional and elegant fashion are available here as well as business gifts in leather and brass.

The Royal Cigar Company (J9), 48 Forsyth St. NW; 524-9069. Since 1922 this downtown tobacco shop has offered the connoisseur the best names in pipes and smokers' articles and over three hundred blends of tobaccos. The Royal Cigar Company is one of the few shops in the country to still have a wooden Indian statue at its entry symbolizing the native American's introduction of tobacco to the colonists.

TOYS

Kiddie City (A3), 6285 Roswell Rd. NE; 252-2214. This remarkable children's department store has a prime and extensive selection of toys.

F. A. O. Schwarz (B3), Lenox Square; 233-8241. The Atlanta branch of this famous New York children's toy store is conveniently located in Lenox Square.

Toy Safari (B3), Phipps Plaza; 262-1515. Three locations. Intriguing and elegant toys for children are featured in this specialty shop.

SPORTS

SPORTS TO SEE

Atlantans are sports lovers. Since the mid-sixties, Atlanta has endorsed major league sports, with two of the professional teams owned by ace sportsman and America's Cup winner Ted Turner. The Atlanta Braves, Turner's baseball team, highlighted the 1974 season with Hank Aaron's record-breaking 715th home-run hit. The Atlanta Hawks is the other Ted Turner team, a favorite of Atlantans. The Atlanta Falcons have had a solid following year after year on the football field. Atlanta is also the center of major professional golf and tennis tournaments, motor-racing spectaculars, a steeplechase, and polo matches. Visitors from towns and cities in the southeast gravitate to the city to join Atlantans in one of their favorite pastimes, spectator sports — on the gridiron, or on the diamond, the links or the courts, the raceways or in the rolling countryside.

College Football

College football is dear to the hearts of Atlantans and is played in the heart of the city, the Georgia Tech stadium. Culminating this keen interest in college football is the Peach Bowl, an annual post-season college football game, generally on New Year's Eve, at the Atlanta/Fulton County Stadium. Tickets and information 522-1967.

A favorite rivalry between Morris Brown and Morehouse Colleges, both part of Atlanta University, is played out in October. Information 525-7831.

Golf

Tournaments in the Atlanta area include the Lady Michelob in May and the Atlanta Golf Classic in June. See SPECIAL EVENTS Chapter.

Major Leagues

Atlanta Fulton County Stadium   Courtesy Atlanta Convention and Visitors Bureau

The **Atlanta Braves,** National Baseball League. Games from April through October, at Atlanta/Fulton County Stadium. Ticket and game information 577-9100.

The **Atlanta Falcons,** National Football League. Eight regular home games beginning in the fall, one or two pre-season games, at Atlanta/Fulton County Stadium. Ticket and game information 325-2667. Shuttle buses make transportation to the game an easy and fun Sunday party time.

The **Atlanta Hawks,** National Basketball Association. Games from October through March at Omni Coliseum. Ticket and game information 681-3605. Have a bite to eat at the Omni Center before the game, for an enjoyable evening's outing.

Motor Racing

Stock car racing is a friendly and casual social event in the South. Driver and movie star Paul Newman occasionally turns up in Atlanta to add a bit of glamor to this down-to-earth sport.

The **Atlanta International Raceway** (25 miles south of Atlanta, I-75 to exit 77, south on US 19 and US 41, in Hampton, GA). *CH.* Events include the Coca-Cola 500 in March, and the Atlanta Journal 500 in November, both annual national stock car races. The raceway summer schedule includes motocross and truck and tractor pulls. Tickets and information 946-4211.

Road Atlanta (50 miles north of Atlanta, I-85 to GA 53, near Gainesville, GA). *CH.* Events include the Champion Spark Plug Road Racing Classic in October, International Motor Sports Association GT series, and a Canadian-American series in April and September. Call 881-8233.

Polo

This thrilling sport combines speed, skill, grace, and danger and has been equated to chess in its finesse. The Atlanta Polo Club play matches year-round, with Arena Polo in the winter months.

Their polo field is on Johnson Ferry Road, just across the Chattahoochee River, (A3). Scrimmaging starts in April on Tuesday and Thursday from 5:30 pm to dusk. *NCH.* Matches are played from May every Sunday at 1 and 3 pm. *CH.* Three tournaments a year on Memorial Day, Fourth of July, and Labor Day, plus other benefits attract players from all over the southeast. Women's matches are on Saturday afternoons. Call 252-5712 for further information. Arena Polo is played from December to March at Pine Tree Stables, Shallowford Road in Marietta on Sunday afternoons. *NCH.* Call 475-4404.

Tennis

Major tennis tournaments held in Atlanta include the Atlanta Journal-Constitution Open in August and the Saks Fifth Avenue Kodel Mixed Doubles Championship in May. See SPECIAL EVENTS Chapter.

SPORTS TO DO

Visitors can share the active lives Atlantans lead. Perhaps you have thought of a golf game in the afternoon with a client or tennis/racquetball with your associate, a health club to continue your workouts, a convenient track to run on, some scenic jogging routes, disco roller-skating at night, ice skating, or biking through Atlanta's famous intown and suburban neighborhoods. Maybe you want to spend the day rafting down the Chattahoochee River, fishing, sailing, or boating at Lake Lanier or Lake Allatoona. Here's how, whether you are solo, with a partner, your family, or a group.

Bicycling

The **Southern Bicycle League,** regularly scheduled guided tours and rides of varying distances throughout the hilly city and environs, bring your own bike. 633-8147, 633-5512.

Skate Escape (C3), 1086 Piedmont Ave. NE; 892-1292. One speed and tandem rental bikes available for biking in Piedmont Park in midtown.

Stone Mountain Park (C6), rental bikes for men, women, and children available daily from June through August, on weekends from March through November. Three-speed, tandem bikes, and baby seats also available, 469-9831.

Bowling

Bowling is a long-time popular indoor sport in the South.
Broadview Bowl-O-Matic (B4), 2581 Piedmont Rd. NE; 237-6612.
Brunswick-Express Lanes (C3), 1936 Piedmont Cir. NE; 874-5703.
Steve Jerome's Northeast Plaza Lanes (B4), 3285 Buford Hwy. NE; 636-7548.
Sandy Springs Lanes (A3), 6320 Roswell Rd. NW; 255-7942.

Golf

Atlantans and Georgians enjoy golf year-round. Golf courses generally do not close except for occasional ice storms, or maintenance. Call for starting times, rental clubs, carts, and information. All courses 18 holes except where designated.

City Public Courses
Adams Park (D2), 2300 Wilson Dr. SW; 753-6158.

Bobby Jones (C3), 384 Woodward Way NW; 355-9049.
Browns Mill (E3), 480 Cleveland Ave. SE; 361-9959.
Candler Park (C4), 585 Candler Park Dr. NE; 373-9265. Nine holes only.
North Fulton (B3), 216 W. Wieuca Rd. NW; 255-0723.

Other Public Courses
Stone Mountain Park (C6), Stone Mountain; 469-9831. Designed by the renowned golf course architect Robert Trent Jones.
Sugar Creek, 2706 Bouldercrest Rd. SE; 241-7671. Operated by DeKalb County.

Health Clubs

The national chain health clubs and exercise centers are everywhere in Atlanta. Check the yellow pages if you desire one of these. We list some preferred clubs.

Adventures International (J10), Atlanta Hilton Hotel, Courtland and Harris Sts.; 659-2000. Open to visitors to Atlanta. Includes complete Nautilus-equipped gym, saunas, outdoor track, full exercise room, outdoor swimming, steam, sauna, jacuzzi, and four tennis courts. Open from 7 am - 10 pm, seven days a week. Facilities for men and women, and a lounge with snacks.

American Fitness Center (A3), 6780 Roswell Rd. NW; 394-0090. Eight other locations in Druid Hills, Chamblee, Norcross, Stone Mountain, Smyrna, and Forest Park. A full service center for physical fitness in Metro Atlanta.

Arden Zinn Studio (J9), Peachtree Center Shopping Gallery, 875-9088; (C3), 1874 Piedmont Rd. NE, 875-9088; and many other metro locations. This club offers exercise classes at various times during the day. Special 'Ardenics' cater to women.

Athletic Center of Atlanta (I10), 615 Peachtree St. at North Ave.; 873-2633. Take advantage of a 100-yard tartan-surface indoor track, Nautilus machines, massage therapy, sauna, lockers. Open Mon-Fri from 6 am - 8 pm; Sat 8 am - 3 pm. Co-ed facilities.

Court South (B3), Around Lenox; 262-2120. Four other locations: Downtown at the Omni, Sandy Springs, Marietta, Akers Mill. Racquetball is featured with indoor jogging tracks, Nautilus, complete spas, exercise rooms with instructors, tanning solariums, and massage therapy.

Westin Peachtree Plaza Health Spa (J9), Westin Peachtree Plaza Hotel, 210 Peachtree St.; 659-1400. Facilities at the Westin Peachtree Plaza include an indoor swimming pool, gym with universal equipment, and sauna. Opened to visitors at $5.75 per day or $15.00 per week.

YMCA (J9), Downtown Branch; 145 Luckie St. NW; 525-5401 and eleven metro locations. Call for current offerings.

Hiking

Hiking in and around Atlanta can be planned as a leisurely outing or a course of strenuous activity.

Chattahoochee River National Recreational Area (A2), a relatively undisturbed and beautiful national river area in the heart of metro Atlanta. A day-use park open seven days a week. Trail maps of hiking areas and information available from the Information Center at US 41 and the Chattahoochee River (one mile west of I-75 north, near the Perimeter I-285). Perfect for a picnic lunch and short hike. 952-4419.

Fernbank Science Center (C4), 156 Heaton Park Dr. NE; 378-4311. Two-mile nature trail with shrubs and trees labelled. Maps available at the Forest Gate behind the center. Open daily 2 - 5 pm, Sat 10 am - 5 pm.

Kennesaw Mountain National Battlefield Park (Ga 120 about 25 miles north of Atlanta); 427-4686. Four hiking trails and an historic Civil War mountain to climb.

Stone Mountain Park (C6), (7 miles east of I-285 on US 78); 469-9831. Nature trails and a 1.3-mile hike to the top of the granite mountain for a wonderful view of the whole park and nearby Atlanta.

Horseback Riding

The Atlanta area is beautiful horse country, with outstanding trails. The area has over twenty excellent stables, which offer riding lessons in Western, saddle seat, and hunt seat as well as boarding facilities. Only a few of these have horse rentals, which we list below.

Chattahoochee River Barn, 10265 Highway 141 (Duluth); 476-2301. Trails over 900 acres on the banks of the Chattahoochee River; English and Western saddle, beginners, and experienced riders.

Danner's Stables, 5438 Brown's Mill Rd., Lithonia; 981-8963. Hunt seat and Western lessons and horse rentals for supervised trail rides.

Lanier Stables, Lake Lanier Islands (Buford). A five-mile trail around the lake, over hills, and through creeks led by a guide. Horses for all riders, English and Western saddles. Pony rides and pony-cart rides for children, evening hayrides in summer, and horsemanship classes. Open March 15 to December 20, 9 am until dark. Call 945-6164.

Paradise Manor Stables, 5 Lilburn-Stone Mountain Rd., Lilburn; 921-9821. Boarding and riding lessons only.

Statebridge Stables, 3905 Kimball Bridge Rd. (Alpharetta); 475-4470. Trails over 1000 acres, English and Western saddles, beginners and experienced riders.

Hunting

Georgia is known as prime quail hunting territory.

Callaway Gardens Gun Club and Hunting Preserve, Pine Mountain, Ga. (1 1/2 hours drive on I-85 south of Atlanta). Hunting season at Callaway Gardens lasts from October 1 through March 31. This verdant Georgia resort includes a hunting lodge on 1000 acres of preserve. Parties of two to three quail hunters, with dogs and guides, cost $100 per hunter per half-day hunt. Guns are available at no charge; shells can be purchased at the lodge. There is a guarantee of 10 birds per hunter, $5 for each additional bird. Deer stands are available for rental also. Skeet and trap shooting are offered year-round. The Gun Club and Hunting Preserve are open seven days a week during the hunting season. Call the hunting preserve for advance reservations at 688-8542.

Ice Skating

Parkaire Olympic Ice Arena (A3), 4859 Lower Roswell Rd. SE, Marietta; 973-0753.

Stone Mountain Ice Chalet (C6), Stone Mountain Park; 469-9831. Open daily all year, the Ice Chalet has instruction, hockey leagues, and pro shop.

SPORTS

Racquetball

This is a new sport which has proliferated in Atlanta.

Court South. See Health Clubs above.

The Racquet House at Parkaire (A3), 4951 Lower Roswell Rd., Marietta; 971-1700. Member of the National Court Club Association of America. Racquetball, Nautilus, and health facilities. Guest fee.

Terminus Racquetball Club (A2), 1775 Water Pl. NW; 952-3200. Lots of racquetball in this Marietta location plus squash, tennis, swimming, aerobics, and other exercise classes.

Rifle Ranges

These places welcome out-of-towners.

DeKalb Public Firing Range (D6), 3905 N. Goddard Rd., Lithonia; 482-8965. Open seven days a week.

The Marksman (A6), 6296 Dawson Blvd., Norcross; 449-3838. Open seven days a week.

Roller Skating

Roller skating has been popular in this area of the south with each generation learning on the city sidewalks and most recently rolling on bright skates to the sounds of disco in the roller rinks.

Jellybeans, 3850 Stone Rd. SW; 346-1111.

Playland Roller Skating Center (B5), 4405 Buford Hwy., Chamblee; 457-8811.

Stone Mountain Park (C6); 469-9831. Skate on trails through the woods or on the rink.

Running

Runners are quickly reminded that Atlanta is a city of hills and dells, ups and downs, so pace yourself to accommodate the terrain and enjoy the scenic routes.

The Atlanta Track Club, 3224 Peachtree Rd. NE; 231-9064. Co-sponsors with the Atlanta *Journal* and *Constitution* of Atlanta's Peachtree Road Race on the Fourth of July. 25,000 runners compete, making this the largest road race in the U.S. Everyday of the year runners can be seen on the streets and in the parks.

Phidippedes, a specialized running equipment store with workshops, programs, advice and comprehensive information about the Atlanta running scene. Stores at a variety of locations in Atlanta, 875-4268.

Tennis

Atlanta is a tennis town. Bring your racquet and play tennis year-round on its numerous courts, both public and private.

Public and City Municipal Courts

The following fine Atlanta tennis centers offer excellent facilities and lessons and are staffed with a tennis professional. *CH.*

Bitsy Grant (C3), 2125 Northside Dr. NW, the city's major tennis center, 351-2774.
Chastain Park (B3), 110 West Wieuca Rd. NW; 255-9798.
Eastlake Indoor Tennis (D4), 2573 Alston Dr. SE (East Lake Country Club); 373-2212.
McGhee Tennis Center (D4), 1 Beecher Rd. SW; 752-7177.
North Fulton Tennis Center (A3), 500 Abernathy Rd. NE; 256-1588.
Piedmont Park (C3), Piedmont at 12th St. NE; 872-1507.
Stone Mountain Park Public Tennis Center (C6); 469-4843.
Washington Park (D3), 1125 Lena St. NW; 523-1169.

For other city courts call 658-7277.
For Fulton County courts call 572-2526.
For DeKalb County courts call 371-2548.
For Cobb County courts call 424-0204.
For Gwinnett County courts call 448-4464.

Water Sports

Atlanta has two large manmade recreational lakes within 35 miles of its city limits (approximately 45 minutes driving time) plus several others to the south.

SPORTS

Lake Sidney Lanier, named after the nineteenth-century Georgia poet, is northeast of the city. This is the most popular lake in the nation that is supervised by the U.S. Army Corps of Engineers with 15 million visitors annually.

Lake Allatoona, also an Army Corps of Engineers lake, is 30 miles northwest of Atlanta. Located on the western shore of the lake is an excellent Georgia State park, Red Top Mountain, with full recreational amenities.

These two large bodies of water provide flood control for the area, power generation, conservation, and extensive recreational facilities for water sports. For further information and maps call:
Lake Lanier Resource Manager 1-945-9531.
Lake Allatoona Resource Manager 1-382-4700.

The **Chattahoochee River** is the third major area for water sports in Atlanta. The river continues from the Buford Dam at Lake Lanier through the north and northwest sections of metro Atlanta. In 1978 the Chattahoochee River National Recreation area was established providing protection for this great river which flows from the Georgia mountains to the Gulf of Mexico. Atlantans draw not only their city water from the river but draw many pleasurable hours sporting in the waters of the Chattahoochee and relaxing on its banks.

Canoeing

Blue Ridge Mountain Sports, Lenox Square NE; 266-8372. Canoe and camping equipment rental, clinics in canoeing and kayaking, also rock climbing and backpacking. Canoe and hiking trips.

Georgia Canoeing Association, P.O. Box 7023, Atlanta, GA 30357. For open canoe, deck canoe, and Kayak clinics and organized group trips on Georgia's beautiful white-water and flat-water rivers this is an outstanding association for membership.

High Country Inc., four locations; outfitter location at (A2) 6300 Powers Ferry Rd. NW; 955-1866. Rental canoes and rafts; shuttle service from the outposts on the Chattahoochee River; clinics in canoeing, kayaking, rock climbing, white-water rafting, and backpacking; wilderness, paddling trips and various other outdoor programs and trips. The official concessionaire for the area.

Lake Lanier Islands, Lake Lanier (I-85 north to GA 365, follow signs); 945-6701. Canoe and kayak rental at the beach, May through September.

Fishing

The Chattahoochee River, Lake Lanier, and Lake Allatoona are fished mainly for trout, bream, bass, and crappie. The devout fly fisherman can be seen tubing the river or casting into the shoals for the elusive trout, and fishing boats, trailed from city to the lakes each weekend, wander in and around the coves and points on the lakes' shores. Fishing is permitted from all shorelines unless otherwise designated. A Georgia fishing license is required for fresh-water fishing. Licenses are sold at Oshmans Sporting Goods, the Fish Hawk, and Reeder and McGaughey.

Cast and Catch Enterprises, Aquatic Center, Lake Lanier Islands, year-round fishing boat rental, bait sales, and tackle rental. Drivers license required. Write Cast and Catch Enterprises, P.O. Box 356, Buford, GA 30518; or call 945-3328.

Little River Landing, Lake Allatoona, Route 4, Highway 205, Canton, GA; 577-7739.

For further information and maps on fishing in the Atlanta area and in the State of Georgia contact the Georgia Game and Fish Division, 270 Washington St. SW; 656-3530 or The Fish Hawk, 283 Buckhead Ave. NE; 237-3473.

Motor Boating

Lake Lanier Islands; 945-6701. Pontoon boat rental, March through November, houseboat rental all year.

Rafting

Rafting on the Chattahoochee is a popular weekend recreation for Atlantans.

Chattahoochee Outdoor Center (A4), 1900 Northridge Rd., Dunwoody; 394-6622. The COC makes raft rental, transportation, and food service easy and enjoyable. Shuttle buses retrieve rafters and rafts at take out points. The COC works with the National Park Service to create an urban outfitter post that serves the public with careful professionalism.

High Country, Inc. (A3), Johnson Ferry Rd. NW; 955-0880. See Canoeing above.

Rowing

The Atlanta Rowing Club hosts regattas on the Chattahoochee and has sculling and rigging clinics; 939-1981.

Sailing

Lanier Sailing Academy, Ltd., Lake Lanier Islands, sailboat rentals include Sunfish, Hobie Cats, small and large day-sailers, and cruising auxiliary sailboats. Deposit required; advance reservations necessary. Write Lanier Sailing Academy, Ltd., 1105 Spalding Dr. NE, Atlanta 30338; or call 945-8810.

Swimming

Swimming pools are available at most hotels. City of Atlanta pools are located in three different quadrants of the city. Call 658-6317 for other city locations.

Adams Park (D2), 2300 Wilson Dr. SW.
Chastain Memorial Park (D3), 216 W. Wieuca Rd. NW.
Piedmont Park (C3), Piedmont Ave. and 14th St. NE.

The YMCAs in metro Atlanta have fine swimming facilities and programs. Most also have an infant aquatics class. Call the Northside Family YMCA at 261-3111 for a reference to the Y in your area.

Manmade swimming beaches are located at:
Lake Lanier Islands, Lake Lanier (I-85 north to GA 365, follow signs), bathhouses on the beach, water slide.

Red Top Mountain State Park, Lake Allatoona. (I-75 north to Northside Dr. exit, left at light, continue north on US 41 to exit 123 which goes to Red Top Mountain State Park).

Stone Mountain Park (C6) (seven miles east of I-285 on US 78, Stone Mountain Freeway). See SIGHTS Chapter.

Water-Skiing

Makin' Spray, Inc., at Stouffers PineIsle Hotel, Lake Lanier; 945-9550. Water-ski school and water-ski tow service, which includes boat, driver, equipment, and gas. Master Craft tournament ski boats, largest ski shop in the southeast; windsurfers and sailboards also available. May to October 9:30 am to dusk, daily.

If you have the equipment there are many other fine lakes. Call the State Parks Department, 656-3530.

Downhill Skiing, Team Sports, and Car Rallies

Downhill Skiing

Atlanta Ski Club, over 5000 strong is the largest ski club in the country, offering social gatherings year-round and group trips in winter to ski resorts from the Rockies, to Canada, to Europe. ASC also runs a unique ski-school at the Vinings Ridge Ski Area in northwest Atlanta, only 15 minutes from downtown, offering instruction on the artificial slope, with an astro-turf base covered with polyethylene beads — the perfect practice between September and December for the winter ski trips. Call 892-1286.

Rugby

Rugby is relatively new to Atlanta, but it is now played with gusto with both men's and women's teams.

The **Atlanta Old Rugby Club** (B3), North Fulton High School, 2890 N. Fulton Dr. NE; 237-0007. Fall season from September through December, spring season from February to May.

Atlanta Women's Rugby Club (B3), North Fulton High School; 874-4576.

Soccer

Soccer is now well established in Atlanta as a recreational sport and as an integral part of the athletic curriculum of the schools.

Georgia State Soccer Association Inc., (A4), 20 Perimeter Park Dr. NE; information regarding leagues and schedules of games, 452-0505.

Softball

Every warm weekend you will see softball played in all the Atlanta parks.

City of Atlanta, Supervisor of Athletics, for information on leagues, schedules and locations of adult softball, youth baseball, youth basketball, football, and track call 658-6317.

Sports Car Rallies
For sports car enthusiasts call the Georgia Sports Car Club, 923-0464. Monthly road rallies (except December).

Further Information

For custom-designed sports programs for companies and conventions we recommend:

Corporate Sports Unlimited, P.O. Box 20424, Atlanta 30325; 355-1101. A professional staff provides the facilities, transportation, equipment, and food for corporate and convention sports activities. Specialty is a Super Sports Day. All sports included.

Further information on outdoor-recreation programs within Atlanta and the State of Georgia:

Georgia Conservancy, Inc., 3110 Maple Dr. NE; 262-1967. An advocacy organization sponsoring special field trips and hikes in ecologically sensitive or historically significant areas.

State of Georgia Department of Natural Resources, 656-3530. Providing information on state parks, hiking, camping, hunting, and fishing as well as licensing requirements.

U.S. Forest Service, 881-2384. Providing hiking and camping information on the Chattahoochee National Forest and the Appalachian Trail, which begins in the North Georgia Mountains.

SPECIAL EVENTS

The Atlanta calendar is overflowing with exciting events for the whole year, but some are special annual events around which Atlanta traditions are formed and celebrated. They are as seasonally anticipated as the dogwood blossoms in spring and the changing of the fall colors. These two beautiful seasons in particular generate innumerable home tours, garden tours, arts, fairs, folk festivals, and sporting events. Of special note are the outstanding Atlanta Symphony concerts during the summer months in Piedmont and Chastain Parks. Bring your picnic supper and enjoy a warm summer evening of fine music under the stars.

We are selecting annual highlights, those peak experiences that claim a hold on Atlanta's own citizens year after year. Be aware that special events stay in the same season but will shift sometimes from month to month during the change of years.

January

Atlanta Boat Show, Civic Center Auditorium (I11); 523-1879. The Boat Show is a late winter magnet for all the sailors and boatmen yearning for the next spring sail or pleasure trip on the nearby lakes, rivers, and the further waters of the Atlantic or Gulf. Every sort of boat is on display, with lucky draws and prizes for a chosen few. A full week of the nautical world.

February

Annual Children's Festival, Atlanta Memorial Arts Center (G11), 1280 Peachtree St. NE; 892-3600. For over a decade the Children's Festival has attracted kids from Atlanta, with the Atlanta Symphony programs, high school jazz bands, a performance of the Alliance Children's Theatre, clogging, art exhibits, face-painting, and sundry other forms of celebrating young life.

SPECIAL EVENTS

Atlanta Mardi Gras (B3), Phipps Plaza; 261-0074 or 898-1132. Atlanta's Original Mardi Gras benefits the Alliance Theatre Guild and offers a pre-Lenten feast of music, dance, gambling, costumes, entertainment, and an opulent repast.

Camellia Show and Fine Arts Show, Lenox Square Shopping Mall (B3), 3393 Peachtree Rd.; 233-6767. The pride of camellia growers and the work of local artists continue to make February a month to celebrate natural and manmade manifestations of the beautiful.

DeKalb County Mardi Gras for the Arts (C6), 1501 Rock Mountain Blvd.; 378-2637. A warehouse in Stone Mountain becomes the space for Mardi Gras festivities for a weekend in February. Jugglers, magicians, mimers, street performers, and entertainment galore greet the revelers.

March

Coca-Cola 500, Atlanta International Raceway (F4), Hampton, GA; 946-4211. Pack a picnic lunch of beer and sandwiches and join the noisy fun-loving crowd at this daddy of national stock-car racing.

Kite Day, Stone Mountain Park (C6); 469-9631. The March winds scoop the competitors' kites high into the sky above Stone Mountain. The kite flying endurance contest has a 24-hour record for you to challenge, and the kite giveaway will distribute 500 free kites to children 12 and under.

Mr. Pibb Motocross, Atlanta-Fulton County Stadium (L8); 522-7630. The stadium is piled high with dirt mounds and trails for the roaring maneuvers of these dare-devil motorcyclists.

St. Patrick's Day Parade. The Irish have their way and their day down Peachtree Street, sporting the green with floats and bands and lots of Irish chatter, jokes, green beer, and good will.

Virginia-Highlands Bungalow Tour (C4). This inner-city area has an annual tour of its architecturally dominant style — the early twentieth-century bungalow. Call 522-4345, the Atlanta Preservation Center, for information.

April

Ansley Park Tour of Homes (C3); 522-4345. This charming early twentieth-century suburb opens its homes and gardens to visitors during the height of the fall brilliance. Ansley Park is an attractive neighborhood of curving streets, gentle hills, and interior parks, between the Arts Center and Piedmont Park.

Atlanta Dogwood Festival; 892-0539. The triumphant blossoming of the dogwood heralds in the rites of spring. Atlanta's splendid festival features house-and-garden tours, exhibits, art shows, a grand parade, and a gala ball to honor the Dogwood Queen and her court. The city is awash with pink and white dogwood blossoms, a wonderland setting for these city-wide festivities.

Atlanta Hunt and Steeplechase, near Cumming; 233-5332. Part of the southeastern circuit, the steeplechase brings together distinguished horses and riders, while spectators lunch on grassy knolls and enjoy watching each other's gourmet picnics, complete with dinner-party trappings, right down to silver candelabra propped on car hoods. Dress includes everything from British tweeds to morning coats and long dresses. Late March or early April. Tickets must be purchased beforehand. Call for information.

The Atlanta Music Club Spring Promenade, Atlanta Music Club, 3121 Maple Dr. NE; 233-2131. The club tour features six Atlanta-area gardens, a chance for you to see some of the prize gardens of a city known for its lush natural growth.

Inman Park Festival and Tour (D4); 681-2798. This historic district's nationally recognized tour of homes opens its restored turn-of-the-century houses to the public. The festival includes a children's fair, bazaar, art show, music, and street circus.

Midtown Tour of Homes (C3); 522-4345. The midtown area is bounded by Ponce de Leon and 10th Street, Monroe Drive and Peachtree Street, and the tours include a variety of architectural styles from the late nineteenth century to today's condominium.

Norcross Heritage Festival (A6); 449-1776 (City of Norcross). The old-town section of Norcross was placed on the National Register of Historic Places in late 1980. Tours include homes and historic buildings from 1835 to the early twentieth century.

May

Arts Festival of Atlanta, Piedmont Park (C3); 885-1125. For two weekends and the week in between, Piedmont Park is the stage for Atlanta's outdoor arts festival, featuring visual art in all media, demonstrations, and many of the city's finest in the performing arts. The festival schedule is filled with events for adults and children during the day and each evening. Marionettes, jugglers, mimers, jazz, blues, country music, the symphony, chorales, and visual art from the most sophisticated to the gypsy section — all are part of this great festival of art for the people.

The Decorators' Show House. Each year the Junior Committee of the Atlanta Symphony procures a fine old house for three weeks, and Atlanta's exciting decorators design, decorate, and accessorize individual rooms. A chance to see current interior design trends and gather ideas for your own home, as well as seeing one of the city's lovely old houses.

Easter Sunrise Services and the **Great Egg Hunt,** Stone Mountain Park (C6); 469-9831. Sunrise services are held from the top and at the base of the mountain — a spectacular beginning to Resurrection Day. The world's largest egg hunt follows in the afternoon with 20,000 hard-boiled eggs for children 3 to 9 years of age.

The Lady Michelob Golf Tournament, Brookfield West, Willow Run, Roswell; 998-1213. This is a major stop in the Ladies Professional Golf Association Tour, and many of the top players in the country will be here.

Metropolitan Opera, Atlanta Music Festival Association, Civic Center (I11); 262-2161. The Metropolitan Opera comes to town from New York for a week each May, delighting the local music connoisseurs and those who make a special visit to Atlanta from points all over Georgia to hear the world's best opera. Opera parties, formal attire, and constant "opera" conversation attest to the vitality of the Met's week in Atlanta. Tickets are hard to come by; box-office lines are long. Look at the want ads in May and listen for ticket-exchange broadcasts on Atlanta's classical music stations.

Saks Fifth Avenue Kodel Mixed Doubles Championship, Phipps Plaza (B3); 261-7234. *NCH.* In the parking lot of Phipps Plaza, Saks sets up a tennis court inviting top local doubles' players to compete. Stop by after shopping to see the matches.

June

The Atlanta Dance Festival, 1280 Peachtree St. NE; 658-6691. This two-week festival features diverse works by many choreographers. Although mostly Atlanta dance companies, the festival also includes non-Atlanta groups.

The Atlanta Golf Classic (A3), part of the Professional Golf Association tour, at the Atlanta Country Club, Country Club Rd. SE, Marietta. Be sure to get tickets early for this popular event which brings big names to vie for big prizes. Call 255-0790.

The Atlanta Jazz Festival, Atlanta Stadium (L8); 876-5470. The Jazz Festival, in June or late May, holds court to the most brilliant jazz musicians and groups in the nation.

The Atlanta New Play Project. Sponsored by Atlanta area theater groups, the New Play Project offers playwrights the opportunity to present their works. After the first showing, post-production discussions are held with guest critics, and the plays are revised for the second week. Call the different theater groups for more information.

Chastain Park Concerts (B3), Atlanta Symphony Orchestra. See PERFORMING ARTS Chapter.

Dahlonega Bluegrass Festival, Hwy. 60 S., Dahlonega; 864-7203. Held the 4th weekend in June, come hear the nation's top bluegrass bands. Camping facilities available.

Fox Film Festival (I10), 660 Peachtree St. NE; 881-1977. During the summer the fabulous Fox Theatre sponsors a series of 12 screen classics. For an extra treat, the Mighty Moeller organ is played prior to the screenings.

Light Up Atlanta. This annual event draws thousands downtown for street dances, live entertainment, outdoor vendors, and fireworks. Call 874-FEST.

WPLO Fishing Derby (A2), Holiday Rd. at Lake Lanier Islands; 945-6701. Amateur fishermen win trophies for everything from largest bass to most fish caught by anglers under the age of five.

Piedmont Park Free Concerts (C3), Atlanta Symphony Orchestra. See PERFORMING ARTS Chapter.

SPECIAL EVENTS

July

Atlanta Braves' Game and Fireworks (L8); 577-9100. Almost every Fourth of July, the Braves play in Atlanta. The evening game is followed by fireworks. It's the all-American way to celebrate the Fourth.

Fantastic Fourth Celebration, Stone Mountain Park (C6); 469-9831. Days and evenings of entertainment, gymnastics, dancing, banjo-plucking, jazz bands, stage shows, clogging, Bar-B-Que, and the Atlanta Symphony family concerts are offered around the key salute to national independence — the incredible fireworks display from the top of Stone Mountain on the Fourth of July.

Peachtree Road Race; 231-9064. Fourth of July. One of the largest foot races in the country moves like a massive snake down Peachtree from Lenox Square to Piedmont Park. The heat and hills challenge the 25,000 runners to their limits. Join the runners or spectators lining Peachtree Street as they cheer friends toward their coveted Peachtree Road Race T-shirts.

Salute to America Parade; 897-7385. Fourth of July. This is the super-parade of Atlanta, sponsored by WSB-TV, with the stars and stripes being marched and played and displayed for miles along Peachtree Street.

Stay and See Georgia Week, Lenox Square Mall (B3); 524-8481. The Georgia Chamber of Commerce and Lenox Square sponsor this six-day long presentation of touring and vacationing possibilities to help you plan your next trip within the state. Sixty-five or so exhibitors from all over Georgia display their best, inviting you to explore the seashore, the mountains, and the piedmont of Georgia.

August

Atlanta Journal-Constitution Tennis Open, WCT Peachtree World of Tennis, Norcross, GA (A6); 449-6060. Two major Atlanta papers sponsor this men's professional tournament on the Volvo Grand Prix circuit.

September

American Association of University Women's Book Sale (B3), Lenox Square; 233-6767. During September, this Association sponsors a wonderful used-book sale for the amateur or professional collector.

Atlanta Greek Festival (C4), Greek Orthodox Cathedral of the Annunciation, 2500 Clairmont Rd. NE; 633-5870. The Atlanta Greek community has its annual festival complete with Greek dancing, dinners, exhibits, shops, wines, and warm Mediterranean merriment.

Grant Park Tour of Homes and Festival (D4), Grant Park; 622-6366. During the third weekend of September, residents of the Grant Park area open their doors to illustrate the various stages of renovation of the area's Victorian cottage-style homes. A street festival accompanies the neighborhood celebration.

Oktoberfest, Helen, Georgia; 1-878-2181. Alpine Helen, Georgia, fashioned after the original Oktoberfest in Germany, has a festival which lures Atlantans with its blazing autumn spectacle of the North Georgia Mountains and the foods, wine, beer, and entertainment of our little Bavaria.

Powers Ferry Crossroads Country Fair and Arts Festival. Take I-85 south to Newnan exit. Take Georgia Highway 34 through Newnan. Ten miles beyond see the signs. Annually for over ten years, this festival has displayed the crafts and talents of southern craftsmen in the country setting of the old Powers plantation, where grist and sorghum mills have been restored under the big oaks of middle Georgia. Expect bluegrass bands and barbeque, clogging and fried chicken, and a fine summer treat.

October

High Museum Antique Show, usual location is the Atlanta Apparel Mart (J9); 892-3600. Antique dealers from across the United States sell their furniture and porcelains and fine accessories to benefit the museum. The weekend activities include lectures in the decorative arts, home tours, wine-tastings, and galas.

Scottish Festival and Highland Games, Stone Mountain Park (C6); 469-9831. Georgia descendants included Scottish stock migrating south from the Appalachians. The third weekend in October the Scottish folk from over 50 clans, clad in Scottish garb, flock to Stone Mountain to celebrate their heritage. The call of bagpipes, the Scottish sword-dance, the tossing of the caber, and other athletic games are some of the activities of this ethnic festival, which shows all its colors in Sunday's Parade of Tartans.

November

Atlanta Journal 500, Atlanta International Raceway (F4), Hampton, GA; 946-4211. Major stock-car racing comes again, this time a cooler day at the track for the driving elite and the multitude of fans.

Follies and Holiday on Ice, Omni Coliseum (J8), 100 Techwood Dr.; 681-2100. Even before commercial ice rinks came to the southern clime, Atlantans looked forward to the traveling ice shows with their show-biz mastery of this graceful northern sport.

Lighting of the "Great Tree," Rich's Department Store (K8), 45 Broad St.; 586-4636. Thanksgiving Day, Atlanta style, has traditionally included the lighting of the magnificent huge evergreen tree atop the bridge that connects the two buildings of Rich's downtown department store. As the tree lights are turned on the tiers of the bridge are illuminated, and massed choirs from Atlanta-area schools sing carols to the spectators below. The evening event is a spectacular stirring introduction to the Christmas season. Park in the Rich's parking garage on Alabama St. or in the Deck parking on Spring St. across from Rich's.

December

Christmas at Callanwolde, Callanwolde Fine Arts Center (C4), 980 Briarcliff Rd. NE; 872-5338. The old Candler Mansion is put in the hands of the area's best interior designers for the Christmas tide. Period decorations from Christmases of the past renew the holiday spirit of today.

Festival of Trees. This event has become one of the largest events in Atlanta during the festive yule season. Look for this year's location and take delight in the varied ornamented trees and help support one of Atlanta's children's hospitals at the same time.

Holiday Tour of Homes; 255-2136. First weekend in December. The Atlanta Chapter of the Freedoms Foundation at Valley Forge sponsors a Christmas home tour, featuring interiors aglow with the season's symbols, lights, and trimmings.

The *Nutcracker,* at the Fox Theatre (I10). Every year the Atlanta Ballet Company puts on this seasonal favorite. A must for children and adults alike. Call 873-5811 for tickets and information. Performances in early- to mid-December for four days.

Peach Bowl, Atlanta-Fulton County Stadium (L8); 525-2971. Atlanta's post-season college football game is usually played on New Year's Eve. A high-kicking, high-spirited parade down Peachtree Street precedes the battle on the football field.

Entrance to the Candler Building, downtown Atlanta   Marge McDonald

SELF-GUIDED CITY TOURS

We include two city tours, which you can do on your own, one a walking tour of downtown Atlanta and the second a driving tour of metro Atlanta. If possible take along a reader/navigator for the driving tour; you will both enjoy it more. For walkers, we suggest some comfortable shoes; a companion can make it doubly fun. Allow two to three hours for each tour. In both cases Atlanta awaits your visitation into her throbbing, inner-city core and into the broad sweep of her development north on Peachtree Street.

DOWNTOWN WALKING TOUR

Introduction

Downtown Atlanta continues to be at an impact stage in its many evolutions as a city. The central focus of the downtown area was redistributed by the mega-complexes of the 1960s and 1970s. The Omni mega-structure anchored the western side of downtown and Peachtree Center took the top of the hill north of Five Points, which has traditionally been the designated center of downtown. Meanwhile, the Georgia State University complex expanded to the southeast. The 1980s signal a time of filling in the stretches between the mega-structures, rejuvenating fine old office buildings in downtown, and adding a rapid-transit system, city parks, malls, and historic districts to tie the core city together once more. In a sense Atlanta is being remolded and seen in new perspectives. A new northern vista appears, for instance, at Peachtree and Houston Streets as the revered Coca-Cola sign was dismantled, and the Georgia Pacific Center took its place on the Peachtree corridor. The MARTA land clearance made coming South into town on West Peachtree Street a thrilling sight, and standing at the corner by the new public library,

188   MARMAC GUIDE TO ATLANTA

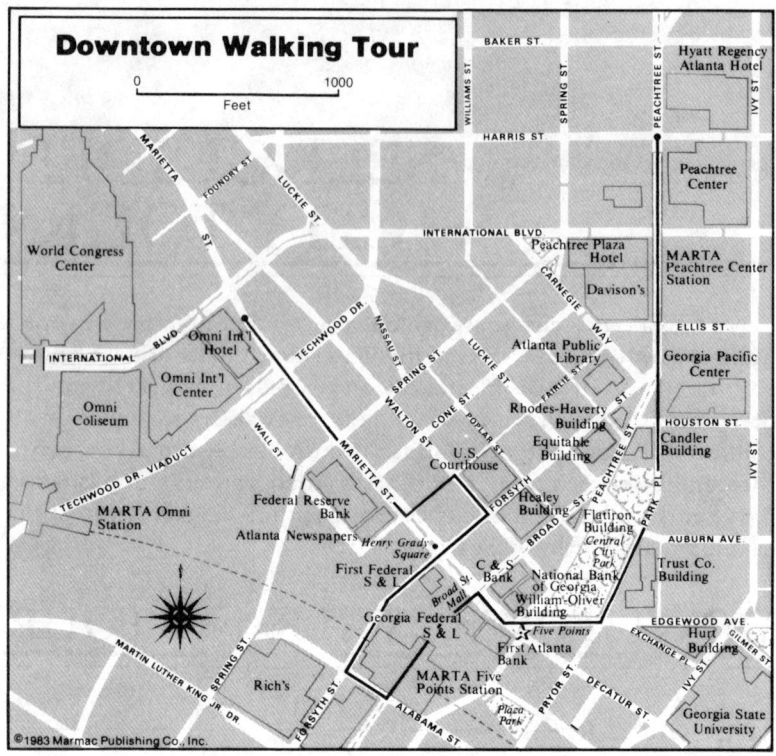

the beauty of the Carnegie Building's ornamental upper frieze and triangular shape are silhouetted against the perfect glass cylinder of the Westin Peachtree Plaza Hotel.

Atlanta's history, past and in-the-making, will be apparent in our downtown tour, and you will have many opportunities to stray from this chosen path (some at our suggestion) to enjoy a special lunch and to indulge in some random shopping. Allow two hours at an easy pace in the morning. We strongly advise a walk-in visit as well as sidewalk view of all the structures and places on this tour. You will then see the city inside out and be in for many pleasant surprises.

The Starting Point

Peachtree Center is our starting point at **Harris and Peachtree Streets.** This coordinated cluster of buildings in Atlanta by architect/developer John Portman started an innovative trend in urban development. Facing the Hyatt Regency Atlanta Hotel, the office towers and Peachtree Center's exciting multilevel mall are to your right with shops, restaurants, and the Peachtree Center plaza. A visitor information booth is conveniently located on this street level plaza and you will see the entrance to the new MARTA Station. The western half of Peachtree Center includes the Merchandise Mart and the Apparel Mart, the two largest wholesale marts in the southeast. Moving south on Peachtree weave through the many large street sculptures. Portman's dramatic Westin Peachtree Plaza Hotel, the site of the first governor's mansion in Atlanta, is on your right and just beyond is Davison's department store with its garlanded arched windows and striped convex awnings. Davison's is a proud 1920s landmark on Peachtree Street. Across the street is the new Ritz-Carlton Hotel, built by an Atlanta-based company that is also owned by an Atlantan. This small, luxurious hotel, one of two in the city, is swathed in elegant pink marble and is well worth a trip inside to sit in the lobby, have a drink, and relax.

From Davison's

You are beginning your descent down **Peachtree Street toward Five Points and Central City Park.** At **Carnegie Way** on your right is the triangular Carnegie Office Building erected in 1926, and on the right corner at **Carnegie Way and Forsyth Street** stands the impressive Atlanta Public Library by international architect Marcel Breuer, dedicated in 1980. The library plaza is an excellent pause-and-view point.

Across from the library on Peachtree Street the new Georgia Pacific Center and Tower, opened in 1982, dominates the skyline. This was the site of Atlanta's first Opera House, the De Give Opera House built in 1893. In 1932 the building was converted into an art-deco movie palace, Loew's Grand. Here, the classic movie, *Gone With the Wind* premiered in Atlanta a few years later to thousands of Atlantans cheering the arrival of Scarlett O'Hara and Rhett Butler.

From Georgia Pacific Plaza

On the right side of Peachtree you pass the handsome 1929 Rhodes-Haverty Building with Brooks Brothers occupying the first two floors. Just beyond is the new Equitable Building, a black steel-frame structure covering a full city block. These two buildings, side by side, contrast Atlanta of the 1920s and Atlanta fifty years later in the 1970s.

At 127 Peachtree on your left, the Candler Building, built in 1902, rises seventeen stories high, Atlanta's most elegant and earliest skyscraper. Asa Candler, founder of the Coca-Cola Company built Roman baths in the basement, and covered the surface with white Georgia marble and elaborate sculptural programs. The ornate frieze above the first story incorporates heroes of the arts and sciences including Shakespeare, Wagner, Michelangelo, and Benjamin Franklin among others. Inside, on the staircase landing, the sculptured bust of Asa Candler is flanked by low-relief portraits of his mother and father. This prestigious building has been beautifully restored to its original elegance.

At Central City Park

Central City Park is in full view now. Stop and take a long look at this breathing space in the heart of the central business district. To your right is the tailored Flatiron Building named after its triangular shape, eleven stories high, built exclusively of stone and brick, with a series of stately bay windows and Greek pilasters fronting Peachtree and Broad Streets. The Flatiron Building is the oldest tall pre-steel building in the southeast, designed in 1897 by Bradford Gilbert who later designed New York City's famous Flatiron Building.

Viewing the Flatiron Building from the apex of its triangle, look at the vertical pastel-striped urban wall by David Berry Lewis and the office towers of downtown layered beyond. Atlanta's business and art communities have coordinated this urban walls program.

Now it's time for a **walk around the park.** The land for Central City Park was given to the city by Atlanta's "anonymous" donor, otherwise known as Robert Woodruff, the philanthropic Coca-Cola heir. At the north end is a combination public amphitheater, fountain, and garden designed for concerts and informal gatherings. **Go left on Auburn.** The Martin Luther King, Jr. Historic District lies about ten blocks east on Auburn Avenue. For a detour here see the SIGHTS Chapter. Park Place office building is ahead on your left.

Turn right on Park Place. The Trust Company of Georgia Building faces the park on the site of the original Equitable Building, which was Atlanta's first steel-frame structure. The columns and marble sign of this former building, which was designed in 1891 by

Chicago architects Burnham and Root, and which the Trust Company later occupied, are set in front as weighty tokens of this past era in Atlanta's history. The secret formula of Coca-Cola, the world's most popular soft drink, is stored in the vaults of this Trust Company Bank.

At the corner of Edgewood look to your left at the Hurt Building. One of Atlanta's first developers, Joel Hurt, built this office in 1913. Notice the curved Corinthian portico and the colorful terra-cotta designs in the upper stories. Hurt also built Atlanta's first garden suburb, Inman Park, and connected the Hurt Building downtown to the residential area with his own streetcar line. Inman Park is now a historic district, alive with Victorian restoration.

To the right of the Hurt Building you will see another Urban Wall, a bouncing figure composition of bright dots by Savannah artist Larry Connatser. Directly behind the Hurt Building is the Georgia State University complex, another short detour option.

The Five Points Intersection

Turn right on Edgewood and take a long look back across the park. You are at **Five Points** when you reach the intersection of Decatur/Marietta, Edgewood, and Peachtree. Five Points is the dead center of the downtown business district. You are in the midst of the south's largest and most prestigious banking and financial institutions. The National Bank of Georgia, the Georgia Federal Bank, and the First Atlanta Bank Building and Tower are concentrated at the Five Points intersection, with other Atlanta banks and financial institutions within short blocks. On the northwest corner of Peachtree and Marietta Streets look carefully at the William-Oliver Building, built the year of the stock-market crash in 1929, with zigzag and semicircular art-deco ornamentation on the exterior and ornate brass grills, elevator doors, lighted brass arrow indicators over the elevators, and a celestial ceiling mural in the interior.

Promenade on Marietta Street

You are now walking **northwest on Marietta Street** passing the Citizens and Southern Bank Building on your right at the corner of Broad Street. The exterior classical features are complemented on the inside by a floor copied from the Pantheon in Rome, Italy. The original solid-bronze banking tables and chandeliers, as well as the beautifully proportionate marble interior, are a treat for bankers and visitors. The building was redesigned in this classical fashion in the late 1920s by Atlanta's classical architect Phillip Schutze.

Walk left at Broad Street in between the soaring First National Bank and First Federal Savings and Loan Building with its softly contoured stories. You are in the wide Broad Street pedestrian mall with its focal sculpture and potted trees leading you to the Five Points MARTA station and beyond to Rich's department store on Alabama Street. Rich's was Atlanta's first department store, now a venerable institution in Atlanta. After an excursion through Rich's **return to Marietta Street via Forsyth Street.** As you move over the elevated Forsyth Street look to your left and see the Omni International complex, our final destination. The rust-brown truncated caps of the Omni Coliseum and the steel scaffolding of the covered mall are clearly visible on the skyline.

At the **joining of Marietta and Forsyth is Henry Grady Square** with the statue of Henry Grady, one of Atlanta's great newspaper editors and promoter of the New South. Grady called Atlanta "a brave and beautiful city," a phrase which characterizes the city even today. The First Federal Savings and Loan Building on your left houses a duplicate of the law office used by President Woodrow Wilson, who practiced law in Atlanta, that is open to the public.

The Fairlie-Poplar Historic District

Cross Marietta on Forsyth for a short excursion into the Fairlie-Poplar Historic District, which is undergoing extensive restoration. At 57 Forsyth Street the Healey Building adds a neo-gothic accent to Atlanta's pack of skyscrapers. Built in 1913, the building will surprise you with its refreshing rotunda and courtyard, reminiscent of the medieval cathedral style.

Turn left on Walton Street. The massive low classical structure at the corner is the U. S. Courthouse, formerly the U. S. Post Office and the 1848 site of the First Baptist Church. At the back of the building on Fairlie Street see the original steel loading dock for the postal service. At 60 Walton Street the Western Supermarket occupies a turn-of-the-century building, which has been completely restored in this busy section. You can't miss its deep-red exterior. The Walton block gives the tourist an excellent feel for Atlanta circa 1900. Atlanta 1980 looms high above.

From Marietta Street to the Omni

Turn left on Fairlie, return to Marietta and **cross the street.** Take a right on Marietta. As you look back at the Western Union Building's flank the urban wall by Brian Randall is in full view. The trompe l'oeil windows and Gargantuan Kudzu vines should prompt a few smiles. Kudzu, the oriental plant that was originally used by Georgia farmers to hold land from washout, is rumored to grow at a rate of one inch overnight. There are many jokes about Kudzu's creeping capability, even in this world of supreme technology, and even in this downtown district of financial prowess.

On to the Federal Reserve Bank and the new Atlanta Newspapers Building, both of which will host prearranged tours.

Continue on Marietta until you reach the Omni International. Here you are in a mini-city domed by skylights with scores of gift shops, luxury boutiques, and international stores. The Omni sports coliseum is a few steps beyond as well as the World Congress Center. And restaurants from fast-foods to yogurt stands, from Chinese to Italian, from moderate to expensive will satisfy your appetite at the end of this tour and provide time and space to sit and reflect on this metropolitan southland we call Atlanta.

For an alternate luncheon suggestion and a tandem train ride, hop the MARTA train at the Omni station, west to the Decatur station, which features the work of urban wall artist Larry Connatser. As you ascend from the station, on your left is a delightful little restaurant called Conversations. There you can also conclude your downtown tour in one of the older satellite towns encircling Atlanta.

For guided walking tours around preservation interests in old Atlanta in the commercial and residential sections, we highly recommend the Atlanta Preservation Center, in the Healey Building, 57 Forsyth Street NW, Suite 302, Atlanta 30303. Call 522-4345.

METRO DRIVING TOUR

With two to three hours of driving time here is your chance to see a big picture of Atlanta, one which includes the downtown arenas of business, government, and trade, the cultural midtown, and the acclaimed residential sector in the northwest. Our tour will begin at

Peachtree Center, proceed north on Peachtree Street, and then return to town via I-75 to complete the downtown survey. You will be following the daily cycle of many Atlantans who live in the immediate suburbs and work in the downtown area.

The Starting Point Peachtree Center

We start **north at Peachtree Center.** At the Baker Street intersection Peachtree splits into West Peachtree and Peachtree. **Take Peachtree Street on the right.** At the next intersection you will become conscious of two large churches: the gray granite First Methodist Church with the red doors on your left, and on Ivy Street and Peachtree to your right, the brownstone Catholic Church of Sacred Heart. Peachtree Street will present the stations of the churches as residential communities developed from downtown to Buckhead, an exciting series of architectural styles, denominations, and sites.

Driving up Peachtree

After crossing Ralph McGill Boulevard, renamed in the 1970s after the late editor of the Atlanta *Constitution,* you will pass over I-75/I-85. To your left you can see the Peachtree Summit building and its accompanying MARTA station. On your right look for St. Luke's Episcopal Church and in the next block the Atlanta Museum and Elliott's Antiques. (Swing around the block to your right to see Elliott's Japanese Zero airplane in the back parking lot.) **Continuing on Peachtree** further on the right is a great little restaurant, the Pleasant Peasant, and beyond that the beginning of the Atlanta Theater District, which will extend to 14th Street.

You have approached North Avenue. As you ease across the intersection look left down North Avenue and catch a remarkable vista of the tall white Life of Georgia rectangle, its cylindrical neighbor the C&S Bank, and, in the far reaches beyond, the Georgia Tech campus and the new Coca-Cola Company building. You are riding the Peachtree ridge where the ground falls off on either side.

Entering Midtown

At the next traffic light at Ponce de Leon you pass the curved facade of the Ponce de Leon Apartments (1913), the columned

Georgian Terrace Hotel (1911), and the York Hotel on the right. On your left is the Fox Theatre, an intriguing visual counterpoint to the colossal Southern Bell tower behind. The Fox's 1920s moorish onion domes and extravagant trappings are enjoyed as much today as in the heyday of the flappers and their films.

After Ponce de Leon Avenue the streets intersecting Peachtree will begin to be numbered. On your left is the impressive First Baptist Church, which was originally on the site of the U.S. Courthouse downtown. We are following the northern course of the residential development out Peachtree.

From 5th Street to 14th Street Atlanta shows some reminders of the 1960s hippie colony in Atlanta. Named "The Strip" during those turbulent times, the area is now part of the Peachtree Walk project and receiving some tender, loving care from various organizations and businesses. Before the 1960s, the area was a small village with the locus at 10th Street. At 11th Street Brother Juniper's, run by a Catholic brother and helpers, serves some of the city's best natural-food sandwiches, soups, and breads in a lovely atmosphere of hanging plants and hand-painted menus.

From Colony Square to Pershing Point

You have arrived at midtown's major center, Colony Square at 14th Street. Along with the Omni and Peachtree Center, Colony Square was conceived as a multi-purpose center in the 1960s. The complex includes the Colony Square Hotel facing 14th Street, two office towers, a skylighted retail mall with fine restaurants, and two condominium towers.

Across from Colony Square to your left is the American Telephone and Telegraph Building (AT&T), poised at an angle to the street and to the blue-domed First Church of Christ Scientist. At 15th Street the trilon sculpture fountain by Steffen Thomas is surrounded by an island of seasonal flowers typical of others in the Ansley Park neighborhood to the east.

A Short Detour

If you want a quick tour of this turn-of-the-century restored neighborhood **take a right at the fountain on 15th Street** and an **immediate left on Peachtree Circle. Right on Westminster, left on Prado, right on Peachtree Circle.** Follow Peachtree Circle staying to the left until it joins Peachtree Street once again. **Turn right at the Gulf Station.**

Back to Peachtree Street

Proceeding north on Peachtree from 15th Street, the impressive Robert W. Woodruff Arts Center is on your left. The center brings together under one roof the cultural powers and performances of major Atlanta Arts organizations — the High Museum of Art, which is located next door in its own independent structure, the Atlanta Symphony, the Atlanta School of Art, and the Alliance and Studio Theatres. This is the magnetic center of the arts in Atlanta. Just past the center on your right is one of Atlanta's most exquisite restorations, the Reid House Condominiums, built originally by another esteemed Atlanta classicist Neil Reid.

West Peachtree rejoins Peachtree after a few blocks at Pershing Point, a small triangular park to your left named after General Pershing, its monument listing the names of Atlantans who died in World War I. The Rhodes Memorial Hall, formerly the Rhodes' family residence in 1903, now a branch of the Georgia Archives, is on your left at the Peachtree Circle intersection.

Just before Peachtree crosses I-85 look on the right for The Temple, one of Atlanta's oldest Jewish congregations, designed by Phillip Schutze. Immediately after you pass I-85 the small, distinctive Brookwood Station, Atlanta's only surviving passenger railroad station, is on the left, another architectural contribution by Neil Reid.

Brookwood Village

At Collier Road the numbered streets end. Collier and Peachtree is the village center of the Brookwood Hills neighborhood. Three fine restaurants, Cloudt's, Clarence Foster's, and McNeeley's afford excellent resting places and cool drinks. The peak of the hill at Piedmont Hospital one block north is Atlanta's "heartbreak hill" for the Peachtree Road Race runners coming from Lenox Square toward Colony Square.

Buckhead's Beautiful Houses

At the bottom of this long hill, about one mile, is Peachtree Battle with the Peachtree Battle Shopping Center to the right. **Take a left on**

Peachtree Battle past the neighborhood school. **Take your first right on Habersham, go right on Cherokee** and then **left on Andrews** to the portals of the Atlanta Historical Society. The Swan House, a beautiful Palladian villa, also by Phillip Schutze, is open for tours as is the plain Georgia farmhouse, the Tullie Smith House. The Swan Coach House is now a charming restaurant and gift shop. McElreath Hall usually has an exhibition of some significance. **Go out the rear gates** of the Swan House, **left on Slaton,** and then **left on West Paces Ferry.**

You are now in one of the most beautiful residential areas in the United States. On your right is the Cherokee Town Club, originally a family home, now a private club set far back from the street in the wooded site. Further on the right, past Habersham, the neo-classic, brick Governor's Mansion with its long grassy knolls and spectacular flower gardens is open for tours (see SIGHTS). With this brief introduction, enjoy your wandering into the residential heart of the northside. Just past the Governor's Mansion **take a right on Tuxedo,** after half a mile **bear right at the fork,** cross over Valley, **left on Blackland, left on Northside, left on Valley,** cross over Tuxedo, **right on Habersham, right on West Paces Ferry.** West Paces Ferry will take you to I-75. **Take a left at I-75 South.**

The Martin Luther King Historic District ——

Exit at Courtland. Turn right on Courtland. Proceed five blocks, and **turn left on Auburn.** You are now entering the Sweet Auburn Historic District, an area of totally black-owned businesses and part of Atlanta's black heritage tour. The Big Bethel AME church (1890s) at 220 Auburn, with its powerful circular and square towers, is known for an equally powerful choir. The **Jesus Saves** sign on the tower is visible from all over the city. After passing under the expressway, you are approaching the Martin Luther King, Jr. Historic District, the Ebenezer Baptist Church, on your right, where Martin Luther King, Jr. preached, the offices of the Southern Christian Leadership Conference, the burial site and memorial hall for the slain civil-rights leader, and native Atlantan, the King Community Center on your left, the Center for Social Change headed by Coretta Scott King, and further up Auburn at Number 501, the frame Victorian house and birthplace of Dr. King is on your right.

Turn left on Hogue just past Dr. King's home, **left on Irwin** and **right on Boulevard.**

Take a left in the middle of the bridge, **left fork to I-75/I-85 South,** exit Martin Luther King (MLK) Blvd. about 1 1/2 miles.

Capitol Hill

You have now entered Atlanta's capital complex of city, county, and state governments.

We are going to make a loop around the Georgia State Capitol, the bright-domed neo-Renaissance building at the summit of the hill. The dome is pure gold, mined in the North Georgia hills near Dahlonega, the open rotunda of the Capitol rising 237 feet. The Georgia State Museum of Science and Industry in the Capitol is part of the tour available. Statues of Georgia statesmen, Thomas Watson, Eugene Talmadge, and others form points of political interest among the magnificent manicured gardens on the capitol grounds.

Turn left at Washington Street for the frontal view of the Capitol. Facing the statehouse is Central Presbyterian Church, a neo-Gothic structure built in 1884 on the site of the former church with a congregation that dates to 1860. The two-block capitol area has three major churches of historic significance, another reminder of Atlanta's original residential areas and the characteristic formation of large congregations within the city.

As you **turn left on Mitchell Street** look to your right. Atlanta's City Hall takes up the entire block with its neo-Gothic structure (1930). The site has been important in Atlanta's history, first as the headquarters for General Sherman in 1864, then as the original site of Oglethorpe University in the 1870s, and later as the site of Atlanta's Boys' and Girls' High Schools.

You are making your final turn around the Capitol with a **left on Capitol Avenue,** back to **Martin Luther King Jr. Drive. Take a left.** Two blocks further at the Central Avenue intersection you will see the Fulton County Courthouse to your left and facing it the Shrine of the Immaculate Conception. The Shrine stands on the site of the original church, whose pastor, Father O'Reilly is credited with influencing Sherman to spare the churches in his burning of Atlanta. A plaque in City Hall commemorates Father O'Reilly.

Turn right at Central. The entrance to the former Underground Atlanta, the "city beneath the city" is just to your right. You are on the viaduct crossing the railroad tracks that came through this center of town in the mid-1800s. Remember Atlanta started as a brawling railroad town, took its first name after the railroad phrase Terminus, and was the railroad and supply hub of the Confederacy. Underground Atlanta still holds the real key to the city — the zero-mile post, with its historic marker designating the terminus of the Western and Atlantic Railroad and the central point from which the city was measured in all directions.

Proceeding on Central to Decatur Street the warm Urban Wall abstraction by Tony Greco is on your right. The arts and business communities of Atlanta joined forces to see that the blank walls of office buildings became a ground for creative expression and a source of visual pleasure for the public. Atlanta presently has eight urban walls in the downtown area.

The Downtown Business District

Before **turning left at Decatur Street,** which changes its name to Marietta Street, look to your right at the second largest complex in the state's university system — Georgia State University, a non-residential urban-centered academy. Decatur Street takes you to the center of the downtown business district, Five Points. Here Peachtree, Marietta, and Edgewood converge. Here stand the giants of Atlanta's financial world, their buildings signed at the upper stories and at the street level with logos and names from their past and present histories — the First National Bank of Atlanta, the Trust Company of Georgia, the National Bank of Georgia, the Fulton Federal Savings and Loan Association, and many others.

At the Five Points intersection Central City Park opens up to your right, a large green space in the heart of the city, donated by Atlanta's "anonymous" donor and Coca-Cola heir, Robert Woodruff. This is a place for pedestrian cross-over, lunch breaks, occasional soap-box preaching, and sitting or stretching out in Atlanta's temperate weather.

Continue on Marietta. At the Broad Street intersection look left on Broad at the Broad Street Mall, a tree-lined walking mall with key sculptures leading to the vast Five Points MARTA station. Also notice the new and old office buildings siding Marietta, a study of contrasts in textures, styles, and shapes.

At Forsyth Street, an island with trees and the statue of Atlanta's "New South" editor Henry Grady separates the street. Grady's phrase "Atlanta: a city too busy to hate" spans the post civil war and 20th-century credo of the city's movers and shakers.

Continue on Marietta to Spring Street (just past the glass-sheathed skyscraper). **Take a right. Take the next right on Walton Street,** for a short trip back in time. At 60 Walton Street on your right is the lovely red-faced Western Supermarket and a whole string of restored buildings from Atlanta circa 1890.

Go right at Forsyth. At this intersection notice the stocky low neo-classical building, the U.S. Courthouse, before that the U.S. Post Office, and in 1848 the original site of the First Baptist Church.

From Rich's to the Omni

Cross Marietta Street and continue two more blocks to Martin Luther King Jr. Drive. On your left is the large Five Points MARTA station. A block beyond you pass under the Rich's department store bridge that connects Rich's two buildings and on which stands the Great Tree in all its glory during the Christmas season. Thousands of Atlantans gather at this spot for the lighting of the Great Tree Thanksgiving evening. Rich's is an Atlanta institution, devoted to serving the city and its citizens through flexible sales and credit policies and civic sponsorship.

Turn right on Martin Luther King Jr. Drive. A statue of the Phoenix held aloft by the classical female figure of the city is at the street's center, silhouetted against the sky. This symbol of the City of Atlanta reminds citizens and visitors of Atlanta's regenerative powers, her resolve to rise from the ashes and devastation of the Civil War. The tall white skyscraper to your left is the Richard Russell Federal Building opposite the older U.S. Post Office.

You are now crossing the sprawling yards of the immense Southern Railway System. Directly beyond is the Atlanta University campus. **At Techwood take a right** and proceed to the Omni International. The Techwood viaduct gives you a splendid panoramic view of Atlanta to your right. The Omni complex is a mighty combination of sports coliseum — home of the Atlanta Hawks basketball team, the Omni International Hotel, which anchors one end of the huge enclosed mall of boutiques, restaurants, shops, and theaters; and the neighboring Georgia World Congress Center, site of trade shows throughout the year. The Omni is a city within this great city.

Return to Peachtree Center

Turn left on Marietta, right on International Boulevard and **veer right on Carnegie Way.** As you approach Spring Street we will encircle the Peachtree Center complex. The Westin Peachtree Plaza Hotel, the tallest hotel in the world, rises seventy-three stories high in its cool, glass, tubular form. **Turn left on Spring Street.** Two of the numerous walking bridges span the street and connect John Portman's component buildings, in this instance the parking garage and Apparel Mart, to the Merchandise Mart. At the next intersection, the Apparel Mart covers a full block with its massive walls and external spiral corner stairs. **Take a right at Harris Street. Cross Peachtree to Courtland.** You have just passed through the core of Peachtree Center, the Hyatt Regency's fantastic atrium structure that changed the notion of hotel interiors, the office towers fronting the block, and the wonderful urban mall with its hanging garden ambience, open cafes, boutiques, and assorted shops on multiple levels.

At the corner of Harris and Courtland you will see another integral complex of office towers and hotel, the Atlanta Center with the majestic downtown Hilton Hotel. **Turn right on Courtland,** one block further, **turn right on International Boulevard** and then **right on Peachtree Street.** You have circumscribed Peachtree Center, returned to the point of origin of the tour, and now it's time for a view from the top and a drink in the revolving Sun Dial Lounge atop the Westin Peachtree Plaza, or maybe lunch at Dailey's, one of the many restaurants. The tour is over; it is time to savor fully your comprehensive introduction to Atlanta.

ONE-DAY EXCURSIONS

It seems that all roads lead to Atlanta, Georgia's great transportation center. We suggest you retrace a selected few of these routes, either spend some delicious crisp time in the north Georgia mountains or perhaps in the gentle piedmont and fading foothills southwest of the city, returning at the end of the day to Atlanta. Each excursion is a full day and an overnight if you choose.

Atlantans love these excursions at any time of the year; but the mountains are ablaze with fall color in the month of October, and spring at Callaway Gardens can be breathtaking, with a riot of indigenous flowers and brilliant azaleas.

SOUTH TO CALLAWAY GARDENS AND WARM SPRINGS

(8 to 9 hours)

You are heading south of Atlanta, edging toward the Alabama border, on this day's excursion. The drive is mostly on the swift and easy interstate. Highlighting the tour are the Little White House, the modest retreat of President Franklin Roosevelt, and Callaway Gardens, middle Georgia's premier resort. If you want to stay overnight in this area, Callaway Gardens is ideal.

First to the Little White House

Take I-85 south from Atlanta, **exit alternate GA 27 South, to Warm Springs. Take GA 85W south,** to the Little White House.

Franklin D. Roosevelt, four times President of the United States, died here April 12, 1945. Twenty-one years earlier Roosevelt had come south to Warm Springs for the therapeutic warm pools which aided him in his struggle with the paralysis of polio. He helped develop the

ONE-DAY EXCURSIONS

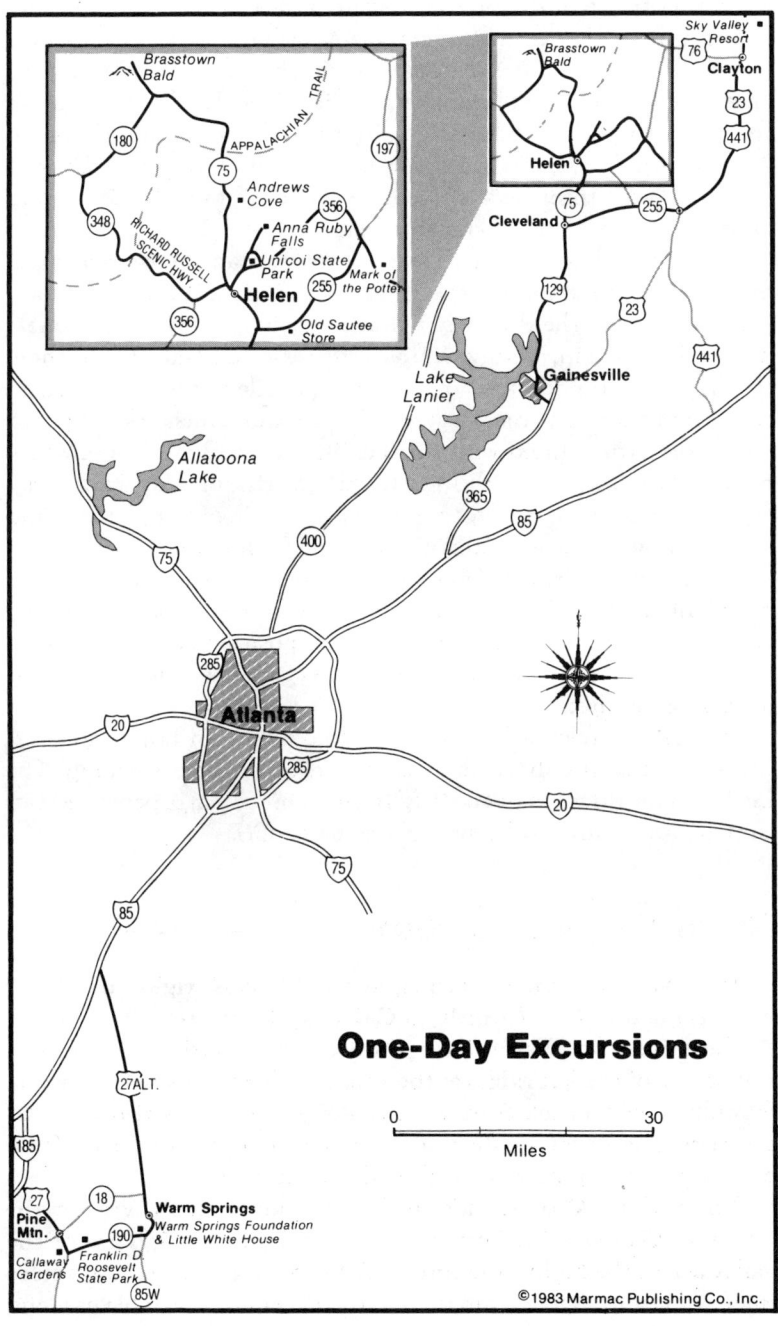

resort for other polio victims, establishing the Georgia Warm Springs Foundation and the subsequent development of health facilities. Before Roosevelt built his house nearby he had used the site for picnics. The Little White House was unlike the palatial quarters of his ancestral home in Hyde Park and the official White House in Washington. Roosevelt chose a simple, rustic dwelling for his Georgia residence, with three bedrooms, an entry, a combination living and dining room, a kitchen, and sundeck.

This personal back-to-basics statement by a man of great riches and high honor is a humbling experience for all visitors. No changes have been made since the President's death — a wheelchair, ship models, his dog Fala's chain, a riding whip in the closet, and gifts from school children and friends are in the pine-panelled interior. A taped commentary accompanies your self-guided tour. Outside see the 1938 Ford Convertible fitted with hand controls, the Guest House where notables from all over the world stayed, the old Warm Springs Stagecoach, the memorial fountain, and the walk of states' stones and flags leading to the Franklin D. Roosevelt Museum.

The museum displays fascinating mementos associated with the president, and a 12-minute documentary movie is shown free of charge in the museum auditorium. The exposure to the private man Franklin is an endearing, personal experience for all visitors including children.

Visitors are welcome to use the picnic tables on the grounds. A snack bar and gift shop are located in the Entrance Building. The Little White House is open daily from 9 am - 5 pm, open one hour later in June, July, and August weekends. *CH.*

On to Callaway Gardens

From Warm Springs take a right on GA 85W, right on GA 190 west, right on GA 27 north to Callaway Gardens.

The drive from Warm Springs to Callaway Gardens is exquisite, riding one of the last ridges at the sinking of the Appalachian chain. Franklin D. Roosevelt State Park is along this route, with over 100 campsites and 21 cottages. Roosevelt was responsible for the planting of many of the pine trees within the park area.

Where GA 190 dead-ends in GA 27, don't miss a visit to the Callaway Garden's Country Store and the panoramic view of the valley across the highway (a fine place for photos). The country store smells of assorted good things from the Callaway vegetable gardens,

Ida Cason Callaway Memorial Chapel, Callaway Gardens   Courtesy Callaway Gardens

along with imported deli items. From slab bacon to escargot, from Swiss chocolates to muscadine preserves and speckled heart grits, this is a place to food shop with zest and imagination. Have a leisurely lunch in the Country Kitchen overlooking Pine Mountain valley. The Country Store is open daily from 8 am - 6 pm, the Country Kitchen daily from 8 am - 5 pm for breakfast and lunch.

Callaway Gardens is one of America's unique horticultural and recreational areas. It was founded by Mr. and Mrs. Cason J. Callaway as a place where all people could find tranquility, natural inspiration, and wholesome recreation. Admission to the gardens is a modest fee, children under 6, Inn and Cottage guests, and annual pass-holders are free. An indepth bus tour of the gardens with a staff naturalist is available daily at 10 am and 2 pm, meeting in front of the Inn. There is a small charge for this bus tour; it is well worth your consideration, especially if your time is limited.

Callaway Gardens has thirteen miles of scenic drives, nature trails, and bicycle paths winding through 2500 acres of woodlands, lakes, streams and ponds, wild flowers, and landscaped areas. Callaway Gardens is lush year-round; in fall the beautiful chrysanthemums and the brilliant foliage, in winter the shiny and berried hollies, in spring more than 600 varieties of azaleas, and the sunny summer produces a rich green growing season.

The Greenhouse Conservatory Complex displays year-round plants native to their climates. Mr. Cason's Vegetable Garden is 7 1/2 acres of delicious fruits, berries, and vegetables. The Ida Cason Callaway Memorial Chapel is a gentle place of repose or organ concerts in the woods by the side of a small pond.

Programs are continuous from the Garden's Education Department. The Southern Highland Handicraft Guild Craftsmen exhibit late November through mid-February. Fall and winter include the PGA Club Professional Championship and special holiday programs. Summer programs feature the Masters Water Ski Tournament in mid-July, the PGA National Junior Golf Championship in mid-August, and the resident Florida State University circus all summer.

Many sports activities are offered at Callaway Gardens. Sixty-three holes of golf, 21 lighted tennis courts, horseback riding, fishing, bicycling, skeet and trap shooting, quail hunting October through March, and swimming and boating at Robin Lake Beach, the largest inland manmade beach in the world.

Obviously a day trip to Callaway Gardens will leave you with a strong desire for more, whether it's the lovely gardens, the superb recreational opportunities, the special events, the country food, or the attractive Inn. The Inn has ample accommodations — 365 rooms with convention facilities for 1000 people. You can also rent a one- or two-bedroom cottage in the woods. See Resorts in the LODGING Chapter. Whatever your needs write to the management at Callaway Gardens, Pine Mountain, GA 31822 or call 1-663-2281.

A Quick Trip Home

Atlanta is not far off; **to return take GA 27 north to I-185** which runs directly into **I-85 to Atlanta.**

… ONE-DAY EXCURSIONS   207

NORTH TO THE MOUNTAINS

(8 to 9 hours)

This full day of touring stretches almost to the North Carolina border, introducing you to the unspoiled setting of the Chattahoochee National Forest, Georgia's tallest summit, a myriad of small craft and artisan shops, and Helen, a charming Swiss-style village tucked in the midst of these beautiful foothills. As a bonus you cross the legendary Appalachian Trail, which follows the mountain chain north to the state of Maine.

Alpine Helen

Take I-85 North from Atlanta, left on GA 365 to Gainesville, left on GA 129 to Cleveland, left around the square, right on GA 75 at the light to Helen.

Helen, a small lumber-mill village at the turn of the century, is now a bustling imitation of a Bavarian village, attracting visitors year-round with festivals, sporting events, dancing, shopping in the many local mountain craftshops and import shops, restaurants, cafes, and tearooms. There are many fine hotels in the town, and during special festivals the hotels fill up rapidly. We suggest advance reservations. This is your first stopping-off place. Enjoy Alpine architecture and ambience here in Helen with its cool stream running right through town, its cobblestone streets, and Bavarian costume.

October is a special season in the mountains, the fall leaves turn brilliant red, ocher, yellow, and orange, and Helen has its equally colorful, Munich-inspired Octoberfest. In the early summer Helen hosts the popular Balloon Race to the coast, with a large entry of brilliant patterned balloons lifting from the Helen balloon-port and forming a grand aerial parade to the east. Summer theater is also part of Helen's activities. The Castle Inn, a turn-of-the-century music hall on the river features vaudeville entertainment in the warm months. Helen has sports to do as well — trout fishing, horseback riding, canoeing, biking, tennis, golf, and plenty of hiking. Write the Helendorf Inn, headquarters for the Balloon Race, for information on Helen's continuing celebrations or for accommodations if you decide to spend the night, at P.O. Box 86, Helen, GA 30545 or call (404) 878-2271.

Helen, Georgia *Courtesy Georgia Tourist Division*

Georgia's Highest Point

From Helen, **proceed on GA 75 north, left on GA 356, right on GA 348,** the Richard Russell Scenic Highway, named after the illustrious late U.S. Senator from Georgia. About six miles down the highway you intersect with the Appalachian Trail at Tessnatee Gap. Park by the roadside, take a ten-minute stroll among the earnest backpackers and know that you are treading where native Americans and all generations of settlers after them have made their way from one end of this nation to another.

The Richard Russell Highway is a spectacular drive in North

Georgia, the mountains breathlessly beautiful and close. **At GA 180, take a right to Brasstown Bald.** The signs point the way. Brasstown Bald is 4784 feet above sea level, Georgia's highest point. Take a bus to the top in the summer months. On a clear day you can see four states from this pinnacle, Georgia, North Carolina, Tennessee, and South Carolina. The Visitors Center has an entry fee and is open May 1-October 31.

Unicoi and Waterfalls

From Brasstown Bald **turn left on GA 180 which becomes GA 66, right on GA 75, left on GA 356** to Unicoi State Park, one of Georgia's most modern state parks designed for individual and family use, as well as conferences and retreats. Accommodations are moderate to inexpensive, another excellent place for an overnight. The Lodge is contoured into a forested hill above a large recreational lake surrounded by attractive contemporary rental cabins and campgrounds for tents and trailer camping. Unicoi has continuing programs around environmental themes, crafts, folk singing, and water sports. Write Unicoi at P. O. Box 256, Helen, GA 30545 or call 878-2824 for information and reservations.

Just a mile before you reach Unicoi you will see a sign to Anna Ruby Falls and Andrews Cove area, a super side trip to one of the many splendid waterfalls in the Chattahoochee National Forest.

The Mark of the Potter and Old Sautee Store

From Unicoi **continue east on GA 356, right on GA 197, bear left at the fork** to continue **on 197** to Mark of the Potter. This converted old corn mill on the Saque River is now a craft shop brimming with the creativity and energy of its owners Glen and John LaRowe, who display the ceramics of Georgia's potters, run a pottery school, and open the whole potting process to the inquisitive delight of visitors. The millpond under the upstairs porch is filled with Georgia's finest and fattest trout, who eagerly show their rainbow sides at feeding time. This is a gem of a place.

Right on GA 197, left on GA 255 to the Old Sautee Store, with its collection of eighteenth- and nineteenth-century memorabilia, farm tools, player piano, posters, and signs, a remarkable museum/store.

You can poke around endlessly in the old section and then move into the modern import shop for Icelandic sweaters, Scandinavian wares, and even a steaming cup of glogg during the Christmas season.

Follow GA 17 to GA 75 to Cleveland, to GA 129 to Gainesville, right on GA 365 to I-85 to Atlanta.

A Side Trip to the World of *Deliverance* —

From Cleveland take GA 115 E to Clarksville, US 441 N to Clayton. En route you will pass by Tallulah Gorge where the "Great Wallenda" made his epic tightrope walk in 1970. Stop and see just what a terrifying prospect this must have been despite the stunning beauty around you. Drive on to Clayton, and you will be passing close by the Chattooga River where *Deliverance* was filmed, starring Burt Reynolds. The experienced or the adventurous can raft down the river with a guide. Inquire Southeast Expeditions Inc. at local number 327-0433.

Clayton is a typical Georgia mountain town. Potters and good country restaurants abound — stop by at the Rabun County Chamber of Commerce Visitors' Center. About ten miles to the east of Clayton is Sky Valley, near Dillard, a popular year-round resort with the only skiing in Georgia. See LODGING Chapter under Resorts.

NEW RESIDENTS

Atlanta is your new home. Welcome to this spirited place. You will be busy locating housing, opening bank accounts, moving furniture, maybe relocating family, and bringing a multitude of items from your life in another city to your new residence. During this transition time you will be establishing your first ring of social and business contacts in Atlanta. We offer a selected group of data and organizations that, together with the rest of this book, will get you off to a fresh and efficient start.

Welcome Services

Atlanta Hospitality League, P. O. Box 720163, Atlanta, 30358; 252-3591. The league provides new resident information, discount coupons from merchants in your area, and a representative who will visit you in your home and tell you what's where in Atlanta. A nice personal touch.

Welcome Wagon; 955-8770. This nationally recognized organization will assist you in settling in and introduce you to merchants and products in your new location.

AN INTRODUCTION TO ATLANTA LIVING

Atlanta is synonymous with growth. The city continues an unabated course of development as a key business and commercial center. At the same time the quality of life in Atlanta receives national acclaim, of 25 major cities in the United States, Atlanta has the lowest cost of living, the city government maintains a balanced budget, and the climate is excellent.

Atlanta is the sixteenth largest city in the country and the greater 15-county area has 83 incorporated towns and cities with over 2 million people. Wherever you live — in town, within the perimeter or beyond the perimeter — you will join in the experience of creating Atlanta's identity.

Atlanta has always been seen by Georgians in other cities, especially the older towns such as Savannah, Columbus, and Augusta as the "New South." And that term does fit this marvelous city, host to people from all parts of the South. Its magnetism has equally drawn people from throughout the country and now is attracting an international population. The mix seems to be the making of Atlanta.

Atlantans' love of outdoor living and entertaining in their homes has extended to the availability of outdoor cafes, well suited to the moderate climate. People enjoy picnicking in the city parks and at the surrounding lakes on the weekends, and sports activities of all kinds keep Atlantans on the run and fit and trim. A cultural surge is taking off in the visual and performing arts. A theater "district" has emerged, the Atlanta Symphony Orchestra is receiving national recognition, the High Museum of Art opened its landmark building in 1983, and galleries proliferate. The demand appears unsatiable. Other rings of residential and commercial development ripple out again and again from the city and the "New South" town wears another necklace of enchantment.

GEOGRAPHICAL PROFILE

Atlanta is situated in the foothills of the southern Appalachian mountains in north central Georgia, over 1000 feet above sea level. To see how far inland Atlanta is located from the Atlantic Ocean, Chattanooga, Tennessee is due north, about an hour-and-a-half drive. The ocean is over a five-hour drive to Savannah, the Golden Isles of St. Simons, Jekyll, Sea Island, or Hilton Head, South Carolina, the closest and favorite seaside resorts.

To reach the Gulf of Mexico also allow at least five hours of driving from Atlanta to points south such as Panama City and Destin, Florida. The interstate system make the trips possible in this period of driving time.

To the north the mountains provide a haven for refreshment within a couple of driving hours. The Chattahoochee National Forest and small northern Georgia towns and inns are frequented by Atlantans throughout the year; southern ski resorts are active in cold winters, the autumn festivals are as colorful as the changing leaves, and spring and summer are always a refuge for the naturalist and mountain lover.

Nearby manmade Lake Lanier and Lake Allatoona are within an hour's drive. Within two hours is West Point Lake to the southwest on the Alabama border; Lake Jackson to the southeast; Lake Hartwell to the northeast on the South Carolina border; and to the north the multiple lakes in the Chattahoochee National Forest, Blue Ridge, Nottely, Chatuge, Burton, and Rabun. Due west is Birmingham, Alabama, also a two-hour drive through the beautiful rolling piedmont.

ATLANTA INSIGHT

Autos

Auto Insurance

Georgia law requires that drivers of automobiles carry no-fault insurance, and you must have a Georgia Insurance Identification Card in your possession at all times while driving. These cards are issued at the time of purchase of insurance. Check with your insurance agent.

Auto Registration

You must buy your Georgia license tag within 30 days of establishing residency. The cost is $8.00. When you purchase your tag, you must have proof of insurance and proof of ownership of your vehicle; plus, you must pay your vehicle's ad valorem tax (personal property tax) at this time. Call tag offices in your county:

Clayton	478-9911	Gwinnett	962-1424
Cobb	424-8320	Fayette	461-3611
DeKalb	371-2361	Forsyth	577-6432
Fulton	572-3151	Rockdale	922-7750

Driver's Licenses

Out-of-state drivers are given 30 days to obtain a Georgia driver's license. Minimum age for a license is 16 years. A learner's license may be obtained at 15 years of age. If you have an out-of-state license, you're not required to take a Georgia road test, but you must take an eye test and a written exam. A four-year license for driving a passenger car costs $4.50. A learner's permit costs $1.50.

It's helpful if you take your out-of-state license, your fee, and your social security card with you when you apply for a Georgia's driver's license. To find the licensing station nearest you, call the Driver's License Bureau 656-5890.

Emission Control Inspection

Georgia's motor vehicle laws currently require that all gas-burning vehicles less than ten years old in Cobb, DeKalb, and Fulton counties be checked for emission standards once a year. The inspection costs $3.00. It can be done at any of the state-designated inspection stations. Non-gas-burning vehicles, such as diesel cars and trucks, and motorcycles, are exempt from the inspection. To find the inspection station nearest you, call 656-6072 or 656-6243.

Reporting of Auto Accidents

In an accident on a **public** street call the police immediately at the emergency number 658-6666 (Atlanta Police). If location of the cars is essential in determining fault leave the cars in the position at the time of accident and be sure traffic can proceed around them. If the cars are blocking traffic, or causing danger, pull cars over to side of the street.

Have your car registration, insurance cards, and driver's license available.

Police will handle situations where drivers are intoxicated or drugged or where persons need emergency assistance because of bodily injury.

In an accident on a **private** street call police immediately. You will have to fill out a SR-B form within 10 days of the accident to submit to your insurance company. These forms are available at Police Headquarters and precincts.

Banking

Atlanta is a powerful banking center in the Southeast. The city, which is the headquarters of the Sixth Federal Reserve District, ranks ninth in the nation in bank clearings (in 1981, over $185 billion). In 1972 Atlanta became the headquarters of the Fourth District of the Federal Home Loan Bank System.

With the flexibility of current banking laws, banks and savings and loan associations are offering diversified banking services and financial investments. This competitive situation means that interest rates, service charges, downpayments, time-limited programs, and

special premiums are communicated directly to the consumer.
Call the **Georgia Bankers Association** (522-1501) for further information about banks in Atlanta and the South.

Chambers of Commerce

For newcomers, prospective home buyers, and businesses the Chambers of Commerce are helpful in securing information and seeking business contacts. Also, foreign countries are establishing branches of their chambers in Atlanta.
The following is a list of chambers in Metro Atlanta.

Atlanta C of C	521-0845	DeKalb C of C	378-3691
Chamber of Commerce		Fayette County C of C	461-8465
of the United States	393-0140	Georgia C of C	524-8481
Cobb County C of C	427-4227	Gwinnett County C of C	963-4887
Conyers-Rockdale County		Sandy Springs C of C	252-4800
C of C	483-7049	South Fulton C of C	768-7286

Churches, Synagogues, and Temples

Atlanta, Georgia is in an area generally referred to as the Bible Belt, with over 2000 metro churches and with a predominance of Baptist and Methodist churches in a matrix of 71 denominations (Christian and others), 11 synagogues, and numerous religious organizations. As residential growth continues, new churches are established to meet the needs of the new congregations.

Notice that Peachtree Street from the Capitol downtown to Lenox Square is a seven-mile Church Row with bold ecclesiastical structures facing this main artery through the city. These churches and synagogues are landmarks in the historical development of Atlanta.

Churches in Atlanta and in the South are important meeting places for social fellowship and church programs such as day-care, as well as worship. Members also provide an array of urban outreach programs such as food banks, shelter programs, literacy training, counseling services, child care, immigrant work, etc.

Among the major denominational and ecumenical organizations are:

A.M.E. Church Headquarters, 208 Auburn Ave. NE; 659-2012.
American Lutheran Church

Southeastern, 756 W. Peachtree St.; 876-3355.
Atlanta Baptist Association, 1370

Spring St.; 874-5206.
Atlanta Jewish Community Center, 1745 Peachtree Rd. NE; 875-7881.
Atlanta Jewish Welfare Federation, Inc., 1753 Peachtree Rd. NE; 873-1661.
C.M.E. Church Headquarters, 2001 Martin Luther King, Jr. Dr. SW; 752-7800.
Catholic Archdiocese of Atlanta, 680 W. Peachtree NW; 881-6441.
Christian Council of Metropolitan Atlanta, Inc., 848 Peachtree St. NE; 881-9890.
Church of God State Offices, 6179 Buford Highway, Doraville; 448-9300.
Episcopal Diocese of Atlanta, 2744 Peachtree Rd. NW; 261-3791.
First Christian Church of Atlanta, 4532 Lavista Rd., Tucker; 939-4358.
First Church of Christ, Scientist, 1235 Peachtree St. NE; 892-7838.
Georgia Baptist Convention, 2930 Flowers Rd.; 455-0404.
Greek Orthodox Cathedral of the Annunciation, 2500 Clairmont Rd. NE; 633-5870.
Presbyterian Center, 341 Ponce de Leon Ave. NE; 873-1531.
Southeast Conference of the United Church of Christ, 2676 Clairmont Rd. NE; 633-5655.
Southeastern Synod of the Lutheran Churches of America, 756 W. Peachtree St. NW; 873-1977.
Southern Union Conference of Seventh-Day Adventists, 3978 Memorial Dr., Decatur; 299-1832.
Unitarian Universalist Congregation of Atlanta, 1911 Cliff Valley Way NE; 634-5134.
United Methodist Church Headquarters, 159 Ralph McGill Blvd. NE; 659-0002.
United Presbyterian Synod of the South, 1001 Virginia Ave.; 768-4436.

Clubs and Associations

Private clubs are plentiful in Atlanta, many associated with neighborhood recreational facilities or apartment and condominium complexes.

Other private city clubs and country clubs require sponsorship or the courtesy of transfer membership from an affiliate club.

Business associations include the Chambers of Commerce listed previously in this chapter, as well as the following, many of which have chapters throughout the Metro Area.

Atlanta Jaycees	524-3022	Optimist Club of Atlanta	876-8028
Atlanta Lions Club	522-6774	Rotary Club of Atlanta	522-2767
Atlanta Women's Network	577-5635	Women's Commerce Club	872-1091
Civitan Club of Atlanta	521-0467	World Trade Club	525-4144
Kiwanis Club of Atlanta	233-3311	Women Business Owners	422-3565

Join the civic association in your neighborhood immediately. These are vibrant groups in Atlanta — a perfect "starter" for newcomers, politically and socially.

For the sports enthusiast, there are many organizations that provide field trips, clinics, sports and exercise programs, good times, and camaraderie. See the SPORTS Chapter for contacts for a particular sport. The **YWCA, YMCA,** and **Jewish Community Center** provide excellent facilities and curricula. Groups such as the **Atlanta Ski Club,** the **Georgia Canoeing Association,** the **Sierra Club,** and many others have a minimal membership fee and offer many opportunities for making new sporting friends. See SPORTS Chapter.

If you want to exchange talents in barter or tutor or learn, join The **Atlanta Network** (876-8888), a non-profit organization that includes exchange activities from ceramics to auto repair, languages to beer brewing, gardening to backpacking.

Interested in cultural associations? Try Young Careers or the Junior Committee or other programs at The **High Museum of Art,** The **Symphony,** or **Ballet;** adopt an animal at the **Atlanta Zoo;** attend seminars at the **Atlanta Botanical Garden;** take an historic tour with the **Georgia Society for Historic Preservation;** or play in a community orchestra. These are just starters; attach yourself to any cultural organization in the city as patron or participant. See the VISUAL ARTS Chapter and PERFORMING ARTS Chapter for referrals.

Education

Public Schools, Primary and Secondary

Atlanta has 10 school districts in the Metro Area, all on the quarter plan. Ask your real estate agent about the school system in your area and call the **Georgia Board of Education** (656-2446) to obtain specific data: scores on the state tests for reading and math for your school, the teacher-student ratios, teacher salaries, number of students graduating, and college-bound students. Then set an appointment with the school principal to inspect the school and talk about the curriculum and special courses for the gifted and the handicapped. The school system of Atlanta offers the additional advantages of a planetarium, gifted children's programs, and an alternative academic program, the Atlanta Downtown Learning Center.

The Atlanta School system also has six magnet schools that offer specialized sub-schools for Atlanta students: Northside School of Performing Arts, North Fulton Center for International Studies, Grady High School of Communications, Benjamin E. Mays Center for Science and Mathematics, Roosevelt High School Center for

Information Processing and Decision-Making, Harper High School Center for Financial Services.

In addition there has been a marked growth in both popularity and excellence in Atlanta's vocational schools. Call your local school board, listed below, for details.

DeKalb County offers two open-campus high schools and the Fernbank Science Center, which is included in the SIGHTS Chapter. The Fernbank planetarium and center is used extensively by schools in Metro Atlanta and offers the exclusive opportunity for independent studies for students in DeKalb County.

Georgia has public school kindergarten available to five-year-olds. Children entering the first grade must be at least six years old before September 1st of the entering year. School generally opens the week before Labor Day or soon after. Enrollment requires your child's birth certificate and immunization documents, and the latest report card from a transfer student.

Call your local school board for full details concerning county or municipality educational programs.

Atlanta	659-3381	Buford	945-2713
Cobb County	422-9171	Clayton County	478-9991
DeKalb County	296-2000	Decatur	373-5344
Fayette County	461-8171	Douglas County	942-5411
Forsyth County	577-6432	Marietta	422-3500
Fulton County	768-3600	Rockdale County	483-4713
Gwinnett County	963-8651		

Private Schools

Atlanta has over 20 private schools, many with church affiliations. Accreditation is through the **Southern Association of Colleges and Schools,** a good source to check for a prospective student application. Call the Association at 897-6100. The other accrediting agency is the **Georgia Accrediting Commission** at (912) 685-6345. The **Atlanta Area Association of Independent Schools** will provide a complete listing, which is available through any one of the independent schools. A joint-testing admission program is administered by the Association. For information call the Association at Trinity School at 237-9286.

For Catholic parochial schools call the **Atlanta Archdiocese** at 881-9286. For other church schools, call your local church office.

The **Bureau of Jewish Education** can be reached at 873-1248.

Colleges and Universities

Major Atlanta Colleges and Universities are listed under the SPECIAL PEOPLE Chapter.

Government

City Government

Atlanta is governed by a Mayor and an 18-member City Council presided over by a President of Council elected city-wide. Twelve council members are elected from single-member districts; six are elected city-wide from paired council districts. Elections for mayor and council are every four years.

County Government

Counties are governed by Boards of Commissioners comprising four to six elected commissioners with one serving as Chairman.

Congressional Districts

The seven-county area of Fulton, Cobb, DeKalb, Clayton, Rockdale, Douglas, and Gwinnett Counties is included in the five U.S. Congressional districts in Metro Atlanta.

U.S. Senators from Georgia

Senator Mack Mattingly, Republican, 380 E. Interstate North Parkway NW, Atlanta 30339; 952-8686.

Senator Sam Nunn, Democrat, 275 Peachtree St. NE, Atlanta 30303; 221-4811.

Health Care

Health care is readily available in Atlanta in private and government medical institutions and hospitals. The 15-county area has 56 licensed hospitals and a combined bed capacity of over 11,000. The **Emory Medical School** is well known throughout the South for its medical research and training for doctors, dentists, and nurses. Attached to Emory is the prestigious **Yerkes Regional Primate Research Center** which is used for behavioral and drug studies. **Atlanta University** has recently established a Medical School in South Atlanta to add to its already impressive roster of learning institutions. The **Centers for Disease Control** (CDC) of the U.S.

Public Health Service is the nation's number-one research center for tracking communicable diseases.

Most of the following Atlanta hospitals have 24-hour emergency care. We list them by area:

Downtown
Crawford W. Long Memorial Hospital, 35 Linden Ave. NE; 892-4411.
Doctors Memorial Hospital of Atlanta, 20 Linden Ave. NE; 881-8400.
Georgia Baptist Medical Center, 300 Boulevard NE; 653-4000.
Grady Memorial Hospital, 80 Butler St. SE; 588-4307.

Midtown
Piedmont Hospital, 1968 Peachtree Rd. NW; 350-2222.

North
Northside Hospital, 1000 Johnson Ferry Rd. NE; 256-8000.
Saint Joseph's Hospital, 5665 Peachtree-Dunwoody Rd. NE; 256-7120.
West Paces Ferry Hospital, 3200 Howell Mill Rd. NW; 351-0351.

East
DeKalb General Hospital, 2701 N. Decatur Rd.; 292-4444.

Emory Hospital, 1364 Clifton Rd.; 329-7021.

West
Cobb General Hospital, 3950 Austell Rd. SW, Austell; 944-5000.

Northeast
Button Gwinnett Hospital, 255 Scenic Hwy., Lawrenceville; 963-6101.
Gwinnett Community Hospital, 2160 Fountain Dr., Snellville; 979-0200.
Shallowford Community Hospital, 4576 N. Shallowford Rd., Chamblee; 455-6000.

Northwest
Kennestone Hospital, 677 Church St., Marietta; 426-2000.
Rockdale County Hospital, 1412 Milstead Rd. NE, Conyers; 922-8900.

South
South Fulton Hospital, 1170 Cleveland Ave., East Point; 763-5000.
Southwest Community Hospital, 501 Fairburn Rd. SW; 699-1111.

Medical Facilities for Specialized Treatment and Aid:

Alcoholics Anonymous		525-3178
Egleston Hospital for Children		325-6100
Emergency Mental Health by County		
Fulton	572-2626	DeKalb 892-4646
Cobb	422-0202	Clayton 996-4357
Fayette	568-5203	Gwinnett, Rockdale, and Newton 963-3223
Medfirst (Emergency Room)		325-2100
Metropolitan Atlanta Council on Alcohol and Drugs		351-1800
Poison Control Center		659-7273
Rape Crisis Center		659-7273
Sandy Springs Minor Emergency Clinic		252-1900
Scottish Rite Hospital for Crippled Children		256-5252
Shepherd Spinal Clinic		352-2020

Referral Associations

Medical Association of Atlanta	881-1714	Cobb Medical Society	428-2812
Northern District Dental Society	294-3214	DeKalb Medical Society	292-4148
Planned Parenthood	688-9300	Gwinnett-Forsyth Medical Society	887-1573
Clayton-Fayette Medical Society	991-0020	Newton-Rockdale Medical Society	922-8323

Home Decorating

Rich's, Davison's, and most major furniture companies have staff designers, whose services may be complimentary.

Atlanta Decorative Arts Center (C3), 351 Peachtree Hills Ave. NE; 231-1720. Nicknamed ADAC, this center is a major regional hub for wholesale antiques and complete decorator products. You will need your designer or architect for admission, but it's well worth the venture into this great consortium of design houses. If you do not have a designer, they can recommend some to you.

Jury Duty

Jurors are called from the registered voter lists of persons 18 and older. There is no residency requirement for jury duty, and there are no exclusions except for convicted felons who have not had their civil rights restored. Doctors, lawyers, teachers, and those with physical handicaps may ask for exemptions in writing.

There are two levels of court service in the state courts. Jurors are called from the county in which they reside to serve either on the State or Superior trial court in their county for both civil and criminal cases. Jurors are called from the multiple counties of the North Georgia district to serve on the U.S. District Court in Atlanta.

Legal Services

For references call the **Lawyer Referral Service** at 521-0777 or the **Atlanta Bar Association** at 521-0781.

Tel-Law Service at 577-HELP gives general legal information over the phone.

Libraries

The **Atlanta Public Library System** (688-4636) has a central downtown library (One Margaret Mitchell Square) and 24 branches in the city and Fulton County. The system has over 1 million books, 3000 films, and a large selection of magazines, foreign language periodicals, records, cassettes, and framed prints. Telephone reference service is available at 688-4034. Film programs, exhibitions, concerts, and theater programs are offered in the auditorium and meeting rooms. Services are free to residents of Atlanta and Fulton County.

Major county libraries providing community library services are listed below. Call for branch nearest you and for information.

Clayton County	366-0850	Fulton County	688-4636
Cobb County	427-2462	Gwinnett County	963-5231
DeKalb County	378-7569	Rockdale County	483-7756
Fayette County	461-8841		

Local Laws

Liquor Laws

State laws require that you must be 19 to buy alcohol. Liquor, wine, and beer are sold in package stores from 7 or 8 AM to midnight, Mon-Sat, with no sales on Sun. Grocery and convenience stores sell beer and wine also, Mon-Sat.

Bars, restaurants, sports arenas, and other entertainment areas serve liquor, beer, and wine seven days. Alcoholic beverages are sold after 12:30 PM on Sunday. Some restaurants have a license limited to beer and wine, but allow liquor to be brought by the customer in a "brown bag."

Surrounding counties have varying liquor laws.

Property Laws

Atlanta has established firm zoning laws that require certain procedures for changes in residential structures from one classification to another, such as condominium conversion. Variances or minor changes of a structure within the same zoning classification require obtaining a work permit from the city.

Historic Districts have special zoning restrictions. Contact your neighborhood civic association before applying for a work permit to

NEW RESIDENTS 223

be sure your changes are in compliance or to seek the support of your civic association for the variance or zoning change.

Medical

See Health Care above.

Newspapers and Publications

The two major newspapers are **The Atlanta Constitution** (morning paper) 522-4141 and **The Atlanta Journal** (evening paper), 522-4141. The **Atlanta Daily World** is the nation's oldest black-owned newspaper, 659-1110.

Popular neighborhood papers include twenty nine **Neighbor Newspapers,** covering the metro area. We list some in the following areas and the phone numbers.

Northside, Sandy Springs, Vinings; 256-3100.

Chamblee-DeKalb, Clarkston, Decatur-DeKalb, Doraville-DeKalb, Dunwoody-DeKalb, Stone Mountain-DeKalb; 939-8452.

Marietta Daily Journal; 428-9411.

Other small city and neighborhood papers include the **Dunwoody Crier,** 394-4217, the **Gwinnett Daily News,** 963-0311, and **News-Sun** papers, 292-3536.

A weekly newspaper now in its 11th year is **Creative Loafing,** 873-5623 and the city magazine is **Atlanta Magazine,** 256-9800. For foreign publications in Atlanta see the SPECIAL PEOPLE Chapter.

Business news is focused on the newspaper, **The Atlanta Business Chronicle,** 325-2442; and the magazine, **Business Atlanta,** 256-9800.

Pets

Laws require rabies vaccination for pets by a licensed veterinarian. Pets must be confined to owner's property except when on a leash. Dogs running at large will be picked up by the Animal Control Unit, and the owner fined.

Public Services

City of Atlanta Public Services are supplied by the following:
Electric: Georgia Power Co.; 325-4001.
Natural gas: Atlanta Gas Light Co.; 522-1150.
Telephone: Southern Bell Telephone Co.; 529-8611.
Water: City of Atlanta Water Dept.; 658-7220.
Garbage Collection: City of Atlanta Sanitation Dept.; 351-0215. Free curbside garbage pick-up is once a week. The City will provide each residence with a free "Herbie Curbie" container on wheels.

Metro Public Services are provided to the following counties.
All counties:
Electricity: Georgia Power Co.; 325-4001; or Oglethorpe Power Co.; 455-1121.
Natural Gas: Atlanta Gas Light Co.; 522-1150.
Telephone: Southern Bell Telephone Co.; 529-8611.

	Water/Sewer	Garbage Collection
Clayton	961-2130	363-1705
Cobb	422-0222	429-4280 Marietta
		422-3260 Unincorporated
DeKalb	371-2641	294-2100
Fayette	461-1146	461-6029 Fayetteville
		(private garbage collection in county)
Forsyth	(912)	
	994-2512	887-9921
Fulton	658-6500	572-2276
Gwinnett	962-1513	945-6761 Buford
		963-2414 Lawrenceville
		962-1400 Unincorporated
Rockdale	483-4411	483-4411 Conyers
		(private garbage collection in county)

Residential Cleaning

We recommend **Abbott's House and Window Cleaning Co.,** 696-6182, for heavy-duty cleaning chores such as window washing, wall cleaning, and carpet vacuuming.

Our choice for light cleaning is **Mini Maid,** 378-6464, the Marietta-based national cleaning service. On a regular basis a team of professionals will whisk, vacuum, and dust away the daily dirt from your apartment or residence.

Taxes

Individual Income Tax
Georgia requires a tax on all sources of income unless they are exempt by statute. Employers are required to withhold state income tax for both resident and nonresident employees.

Property Tax
Property taxes in Metro Atlanta vary by county and municipality. There are various homestead exemptions in different areas. Call your local tax commissioners.

Atlanta	572-2331	Gwinnett	962-1436
Fulton	572-2331	Fayette	461-3611
Clayton	478-9911	Forsyth	887-9966
Cobb	429-3284	Rockdale	922-7750
DeKalb	371-2111		

State and Use Tax
A state sales and use tax is added to all retail purchases, rentals, uses, and consumption of tangible goods, personal property, and special services. The tax is 3% except for 5% in Fulton County and 4% in DeKalb County, where additional tax is levied to finance MARTA.

TV and Radio
Atlanta is the headquarters of a national broadcasting company, Turner Broadcasting System and its Cable News Network. See MATTERS OF FACT Chapter for complete TV and radio listings.

Volunteering
For people who wish to volunteer their time and talents call **Volunteer Atlanta,** 100 Edgewood Ave. NE; 522-0110. Also call the **Arts Alliance** at 892-3600 if you wish to be involved with the symphony, theater, or museum.

Voting

Voter Registration
To vote in city, county, state, and federal elections, you must be a

U.S. citizen, be at least 18 years old (17 1/2 to register), be mentally sound, and not under conviction of a felony.

To register to vote, apply in person to the Registrar's office in your county 30 days before a primary or general election. Or, call the **League of Women Voters** (874-VOTE) to locate your registration location.

If you want to transfer your registration from another county in Georgia, apply to the Registrar's Office in your new county.

To keep your registration current, you must vote at least once every three years in a primary or in a general election. However, if your registration is cancelled, you will be given an opportunity to reregister.

For information about local elections, call your city or county government in your new area. For your convenience we list the following political party headquarters in Atlanta.

Democratic Party of Georgia, 1627 Peachtree St. NE, Suite 306, Atlanta 30309; 688-1984.

Republican Party of Georgia, 1951 Airport Rd., Suite 200, Atlanta 30341; 458-0293.

ATLANTA REAL ESTATE

An Overview

Atlanta has been on a continuous residential building program with new subdivisions rising among the pine-covered hills and hardwood forests of the surrounding counties. The Standard Metropolitan Statistical Area (SMSA) of Atlanta defined by the U.S. Office of Management and Budget now includes a 15-county complex influenced by and relying upon the Central City that is its economic base. This SMSA total population has increased from 1970-1980 by 27% with the outlying counties of Fayette, Gwinnett, and Rockdale increasing 160%, 134%, and 100% respectively.

The total private construction in SMSA, residential and non-residential, for 1981 was valued at $1,317,580,000. Housing starts continued to hold their pattern even in the 1982 recession.

Multiple forms of housing are available from the single family dwelling to the duplex, triplex, and quadraplex, from apartment to condominium, attached and detached townhouses, in every price range, intown, midtown, uptown, and out of town.

The suburban spread has reached as far as Peachtree City in Fayette County to the shores of Lake Lanier in Forsyth County, from Crabapple in the north end of Fulton County to beyond Stone Mountain in DeKalb County. Future development follows the construction of Interstate 575 north of Atlanta into Cherokee County and beyond.

The older City of Atlanta has spruced up its intown neighborhoods, adding to the National Register of Historic Districts the areas of Druid Hills, Inman Park, Ansley Park, and others.

Styles of housing are mixed with a recent revival of Williamsburg and Victorian traditions in both cluster developments and single homes.

Information and Referrals

The **Boards of Realtors** have information about residential property and realtors in the metro area.

Atlanta 351-9295	Fayette 461-3525
Clayton 477-7579	Gwinnett 963-3253
Cobb 422-3900	Rockdale 922-3039
DeKalb 378-6526	

Other sources include the **Home Builders Association of Metropolitan Atlanta,** 938-9900, the **Atlanta Apartment Hunters Guide,** 261-7078, and the **Georgia Association of Realtors,** 451-1831.

Buying and Renting

Consider the many variables that confront you whether you are seeking a home purchase or a rental unit. The proximity of your housing to your place of employment is important. Since Atlanta is still a "car" town, in spite of the developing rapid-rail system, the school district, the location of private schools, and cultural and recreational facilities, figure in as well. Look at the financial considerations such as tax structure, cost of improvements and utilities, and insurance rates. And finally, feel comfortable in the neighborhood of your choice. As a rule, better apartment complexes in Atlanta have exquisite landscaping, pools, social centers, and even tennis courts.

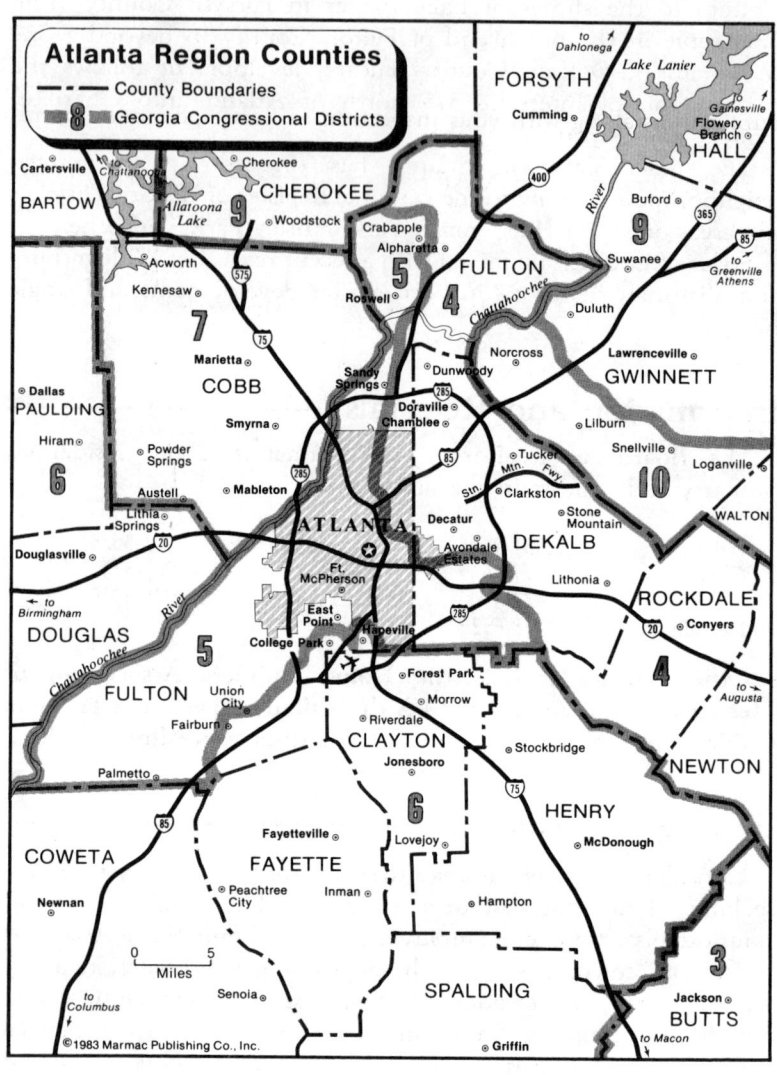

Regional and Neighborhood Profiles

The following is an analysis of some of Atlanta's most recognized neighborhoods to facilitate your choice and introduce you to the many possibilities for settling in. Most civic associations have newsletters; ask your real estate agent to make these available to you. You can sense the spirit of the neighborhoods from these publications along with your inspection of houses, condominiums, and apartments.

Public transportation, MARTA, is available to all parts of the city within the perimeter and beyond to Dunwoody, Sandy Springs, Roswell, Alpharetta, Chamblee, Tucker, Stone Mountain, Fairburn, and the Six Flags area. Cobb County and Gwinnett County are not serviced by MARTA presently. Check with MARTA route and schedule information, 522-4711.

Intown Neighborhoods

The following are renovated neighborhoods less than twenty minutes from downtown in rush hour.

Ansley Park (C3), Fulton County, is a beautiful intown professional neighborhood of restored homes dating from the early 1900s with four interior parks, one with tennis courts. Ansley Park is now on the National Register of Historic Districts and has a very active and influential civic association. The public gardens of Ansley Park have received national awards.

Cascade Heights (D3), Fulton County. Cascade Heights has been a favorite residential area for prominent members of the black community. Luxury homes are featured on ample lots and the area is convenient to the Atlanta University complex and downtown Atlanta.

Grant Park (D3), Fulton County, is a neighborhood in the early process of restoration of its frame Victorian homes. The Atlanta Zoo and the Cyclorama are centered in Grant Park itself, and the neighborhood is a mix of young professionals and old-time residents.

Inman Park (D4), Fulton County, showcases Atlanta's Victorian Homes, the original residences of some of the city's earliest families. Inman Park was Atlanta's first suburb, attached by streetcar to downtown Atlanta. This historic district takes great pride in its neighborhood festivals and continuing restoration. Take Edgewood Avenue east from downtown.

Midtown (C3), Fulton County, is an area of arbored streets, large, small, and multiple family homes and apartments. Midtown is bounded by Ponce de Leon on the south, 10th Street on the north, Peachtree on the west and Monroe Drive on the east. Numerous new "old-style" condominiums and townhouses stand beside original homes from the turn of the century.

Morningside (C4), Fulton County, is an area of homes from the 1920s, many still occupied by the original owners. There are interior parks with playgrounds and tennis courts. The Morningside-Lenox Park Association is active in grounds beautification and neighborhood political and social life.

Virginia-Highlands (C4), Fulton County. The bungalow-style home from the early twentieth century is still alive and well in this neighborhood. The intersection of its two namesakes, Virginia and Highland Avenue has become one of the most popular places for small restaurant dining in the city. It's a low key area of artists, professional folks, and entrepreneurs who understand the beauty of village-living in a city.

West End (D3), Fulton County, neighborhood is an old Atlanta neighborhood in a predominantly black community. Restoration efforts are underway, rendering Peoples Street a model of revived Victorian charm. MARTA trains service the area into downtown.

Buckhead Neighborhoods

Brookwood Hills (C3), Fulton County. Brookwood Hills is a small residential area of fine older homes in a beautiful rolling, wooded section. The neighborhood has its own pool and tennis courts and has walking access to the galleries, eateries, and service stores in Brookwood Village on Peachtree Street.

Collier Hills (C3), Fulton County, is built around the famous Memorial Park at Peachtree Battle Creek. The houses are small, gracefully sited on the hills and in the dells. This is a community where young professionals make their first house purchase and where others return in later life because of the intown convenience and lower maintenance of small residences.

Garden Hills (B3), Fulton County. Homes are generally small and charming, nestled in the wooded terrain of the area. Garden Hills is bounded by Lindberg Drive on the south and Pharr Road on the north, Piedmont on the east and Peachtree on the west.

Peachtree Battle to Northside (C3-B2), Fulton County. From Peachtree Battle extending west and northwest to the Chattahoochee River is one of Atlanta's most celebrated residential areas. Large estate homes, including the Georgia Governor's Mansion rest on imposing properties with long lawns and immaculate landscaping. Northside is the high school. The Bobby Jones public golf course and the Bitsy Grant tennis center afford excellent recreational opportunities.

Peachtree Hills (C3), Fulton County. This cozy neighborhood of small houses and apartments has the advantage of the Peachtree Battle Shopping Center on the west with its neighborhood eateries, boutiques, and shops. The city has a recreation center with multiple tennis courts in Peachtree Hills across from the Atlanta Decorative Arts Center's massive complex on the east side. The Lindberg MARTA station will service the area.

Cobb County

Marietta (A1), East Cobb County, has become a thriving area with fine condominiums and apartments and new exquisite home communities. Simultaneously, the town square in Marietta has a restored and revitalized face, with heightened business activity. Dobbins Air Force Base and Lockheed are two large employers in the area. Marietta continues to grow with the advancing development of Interstate 575 to the north.

Vinings (B2), East Cobb County, has been discovered by more and more folks in East Cobb. This tiny crossroads of antique shops, an inn, and a convenience store is now growing up. Beautiful tracts have residential development down to the river and attractive condos and apartments appeal to singles and couples. Nearby Cumberland Mall and The Galleria provide exceptional shopping.

North Fulton County

Alpharetta, North Fulton County. A fast-developing rural community, convenient to US 400 and the Perimeter complexes.

Crabapple, North Fulton County. In rolling hills and spacious pastures, fine old houses and small horse farms are interspersed with new subdivisions. Centered around a few stores and antique shops, this is a very tight-knit community.

Dunwoody (A4), North Fulton County, a favorite residential area for corporate moves, has the Williamsburg look, with even the Dunwoody Village à la Williamsburg. Dunwoody's prominence nationwide was saluted by the Rand McNally rating as the number one suburb in the United States. The luxury homes are spacious, the natural landscape is respected and enhanced by plantings, with many elegant communities fronting the river. Perimeter Mall and the office complexes nearby make this an ideal area for corporate executives.

Roswell, North Fulton County, is another antebellum town, which used to be considered outside of Atlanta's sphere of influence. No longer. Roswell's town space offers fine shopping and dining and urbanites have found the charm of restoring frame houses, while developers have prospered with condominium building.

Sandy Springs (A3), North Fulton County, is the oldest and most established perimeter community, spreading from both sides of Roswell Road into forested areas of single-family homes, apartments, and townhouses. Sandy Springs is the suburbs at its best, with the convenience of shopping at nearby Perimeter Mall and Park Place. Riverwood High continues to be one of the favorite area high schools.

DeKalb County

Decatur (C4), DeKalb County, is an incorporated city whose history predates Atlanta. The MARTA East Line ends in Decatur which makes the six to eight mile commute ideal. Lovely homes, townhouses, and apartments are available for a relaxed small town lifestyle, only a stone's throw from Atlanta. Agnes Scott College is a central part of the Decatur scene.

Druid Hills (C4), DeKalb County, is the neighborhood of Emory University professionals and students, a lush district originally designed by Frederick Law Olmstead at the turn of the century. This historic district has handsome English Tudor architecture, its prime example the Candler mansion, which is now the Callanwolde Arts Center, a focal point of cultural events in the neighborhood and the city.

Stone Mountain (C6), DeKalb County, is beyond the perimeter to the east of Atlanta. This older community has taken on the restored loveliness of the original village. With the impressive form of Stone Mountain as backdrop, the village affords comfortable living in the frame houses and apartments with full amenities.

Tucker (B5), DeKalb County, is experiencing unprecedented growth of homes in the medium price range. Shopping centers are appearing to service this new influx, Main Street in Tucker is a charming restored center, and the DeKalb school system attracts new residents.

South Metro Atlanta

East Point, College Park, Hapeville (E2), South Fulton and Clayton Counties. These are three long-time Atlanta communities located in the Atlanta airport area, catering to airport personnel and business.

Peachtree City, Fayette County. Peachtree City is a 20-year-planned community south of Atlanta at Georgia Highways 74 and 54. The condominiums and single-family homes are designed around five villages all with walking and biking trails. Full recreational amenities and a school system through high school service over 10,000 residents. Built with private funds, Peachtree City is recognized by the *Ladies Home Journal* as one of the finest planned communities in the United States.

Forsyth and Gwinnett Counties

Gwinnett County is one of the fastest growing metro counties. Communities such as Duluth, Norcross, Snellville, and Lawrenceville have extensive suburban additions and enlarged shopping areas. Land is still moderately priced and available for building. Elegant office parks complement the attractive residential development.

Lake Lanier area, Forsyth County. Since the early 1960s this man-made lake with over 500 miles of shoreline has always been popular as a second-home area and is now a thriving primary living area with route 400 and I-85 making commuting easy into north Atlanta. The country living and accessibility to lake recreation are great drawing cards to Forsyth County.

Counties Beyond

Cherokee, Forsyth, Hall, Paulding, Douglas, Fayette, Henry, Butts, Rockdale, and **Newton** counties are now part of the SMSA of Atlanta, along with the original counties of Fulton, Clayton, Cobb, DeKalb and Gwinnett.

With increased development on the perimeter the outer lying counties are actually close in for commuters to these perimeter locations.

In conclusion, living and working in metro Atlanta can occur with commuting in either direction or living near one's place of work. Take your pick.

HOME AND GARDEN SHOPPING NEEDS

These author's choices will get you started. Many of these listings have several locations.

Air Conditioning Repairs - Conditioned Air Engineers; 352-4040.
Appraisals - Trosby Auction Galleries; 351-4400.
Auto Repairs - See your car dealer.
Blinds and Shades - American Sun Control; 266-1200.
Building Materials - Randall Bros.; 892-6666.
Carpet and Rug Cleaning - Sharian; 373-2274.
Doors - Peachtree Doors; 447-5757.
Electrical Repairs - North Fulton Electric; 875-0449.
Furniture Rentals - Aaron Rents; 873-1455.
Furniture Repairs and Upholstery - Trinity Furniture Shops; 688-4431.
Glass (Auto and Home-Mirrors) - Automobile Glass Co.; 881-1414.
Home Accessories - Abernathy's; 233-6014.
Lamp Repairs - Briarcliff Lamps; 261-0526.

Landscaping, Nursery - Julia O. Martin; 892-8092. Frank A. Smith Nursery; 255-7731.
Leather Cleaning - Ram Leather Care; 483-3454.
Locks - Bullards Lockmaster and Safe Co.; 876-1267.
Painting, Residential - Goodman Decorating; 351-8922. William Thiel; 953-8545.
Paintings Restored - O'Karma Jones Inc.; 874-9461.
Pest Control - York Pest Control; 875-8378.
Picture Frames - Poor Man's Frame Shop; 892-1271.
Plaster Moldings and Character Items - House Parts; 577-5584.
Plumbing - Ansley Park Plumbing; 872-5788.
Pool Services - Craftco Enterprises; 873-4194.
Remodeling - Central Remodeling and Construction Co.; 874-3321.
Rentals (tools, machines, clearing

equipment) - Northside Tool Rental; 233-6722.

Silver Repair (also brass, gold) Estes-Simmons Sliverplating; 875-9581.

Stained Glass - Llorens Stained Glass Studio; 373-7374.

Wrought Iron - Colonial Forge; 873-3114.

LET'S HAVE A PARTY

It's time to try something different for that special occasion. It's time to find a new place on a shoestring budget or with the champagne popping. Let us make a few wild and wonderful suggestions. Or if you want to hire some creative talent to organize your party, call **McClatchey Talent Brokers and Spectacular Events, Inc.** at 355-2225.

Buy the Bus

Ever wanted to just get on a bus and ask your friends to go along for the ride? **MARTA** will do it for a price. You bring the drinks and goodies and plan the route. See you at the bus stop. MARTA Customer Services; 586-5311.

A Christmas Cutting

Have a family party or put together your favorite families to cut your own Christmas tree. Within an hour's drive of Atlanta, to the north in Cherokee County, is **L. R. Ellington,** Route 3, Ball Ground at 479-1286; or, if you are on the southside, call **Mickey Harp** in Fayette County, 2260 Highway 92, at 461-1821. Pack some hot drinks and sandwiches or stop over at a restaurant on the way and toast bringing home the tree. Virginia pines are available at all locations.

Fox Holes

For all you big spenders, contemplate a takeover of the **Fox Theatre.** Maybe the Egyptian Ballroom or the Moorish Grand Salon. Bring in your caterers, bring in your guests, and fill up the holes with a giant party to end all parties. The Fox Theatre; 892-5685.

A Garden for All Seasons

The **Atlanta Botanical Garden** is the perfect setting for your next garden party outdoors. Expand your guest list, hire a caterer, and schedule your time to expose your guests to one of the most beautiful nature spots right in the heart of the city. Atlanta Botanical Garden; 876-5858.

Kid's Time Out

For something different, try pony rides either at your home or at the stables. Four ponies and two stable hands will be provided by **Briarcliff Riding Stables; 634-3564.**

Alternatively, the **Toy Museum of Atlanta** can host 10 to 20 children in the party room, plus provide a tour of the museum. Complete kitchen is a boon for preparation of refreshments, which you must bring yourself. Call 266-8697.

Bobo the Clown will come to your home to enthrall and delight, complete with face-painting, games, and prizes. Call well ahead to 355-8097.

Mind Your Manors

The fine English Tudor manor house built in the roaring 20s by Charles Howard Candler will host a music concert, a festive ball, or catered dinner in one of the many rooms available. **Callanwolde Fine Arts Center;** 872-5338.

OR rent the **Howard School** mansion, a turn-of-the-century classic design by Neil Reid on Ponce de Leon Avenue. The Howard School; 377-7436.

OR rent the **Women's Commerce Club,** built in 1908, with Italian marble fireplaces and now redecorated in peachy tones. Women's Commerce Club; 872-1091.

Paddleboat Party

Stone Mountain park has the boat on the water — all aboard for a **Henry W. Grady Riverboat** ride and a meal catered by the Stone Mountain Inn. What a great party for 150 or a cruise for 300 guests. Stone Mountain Park; 469-9831.

NEW RESIDENTS   237

Plantation Style Party

Gather 50 to 200 of your favorite friends and motor 40 minutes south of Atlanta to **Betty Talmadge's Lovejoy Plantation.** Betty will host a Magnolia dinner complete with strains of the sound track from *Gone with the Wind* and the dining room table presenting a Southern special of fried chicken, Talmadge country ham, grits, turnips, tomatoes, and biscuits. Lovejoy Plantation; 478-6807.

Riverboat on Stone Mountain Lake   *Courtesy Stone Mountain*

SPECIAL PEOPLE

THE INTERNATIONAL VISITOR

International visitors from all the continents of the world arrive daily in Atlanta, the historic gateway to the southern United States. The city has made a concerted effort to transform herself into an international center. The Atlanta Hartsfield International Airport welcomes the foreign traveler in its separate international concourse with full immigration and customs facilities. The First National Bank of Atlanta has a branch office in the main terminal for currency exchanges.

SPECIAL PEOPLE

Consulates and ethnic societies in Atlanta have multiplied rapidly during the last decade as global economics, politics, and cultural exchange have interlaced the peoples of the world. We list aids and resources for international visitors and new residents in Atlanta, beginning with the consulates, trade offices, and ethnic societies.

Atlanta Counsel for International Visitors (J9), 235 Peachtree St. NE, Peachtree Center; 577-2248. This fine group will help you secure translators from their language bank of over 50 languages, introduce you to ethnic groups in the city, exchange and be an over-all resource center for professional and emergency services. The council is responsible for the programming of official international visitors to the city. For assistance call 522-7866 Mon-Fri from 9 am - 5 pm; call the United Way Help Line after 5 pm, 522-7370.

Consulates, Trade, and Tourism Offices

The career consulates have an asterisk (*) beside them. For additional information, call the Atlanta Consular Corps, Louise Suggs, 659-4270.

Austria, 6075 Roswell Rd. NE; 252-7920.
Bahamas Tourist Office, 1950 Century Blvd. NE; 633-1793.
Belgium*, 229 Peachtree St. NE; 659-2150.
Bermuda Department of Tourism, 235 Peachtree St. NE; 524-1541.
Bolivia, 5555 Roswell Rd. NE; 255-8032.
Brazil*, 229 Peachtree St. NE; 659-0660.
Canada*, 260 Peachtree St. NW; 577-6810.
China, Republic of, Coordination Council for American Affairs, 229 Peachtree St. NE; 522-0182.
Colombia, 1588 Alderbrook Rd., Decatur; 634-7748.
Colombian Trade Development Bureau, 5775 Peachtree-Dunwoody Rd.; 257-9238.
Costa Rica, 1232 Arbovista Dr. NE; 457-5656.
Denmark, 225 Peachtree St. NE; 522-8811.

Danish Trade Office, 229 Peachtree St. NE; 588-1588.
Ecuador, 1650 Birmingham Rd., Alpharetta; 475-4751.
El Salvador, 1161 Rennes Ct. NE; 252-8425.
Finland, One Dunwoody Park NE; 446-1400.
France, 1632 Ponce de Leon Ave., Decatur; 378-4226.
French Trade Commission*, 100 Peachtree St. NW; 522-4843.
Germany, Federal Republic of*, 229 Peachtree St. NE; 659-4760.
Goethe Institute Atlanta, German Cultural Center, 400 Colony Square; 892-2388.
Great Britain, United Kingdom of*, 225 Peachtree St. NE; 524-5856.
Guatemala, 4772 E. Conway Dr. NW; 255-7019.
Haiti, P.O. Box 80340, Atlanta 30341; 455-3434.

Honduras, 229 Peachtree St. NE; 659-8675.
Iceland, 1649 Tullie Cir. NE; 321-0777.
Israel*, 805 Peachtree St. NE; 875-7851.
Italy*, 1106 W. Peachtree St. NW; 875-6177.
Italian Trade Commission*, 233 Peachtree St. NE; 525-0660.
Japan*, 400 Colony Square, Peachtree & 14th Sts. NE; 892-2700.
Korea*, 229 Peachtree St. NE; 522-1611.
Luxembourg, 1900 The Exchange NW; 952-1157.
Mexico*, 550 South Omni International; 688-3258.
Netherlands*, 233 Peachtree St. NE; 525-4513.
Nigeria*, 225 Peachtree St. NE; 577-4800.
Norway, 5775 Peachtree-Dunwoody Rd.; 421-7333.
Puerto Rico, Commonwealth of, Economic Development Administration, 235 Peachtree St. NE; 396-2544
Romanian Trade Promotion Office, 229 Peachtree St. NE; 636-6044.
Sweden, 230 Peachtree St. NE; 522-8811.
Switzerland, 235 Peachtree St. NE; 524-4748.

Ethnic Societies

Many of these societies are run by individuals from their homes, so keep calling if there is no answer.

Afghanistan: Afghan Society in the U.S., 676-3884.
Arab Countries: American-Arab Association, 633-1161, 633-0150.
Argentina: La Casa Argentina, 874-1533.
Finland: Atlanta Suomi Society, 373-9919.
France: Alliance Francaise d'Atlanta, 875-1211.
Germany: Goethe Institute of Atlanta, 892-2388.
Greece: Greek Orthodox Cathedral of the Annunciation, 633-5870.
Holland: Atlanta Holland Club, 377-1922.
Hungary: Hungarian Cultural Association of Georgia, 284-7725.
Indo-China: Indo-Chinese American Association, 231-0940.
Italy: Italian Cultural Society, Inc., 761-6214.
Japan: Japan-American Society of Georgia, 872-6443.
Korea: Korean Association of Greater Atlanta, 581-2057.
Latin-American Countries: Latin American Association, 231-0940.
Liberia: Liberian Students' Association, 296-7570.
Norway: VASA Order of America, Nordic Lodge, 482-7987.
Panama: 451-4983.
Philippines: Filipino-American Association of Greater Atlanta, 255-1713.
Puerto Rico: Spanish American Social Club, 972-4824.
Russia: Russian Cultural Society, 658-2265.
Scotland: Burns Club of Atlanta, 252-3857.
Spain: Casa Cultura Iberamericana, 650-2265.
Sweden: VASA Order of America, Nordic Lodge, 373-0174.
Switzerland: The Swiss-American Society, 993-3268.
Thailand: Thai Association of Georgia, 973-6971

SPECIAL PEOPLE 241

Turkey: Turkish American Cultural Association, 973-1615 or 231-3357.
Ukraine: The Ukranian Association of Georgia, 452-4127.
United Kingdom: Daughters of the British Empire, 938-5405.
Vietnam: St. John's Catholic Church, 768-5647.

Bank Hours

Atlanta's banking hours are generally from 9 am to 4 pm, although some banks' branch locations are open on Saturday mornings as well.

Currency Exchange and International Banking

Always try to exchange foreign currency in a bank, which will offer you the most competitive rate. However, after hours the cashier in the major hotels will be able to change money.

When you arrive at Hartsfield International Airport, the First National Bank of Atlanta is open Mon-Fri 9 am - 7 pm, Sat-Sun 4 - 7 pm.

International banking services available in Atlanta include, as well as purchase and sale of foreign currencies and foreign travelers' checks, cable transfers, foreign drafts on overseas banks, foreign collections, import/export financing, acceptance financing, and issue of commercial letters of credit. The following banks are at your service; all have numerous other locations.

Airport—First National Bank of Atlanta (E2), Main Terminal Building, Hartsfield Atlanta International Airport; 768-2856.

Citizens and Southern National Bank (K8), International Dept., Marietta and Broad Sts., 10th Floor, C&S Building; 581-3424.

First National Bank of Atlanta (K8), International Banking Division, Main Banking Floor, 2 Peachtree St. NE; 588-6442.

Bank South (K9), International Banking Dept., 55 Marietta St., 12th Floor; 529-4427.

The National Bank of Georgia (J9), International Division, 34 Peachtree St. NW, 1st Floor; 586-8425.

Trust Company Bank (J9), International Division, 25 Park Place, 10th Floor; 588-7694.

These international banks have offices in Atlanta: Algemene Bank Nederland (Dutch), Banca Nazionale del Lavoro (Italian), Banco do Brasil, The Bank of Nova Scotia, The Bank of Tokyo, Ltd.; Barclays

Bank International Ltd. (British), Canadian Imperial Bank of Commerce, Commerzbank (German), Credit Lyonnais (French), Credit Suisse (Swiss), Kredietbank (Belgian), Lloyds Bank International (British), Standard Chartered Bank (British), Swiss Bank Corporation, Toronto-Dominion Bank, Union Bank of Bavaria.

Customs Allowances

You are allowed to bring into the United States from overseas the following duty free:

One liter of alcoholic beverages; one hundred cigars; two hundred cigarettes. Be aware, however, that state liquor laws supercede the national regulations.

There is a personal exemption of $300; over this amount the next $600 in goods is charged at a flat rate of 10%.

Gifts that are mailed to the U.S. under the value of $25 are duty free; over that amount the recipient will be charged duty.

Driving

Driving in the United States is in the right lane. An international driver's license should be secured through your local automobile association before you leave home. U.S. gallons of gasoline are one-fifth smaller than the United Kingdom's imperial gallon. Gasoline stations along the highways are generally open on weekends or in the evenings, and some remain open 24 hours — watch for signs.

The national 55 m.p.h. speed limit is observed and enforced by the use of police radar observation. In Georgia you are allowed to turn right at a red traffic light except where posted, and the law dictates that you must turn your headlights on when it is raining and call the police immediately when you have an accident.

Electricity

110 volts 60 cycles A.C. Bring an adapter for your razor or hair dryer.

International Publications and Newspapers

The stores listed are in the downtown area. If you are staying near an ethnic neighborhood local stores may have foreign newspapers published in the U.S. in a foreign language.

Atlanta Public Library (J9), 1 Margaret Mitchell Square, corner Forsyth and Carnegie Way; 688-4636. Newspapers and magazines from most countries. Books: fiction, non-fiction, and dictionaries in most languages.

The Bookworm Bookstore (J9), 7 Houston St. (near Peachtree St.); 525-9687. Open Mon-Sat. Newspapers: British weekend, German; magazines: British, French, German.

Eastern Newsstand (J9), Peachtree Center Shopping Gallery, 1st floor, 231 Peachtree St.; 659-5670. Open Mon-Sat. Newspapers: London Sunday Times; magazines: British, French, German, Italian, Spanish.

Georgia State University Library (K9), Washington and Gilmer Sts., accessible from Washington into university courtyard; 658-2172. Open to guests. Most foreign newspapers and magazines are available at Georgia State. A list is on the wall as you enter.

Oxford Book Store (B3), Peachtree Battle Shopping Center, 2345 Peachtree Rd.; 262-3332. Open Mon-Sun, 9 am - 8 pm. Newspapers: London Sunday; magazines: French, Italian.

Rizzoli International Bookstore (J8), 328 Omni International Complex; 688-9065. Open Mon-Sun. Newspapers: British daily; magazines: British, French, German, Italian; books: dictionaries and grammar guides in 80 languages; fiction and non-fiction in French, German, Italian, Spanish.

Medical Insurance

Medical insurance should be secured prior to arrival. There is no national health service.

Money

The U.S. dollar ($) is divided into 100 cents (¢). The coins are the penny worth 1¢ (copper-colored), nickel 5¢, dime 10¢, quarter 25¢, half-dollar 50¢ (all silver colored), and occasionally a silver dollar coin. The bills or notes are all one color — green — and are in denominations of one dollar, five dollars, ten dollars, twenty dollars, fifty dollars, one hundred dollars, and one thousand dollars.

Postage

Mail service is generally good, and letters can cross the country in one to three days. Zip codes must be used for guaranteed delivery. Express Mail is available. Check with the nearest post office for information on rates.

Public Holidays

The following holidays are considered legal holidays in most businesses, including government offices. Banks and businesses will not operate on these days. Some holidays are celebrated on the closest Monday to the holiday in order to give working people a long weekend. This is indicated in the listing.

January 1, New Year's Day.
February 22, George Washington's Birthday, celebrated on closest Monday.
May 31, Memorial Day, celebrated on closest Monday.
July 4, Independence Day.
September, Labor Day, first Monday after first Tuesday.
October 12, Christopher Columbus Day, celebrated on closest Monday.
November 11, Veterans Day.
November, Thanksgiving Day, fourth Thursday.
December 25, Christmas.

Telephone and Telegrams

Most public pay phones require a 25¢ coin deposit, but read the instructions before inserting your coin. When calling long-distance, dial 1, the area code, then the number. Telephone numbers preceded by an (800) number are toll-free in the United States.

To send a mailgram (guaranteed next-day delivery by mail and less expensive than a telegram), telegram, international message, or charge-card money order, call Western Union, 688-9870.

Tipping and Taxes

Tipping is your way of rating and rewarding service. These general guidelines will help you adjust the size of the tip you wish to give. A 15% tip is customarily considered for restaurant service, hotel laundry and valet service, room service, bar bills, and taxi fares. Bellhops and porters generally receive 50¢ per bag. Atlanta counties have a 3% to 5% sales tax on merchandise and food. There is an additional 3% tax on hotel and motel rooms in Atlanta and surrounding counties.

Tour Companies, Foreign Language

TourGals, 262-7660, specializes in group tours with multilingual guides.

Translators

Catholic Social Services, 885-1752, provides assistance for Spanish speaking visitors, Mon-Fri, 9 am - 5 pm.

Georgia State University Translator and Interpreter School, 658-2265. Professionals are available in German, French, Italian, and Spanish, Mon-Fri, 9 am - 5 pm.

HATA, (800) 356-8392 assists you in making travel arrangements in French, German, Japanese, or Portuguese.

Language Services, 3355 Lenox Rd. or 2258 Northlake Pkwy.; 939-6400. Professional translation, interpreters, foreign language instruction, and city tours are all available at Language Services.

TV Channels and Radio Stations Broadcasting in Foreign Language

In Atlanta the language broadcast other than English will generally be Spanish because of the large Cuban population in the city.
WABE Radio FM 90 on the dial — Spanish (check paper for time).
WAGA-TV Channel 5 — Sunday morning Spanish Program.
WXIA-TV Channel 11 — Sunday morning Spanish Program.

METRIC CONVERSIONS

Length

1 millimeter	=	.039 inch (in.)	1 inch	=	2.54 cm.
1 centimeter	=	.39 in.	1 foot	=	0.30 m.
1 meter	=	3.28 feet (ft.)	1 yard	=	.91 m.
1 kilometer	=	.62 mile (mi.)	1 mile	=	1.61 km.

To convert miles to kilometers, multiply the number of miles by 8 and divide by 5.

Weight

1 gram	=	.04 ounce (oz.)	1 oz.	=	28.35 g.
1 kilogram	=	2.2 pounds (lbs.)	1 lb.	=	.45 kg.
			1 ton	=	.91 metric ton

Liquid

		2.11 pints (pt.)	1 pt.	=	.47 liter
1 liter	=	1.06 quarts (qt.)	1 qt.	=	.95 liter
		.26 gallon (gall.)	1 gall.	=	3.79 liters

Temperature

To convert Fahrenheit temperatures to Centigrade (Celsius): Take the Fahrenheit temperature, minus 32 and divided by 1.8 equals the Centigrade temperature.

CONVERSION CHARTS FOR CLOTHING

Dresses, coats, suits and blouses (Women)

British	10	12	14	16	18	20
American	8	10	12	14	16	18
Continental	40	42	44	46	48	50

Suits and overcoats (Men)

American/British	34	36	38	40	42	44
Continental	44	46	48	50	52	54

Shirts (Men)

American/British	14	14 ½	15	15 ½	16	16 ½	17	17 ½
Continental	36	37	38	39	40	41	42	43

Shoes (Men) for ½ sizes add ½ to preceding number

British	6	7	8	9	10	11	
American	7	8	9	10	11	12	
Continental	39 ½	40 ½	41 ½	42 ½	43 ½	44 ½	

Shoes (Women) for ½ sizes add ½ to preceding number

British	3	4	5	6	7	8	9
American	4 ½	5 ½	6 ½	7 ½	8 ½	9 ½	10 ½
Continental	35	36	37	38	39	40	41

STUDENTS

Students visiting Atlanta will find camaraderie at the many colleges and universities in the area. Your most important document as a traveling student is your student identification card, which certifies your student status and helps stretch the travel budget. Always ask if a student discount is applicable for accommodations or transportation systems, at restaurants, at theaters, cultural programs, museums, and at places of entertainment. Be aware of the "Happy Hour" at bars and restaurants, when drinks are offered at half price or discount price. Drinking age in Georgia is 19, except if you are in service uniform when it's 18.

Lodging

Lodging in Atlanta is available for your specific travel needs. Atlanta does not have youth hostel network, however, we suggest the following accommodations for students.

Bed and Breakfast (see LODGING Chapter). This gives you the opportunity to stay with a family in their home.

Cheshire Motor Inn (C4), 1865 Cheshire Bridge Rd., NE; 872-9628. Moderate rates, modest and clean accommodations, and a convenient location between midtown and Buckhead make this a good choice for students. The Colonnade restaurant next door serves plenty of good American fare. Niko's Greek Restaurant is within the block, as well as a number of fast-food places.

Days Inns of America (see LODGING Chapter). Days Inns are on the expressway on the outskirts of the city and are reliable, clean accommodations, well-suited for individuals or a group.

The universities have variable policies concerning short-term room rental to students. If you are interested in applying to an Atlanta area college, the admissions office will see that you are lodged on campus during your visit. Also, film, art, music, reading and lecture programs, social gatherings, and special campus events are worth checking by phone or on the bulletin boards at the student centers and administration offices. Excellent free or $1 films are shown each weekend as a starter. Student cafeterias are always a good place to meet other students over an inexpensive lunch.

Metro Colleges and Universities

Agnes Scott College (C5), College Ave. at McDonough St., Decatur; 373-2571, Ext. 230. Agnes Scott is a women's college, founded in 1889, with an outstanding annual series "The arts at Agnes Scott," special festivals and symposiums, a student theater, and art exhibits and film series.

Atlanta University Center (D3), 360 Westview Dr. SW; 522-8980. A.U. is a confederation of black colleges including Atlanta University, Morris Brown, Clark College, Morehouse College, Spelman College, and the International Theological Center. The center, the oldest and largest consortium of black colleges in the country, offers a wide variety of lectures, exhibits, and programs.

Emory University (C4), 1380 S. Oxford Rd. NE; 329-6216. Emory is located near Decatur, has a Methodist affiliation, funding from the Coca-Cola company, and an excellent reputation for all its art, film, music, and cultural programs.

Georgia Institute of Technology (H9), 225 North Ave. NW; 894-2805. This renowned technical school in downtown Atlanta offers exciting college football, a superb student-run radio station WREK-FM, and a mixture of public programs in the sciences, arts, and film.

Georgia State University (K9), Public Information Department, 129 Sparks Hall, University Plaza SE; 658-3570. Georgia State is Atlanta's large public university in the heart of downtown, with a continuous schedule of film series, art exhibits of national caliber, musical programs, readings, and lectures.

Mercer University (B5), 3001 Mercer University Dr. NE; 451-0331. A private college with a Baptist affiliation, Mercer is a small, liberal arts, commuter college with many students in their mid-twenties.

Oglethorpe University (B4), 4484 Peachtree Rd. NW; 261-1441. North of the city in Chamblee, this small liberal-arts college offers occasional events for the public.

Popular Student Hangouts

Restaurants, bars, cinemas, and music halls are instinctive student haunts. Here are some from the Atlanta area, compiled with the aid of many student friends. Remember, these kinds of places go in and out of business everytime the wind changes direction. See DINING and NIGHTLIFE Chapters.

Bennigan's (B3), Around Lenox; 262-7142. A popular bar decked out in green awnings, brass rails and wood.

Bijou (C3), 1544 Piedmont Rd. NE, Ansley Mall; The Bijou specializes in foreign films with a roster of superior films year after year. Special rates for late shows.

Buckhead Cinema 'N' Drafthouse (B3), 3110 Roswell Rd. NE; 231-5811. Order a pitcher of cold beer and pizza at your table and view fine oldies, film classics, and the best of the new — a popular combination.

The Buckhead Saloon (C3), 330 Piedmont Rd. NE; 231-2326. For a genuine saloon atmosphere in the area, try the Buckhead Saloon. Live music nightly.

Carlos McGee's (B3), 3035 Peachtree Rd. NE; 231-7979. This restaurant-bar, located on the Buckhead Strip, specializes in Tex-Mex style food, margaritas served in pitchers, and live music every night ranging from jazz to reggae to rock. Arrive early on weekend evenings.

Everybody's (C4), 1593 N. Decatur Rd. NE; 377-7766. Directly across from Emory University, Everybody's is a traditional student hangout for pizza, beer, and good times.

Excelsior Mill (C4), 695 North Ave. NE; 577-6455. Lunch or dinner and then a concert at this restored Atlanta excelsior mill will be a fantastic experience. The structure maintains the giant beams, pulleys, and machinery of the original mill. Fresh vegetables are served for lunch — pizza is the specialty, and music in the concert hall on the ground level ranges from jazz and rock to country and blues. Happy hour from 3 - 7 pm, Tues-Sun.

Good Ol' Days (B3), 3013 Peachtree Rd. NE, on the strip in Buckhead, 266-2597; and (A3), 5841 Roswell Rd. NE in Sandy Springs, 257-9183. These two restaurants offer eating and drinking al fresco. The specialties of the house are sandwiches made with Good Ol' Days' delicious flowerpot bread. Live music every evening as students congregate to drink a pitcher of beer in the friendly atmosphere.

Hedgens (B3), 3236 Roswell Rd. NE; 233-1216. Hedgens is for those who are into hard rock.

Houlihan's Old Place (B3), Lenox Square; 261-5323. This popular spot for students offers an atmosphere of Victorian memorabilia and conviviality, soups, sandwiches, quiches, and unusual lunches and dinners.

Houston's (B3), 3321 Lenox Rd. NE, 237-7534; (B3), 3539 Northside Pkwy., 262-7130. Uptown decor of beige and forest green and a full menu of moderately priced food combine to make Houston's one of the most frequented gathering places for students in both locations.

Los Mariaches (B3), 3639 Piedmont Rd. NE; 233-9373. This small restaurant serves lots of tasty Mexican food at moderate prices to lots of hungry students.

The Market (B3), south end of Lenox Square. Here is a natural milling place for everybody in Atlanta, students included. Play the electronic games at Time-Out's grand pinball arcade, top off a movie, a shopping day, or a date with Haagen-dazs ice cream at The Market.

Moe's and Joe's (C4), 1033 N. Highland Ave. NE; 892-9231. This is a long-time bar in the Virginia-Highland section for neighbors and Georgia Tech students. For beer drinkers only — no wine, no liquor.

Moonshadow Saloon (C4), 1880 Johnson Rd. NE; 881-MOON. High-quality bands perform at the saloon, which is located in the Virginia-Highland area near Emory University. Huge photographs of the surface of the moon line the walls with over 500 seats available for the audience. Beer, wine, and mixed drinks are served with snacks.

The Screening Room (C3), 2581 Piedmont Rd. in Broadview Plaza; 231-1924. This theater specializes in top foreign films.

Taco Mac (C4), 1006 N. Highland Ave. NE; 873-6529. Mexican food is the fare. Beer is the real specialty with foreign beers in cartons piled from floor to ceiling. The Taco Mac encyclopedia of beer includes 122 selections, Atlanta's largest. Don't miss this unique opportunity, all you beer drinkers.

Tom Foolery (B3), 3166 Peachtree Rd. NE; 231-8666. This small bar features the antics, pranks, and jokes of 25-year-old Tom who delights his packed audience each evening (except Sun). Come enjoy this incredible trickster and have a lot of laughs.

The Varsity (I10), 61 North Ave. NW; 881-1706. The Varsity is an Atlanta landmark next to Georgia Tech. The shiny red enamel art-deco exterior, the curb service, and the TV rooms are part of Atlanta's history. Chili dogs are a must before Georgia Tech football games. Service is 24 hours. You haven't seen Atlanta until you've been to the Varsity.

CHILDREN

Visiting children will enjoy the many sights described in this guide. Just remember to punctuate your sightseeing time with some fun eating spots like the Varsity downtown or Chick-Fil-A at Lenox Square or an Old Hickory House for some super Bar-B-Q or the Garden Room at Plaza Park for snacks and ice cream by the capitol or finally the Showbiz Pizza, (B5), near Northlake Shopping Mall, where a video arcade and "skee-ball" team up for entertainment before the pizza, together with the animated bear show.

Places children enjoy without question are the Fernbank Science Center, Six Flags over Georgia, the Wren's Nest, the Zoo and Cyclorama, the State Capitol and Museum, the High Museum with a special children's exhibit year-round, the Toy Museum, Stone Mountain, and the Center for Puppetry Arts. You can't go wrong with these kid-pleasing winners. See the SIGHTS Chapter for details.

During the year Atlanta has special treats for young people. **Children's Theater** at the Alliance Theatre and at the Academy Theatre have wonderful productions. The Atlanta Symphony orchestra performs several young-people's concerts during the year, and the summer outdoor pops series at the Chastain Park amphitheater is a charmer.

During the Christmas season, the Atlanta Ballet presents the *Nutcracker* or *Sleeping Beauty* each year and in March there is an extraordinary **Children's Festival** in the Robert W. Woodruff Arts Center.

The new public library downtown has a special reading room for children, with soft sculpture chairs and a carpeted conversation pit for "down-to-earth" storytime. Adventures in looking at the High Museum is an ongoing total-involvement environment for children to heighten their visual awareness of the world around them.

Playgrounds are available through the Atlanta Parks Department. One we particularly recommend is the modern **Playscapes** in Piedmont Park (G12) at Piedmont Drive and 11th Street.

For an unusual excursion into the immediate countryside, take your child to **R. L. Mathis Dairy** (C5), 3181 Rainbow Drive, Decatur; 289-1433. Two sections, the Milking Parlor and the Maternity Ward, are great fun along with the whole tour of the dairy and a visit with the other Mathis animals. A lovely picnic area is available for lunch.

Children can also have a fine time just seeing the city from different perspectives, from the MARTA train as it passes over the downtown cityscape, from the outside elevators zooming up the Westin Peachtree Plaza Hotel, and from the interior bubble elevators of the Hyatt Regency Hotel.

SENIOR CITIZENS

The older traveler is recognized as an integral part of the large traveling population in the United States and abroad. Travel agencies nationwide focus many of their travel promotions and group trips on the interests of the mature traveler, interests that range from fixed-income capabilities to comfortable transportation and accommodations, from available medical facilities to theme tours and social life. These are the same concerns of the older person who is visiting Atlanta.

Discounts for Travel, Events, and Lodging

Most major airlines in Atlanta offer special rates for senior citizens, with discounts as high as one-third of the regular rate. AMTRAK allows 25% off its regular fares for senior citizens, and Greyhound and

Trailways bus service is discounted 10% for bus-traveling senior citizens. Public transportation within the city on MARTA is half-fare.

Special discounts for senior citizens are available frequently for sports events, concerts, tours of homes, theaters, and other attractions. Ask the box office about senior citizen rates or call Atlanta's central ticketing organization, SEATS Administration, 100 Techwood Dr. Viaduct; 681-2100.

Also check the public libraries and arts centers of Atlanta for ongoing cultural programs for older persons.

Hotels and motels generally do not have a lower rate for senior citizens, but inquiries should always be made at the reservations office. An exception to this lodging policy is Days Inns of America, a nationwide motel chain with nine Days Inns or Days Lodges in the Atlanta area. Days Inns offers a special travel program for people 55 and older — the September Days Club. For a one year membership of $10, club members receive a membership card that permits ten percent discounts on rooms, food, and gifts. Bonuses include discounts at major travel attractions, affordably priced tours, a quarterly magazine, and a discount prescription drug program. See Days Inns in LODGING Chapter. Write to **September Days Club**, 2751 Buford Highway NE, Atlanta, GA 30324 for a free brochure and application. Gift memberships are also available.

Another recommended accommodation in Atlanta for older travelers is the Bed-and-Breakfast program listed in LODGING. Staying with an Atlanta family can create a comfortably-paced visit and a personable introduction to this energetic city.

Special Organizations

Two organizations in Atlanta are helpful to the older person as expansive referral sources. The **American Association of Retired Persons** is a non-governmental, non-partisan, and non-profit national organization for men and women fifty-five years of age or older, whether employed or not employed. The $4 annual membership entitles AARP members to over a dozen benefits, which include 10-25% discount rates at participating Holiday Inns, Howard Johnson's, Quality Inns, Ramada Inns, Rodeway Inns, Scottish Inns of America, Sheraton, and Treadway Inns. Again, if you are a card-carrying AARP member, call ahead to inquire at each hotel. AARP membership also aids in car rental discounts as high as 30% at

Hertz, Avis, and National rent-a-car systems. Another travel feature is a custom membership in the Amoco Motor Club. For more information on the AARP and its twenty-five chapters in metro Atlanta call 458-1491 or write to 2872 Woodcock Blvd., Chamblee, GA 30341.

The second organization which offers eleven operational components is the **Senior Citizens Services of Metropolitan Atlanta,** a private non-profit agency and member of the United Way. Although this agency is primarily designed for the needs of older Atlanta residents and newcomers, it serves as an invaluable information pool for older travelers in Atlanta. The Senior Center (H11) is located at 34 Tenth St. NE, Atlanta, GA 30367. Call them at 881-5950.

HANDICAPPED PERSONS

More and more handicapped persons are on the move for both business and pleasure. The wheelchair, the laser cane and sonic glasses for the blind, and the network of dialysis centers, combined with public support and awareness, have opened new pathways of travel and visitation for the handicapped person.

Accessibility and Discounts

The key advice to the handicapped person is always call ahead to check accessibility at your place of destination. Be specific about your needs. This will reassure you of the features of each particular hotel, restaurant, center, theater, or other establishment.

The new Atlanta airport was designed for complete accessibility with ramps, special elevators, restrooms, and parking lots clearly marked with the international logo for the handicapped person. The city bus and rapid transit system is also designed for wheelchair riders. "Lift" buses that assist wheelchair riders to and from work are on fixed routes and on fixed schedules. A minimum of four riders is required by MARTA to establish a fixed route. Call MARTA at 522-4711 for detailed information. MARTA trains have wheelchair parking, and ticket gates at all MARTA rail stations have wheelchair accessibility. MARTA fares are reduced 50 percent for the handicapped.

Lodging for the handicapped traveler continues to improve. The downtown Atlanta Hilton has 144 guest rooms fully equipped for the handicapped, and it has easy front entry and a ramped coffee shop. Some of the other hotels and motels providing facilities include Days Inns, Holiday Inns, Ramada Inn Central, the Marriott, Sheraton Hotel, Terrace Garden Inn, Omni International, and Hyatt Regency. See the LODGING Chapter and again, call ahead about your specific requirements. Days Inns and Holiday Inns, with handicap-coded guidebooks to all their inns, are setting an excellent precedent for all hotel and motel chains. These guidebooks are valuable references especially to the handicapped person who travels frequently.

When attending a concert or theater function at the Robert W. Woodruff Arts Center, the Fox Theatre, Civic Center, Stadium, or Omni call ahead for arrangements. Special rows are available for wheelchairs. Stone Mountain is accessible including a refreshing Steamboat ride on the lake. Six Flags provides assistants for wheelchairs. For special admission rates for the handicapped call Special Audiences at 875-9011 and SEATS at 681-2100.

Services for the Blind

The **Atlanta Area Services for the Blind** (H11), 763 Peachtree St. NE has extensive information for the visually-impaired traveler or newcomer to Atlanta. At the same location is a museum of Touch; the High Museum and Fernbank Science Center offer touch programs for the blind person. The Magic Pan and the International House of Pancakes have braille menus. Call your restaurant for the availability of braille menus. Atlanta law allows you to take your seeing-eye dog into restaurants and food establishments.

Two other services for the blind deserve mention. The **Georgia Radio Reading Service** (C3), 1580 Peachtree St. NW reads current radio programs, newspapers, periodicals, and best-sellers to the blind through a special receiver. Some hospitals also have receivers, and the reading service has sixty-four centers nationwide. Applications for the receiver can be made at the Library for the Blind, 656-2465.

The **Library for the Blind** (D3), 1050 Murphy Ave. SW has thirteen sub-regional free-lending libraries. Cassette players, tapes, talking-book machines, books-on-records from the Library of Congress, magazines-on-records, and cassettes, excerpts from the daily New York *Times,* and Atlanta *Magazine,* as well as large-print books are all available free of charge to certified applicants.

Dialysis Centers

Atlanta has fourteen dialysis centers in the metro area. Travelers who need dialysis while in the city must contact their home nurse or social worker to plan their Atlanta itinerary and dialysis schedule before arrival.

State Park

For a day's excursion from Atlanta or for an overnight stay in a natural area, fully equipped for the handicapped person, visit **Fort Yargo State Park,** Winder, GA 30680. The Will-away Recreational Center within the park offers picnic tables, two beaches, boat rentals, fishing, and cottage accommodations. The park is about an hour from Atlanta, east on US 29. Call 867-3489. This is a beautiful and comfortable site.

Lastly we recommend the **Georgia Easter Seals** office as a central clearing house for information concerning any handicapped person. Call 351-6551.

For wheelchair repairs consult the following:

Abbey Medical (B3), 3112 Piedmont Rd. NE; 261-1344.

Atlanta Orthotics, Inc., (I10), 583 Juniper St. NE; 876-5832.

BITS AND PIECES

Atlanta has its legends that emerge out of oral history, storytelling, and an enthusiasm for a living tradition. Atlanta's own 19th-century author, Joel Chandler Harris, produced the Uncle Remus tales that were told to him by America's first Africans, enriching man's brotherly bond with the animal world. Remember Brer Fox and Brer Rabbit?

But Atlanta continues to evolve.

Did you know that . . .

— Atlanta is 1010 feet (308 meters) above sea level, the highest elevation of any U. S. city east of the Mississippi River.

— Atlanta is the capital of Georgia, one of the thirteen original colonies, and the sixth largest state in the nation.

— "The City of Trees" is a description often applied to Atlanta, which was once designated a "city in a forest" by the U. S. Forestry Service.

— Georgia is the Peach State officially, and beautiful young women are called Georgia peaches, although Georgia's major agricultural crop is peanuts.

— The Cherokee rose is Georgia's state flower, a pale, flat climbing rose named after one of the large Indian nations from North Georgia.

— Georgia is a leader in the production of honey bees. The South Georgia land near the Okefenokee Swamp is a natural breeding ground for the bees, which are exported all over, from Florida to Minnesota for pollinating flowering trees and plants.

— About two juvenile bears a year are still spotted and captured in Fulton, Cobb, and Gwinnett counties, wandering down from the mountains, sniffing the sweet smell of honey. Atlanta, for all its progress, is still not "out of the woods."

— The fashionable northside of Buckhead took its name from a tavern where a buck's head was mounted, a vestige of wildlife since departed to the Chattahoochee National Forest with the bears, or at least most of the bears.

—The Chattahoochee river in metro Atlanta means "flowering stone" in the Creek language, an apt description for nearby Atlanta, a blooming, durable civilization.

—The oldest building in Atlanta is the Freight Depot, built in 1869, which is located in old Underground Atlanta.

—Atlanta's Grant Park was not named for Ulysses S. Grant, but for a Confederate Colonel Lemuel P. Grant. Col. Grant designed the fortifications for the city during the Battle of Atlanta and gave the land to the city.

—The Carillon at Stone Mountain Park is the largest electronic carillon in the world. The original carillon, a gift from the Coca-Cola Company after the 1964 World's Fair, had 610 bells. Stone Mountain has added 122 bells to make the carillon the largest of its kind with 732 bells.

—None of the famous movie *Gone with the Wind* was filmed in Georgia, so a local historian took two bushels of Georgia red clay to the Hollywood studio to sprinkle over the set, and so made it authentic.

—They say that Coca-Cola has made a thousand millionaires in Atlanta. If you had bought one share of Coca-Cola stock in 1919 for $40, you would have owned nineteen shares in 1978 worth $13,500!

—The Omni International was the first land development project of its kind because no land changed hands ... the Omni International City Corporation has a 99-year lease of the *air* over the railroad bed owned by Southern Railway.

—All the trees in the Omni International and the Georgia World Congress Center are planted in artificial soil because real soil weighed too much to be supported on the steel-enforced concrete pillars on which the two complexes are built.

—Atlanta University was first housed in a railroad car.

—The Fox Theatre was originally built as a Shriner's temple, but when the Depression hit they were unable to finish it, so it was sold to William Fox, the movie mogul, who turned it into a theater.

—The Centers for Disease Control (CDC) has been located in

Atlanta since its conception during World War II. Many experiments were conducted in the Georgia swamplands because their topography and climate were similar to the Pacific Islands, and so the laboratories were located in Atlanta.

— Visitors flying in and out of Atlanta's busy airport for years have complained that "Whether you are going to Heaven or Hell, you still have to go through Atlanta."

— Emory University is often referred to as "Coca-Cola U" because of the generosity of the Candler and Woodruff families, closely identified with Coca-Cola.

— The Atlanta Daily World is the oldest, black-owned newspaper in the United States.

— The highest ground in Atlanta is at the Piedmont Plateau in front of downtown Davison's on famous Peachtree Street between Ellis and International Boulevard. This point is a signal watershed where the water runs west toward the Pacific and east to the Atlantic ocean.

— Atlanta is the Dogwood City with a snowstorm of white and pink dogwood blossoms festooning the streets and lawns during the springtime. There is also a special legend of the dogwood. The dogwood was the tree whose wood was chosen for the cross of Christ. The tree was so distressed that this was to be its appointed mission, Christ promised that never again should a dogwood tree grow large enough to produce a cross. It would be slender and gnarled, and its blossoms form a cross, with two long and two short petals. At the outer edge of each petal would be nail prints, stained rust brown and red for his blood, and in the center of the flower a crown of thorns.

— And, of course, the main street is named after a tree and honors a fruit tree with its Peachtree Street. There are over 30 variants and versions of Peachtree — Peachtree Road, Peachtree Street, Peachtree Industrial Boulevard, Peachtree Circle, West Peachtree, Peachtree Crossing, Peachtree Lane, and others. The name first came from the Indian village Standing Peachtree and later was transferred to the government's Fort Standing Peachtree. Why the peachtree? One folktale suggests a huge Peachtree on the site. Another suggests a misinterpretation of the Creek word for "pitch." This later interpretation states that a huge pine tree on the site was blazed by the Indians for the pine resin which was used in waterproofing their canoes. In either case, Atlanta is webbed with the many strands of Peachtree streets.

Peachtree Center *Marge McDonald*

ORDER FORM

Please send me the following Marmac Guidebooks postpaid:

CITY GUIDES. Comprehensive guides to all facets of the city for all kinds of people.

_____ A Marmac Guide to Atlanta   @ $7.95 _____

_____ A Marmac Guide to Houston   @ $7.95 _____
         and Galveston

_____ A Marmac Guide to Los Angeles   @ $7.95 _____

_____ A Marmac Guide to New Orleans   @ $7.95 _____

_____ A Marmac Guide to Philadelphia   @ $7.95 _____

COMING SOON IN 1984.

_____ A Marmac Guide to Memphis   @ $7.95 _____

_____ A Marmac Guide to Nashville   @ $7.95 _____

Total _____

*Postage _____

4% sales tax
if mailed in Georgia _____

TOTAL ENCLOSED _____

*Postage—Enclose $1.20 for postage and packing, plus 75¢ each additional book for Third Class Mail within the continental U.S.A.

TO: TRIPLE M BOOKS
   P.O. BOX 720114
   ATLANTA, GEORGIA 30358

Please pay by check or money order. NO CASH ACCEPTED.

Name_____

Address_____

City_____State_____Zip_____

COOKBOOK ORDER FORM

____ **CHEFS' SECRETS FROM GREAT**   @ $13.95 _____
        RESTAURANTS IN LOUISIANA

____ **CHEFS' SECRETS FROM GREAT**   @ $12.95 _____
        RESTAURANTS IN GEORGIA

____ **CUISINE OF CALIFORNIA**   @ $9.95 _____

____ **SOUTHERN COOKING FROM**   @ $8.95 _____
        MARY MAC'S TEA ROOM

____ **NOTES FROM**   @ $7.95 _____
        MARIE'S KITCHEN

Add $1.50 Postage per Cookbook _____

Total Cookbooks _____

Add appropriate sales tax if
mailed in Georgia _____

TOTAL ENCLOSED _____

Add $3 per copy for orders from Canada and $6 per copy for orders outside North America.

SEND TO: TRIPLE M BOOKS
          P.O. BOX 720114
          ATLANTA, GEORGIA 30358

Please pay by check or money order. NO CASH ACCEPTED.

Name_____

Address_____

City_____State_____Zip_____

NOTES

NOTES